Practical Microsoft®
Office 2010

June Jamrich Parsons • Dan Oja • Donna Mulder

D1115350

CONTAINS A BookOnCD **FOR A FULLY INTERACTIVE LEARNING EXPERIENCE**

Includes a multimedia BookOnCD with the entire contents of the printed book, interactive step-by-step software tutorials, videos, pop-up definitions, practice tests, and more!

COURSE TECHNOLOGY
CENGAGE Learning

Australia • Brazil • Japan • Korea • Mexico • Singapore • Spain • United Kingdom • United States

COURSE TECHNOLOGY
CENGAGE Learning

Practical Microsoft Office 2010

June Jamrich Parsons, Dan Oja, Donna Mulder

Vice President, Publisher: Nicole Jones Pinard

Executive Editor: Marie Lee

Associate Acquisitions Editor: Brandi Shailer

Senior Product Manager: Kathy Finnegan

Product Manager: Leigh Hefferon

Associate Product Manager:
  Julia Leroux-Lindsey

Editorial Assistant: Jacqueline Lacaire

Director of Marketing: Cheryl Costantini

Senior Marketing Manager: Ryan DeGrote

Marketing Coordinator: Kristen Panciocco

Content Project Manager: Lisa Weidenfeld

Art Director: Marissa Falco and
  GEX Publishing Services

Senior Print Buyer: Justin Palmeiro

Photo Researcher: Abby Reip

Cover Designer: Nancy Goulet

Electronic Publishing Specialist:
  Tensi Parsons

BookOnCD Technician: Keefe Crowley

BookOnCD Development:
  MediaTechnics Corp.

Prepress Production: GEX Publishing Services

Proofreader: Suzanne Huizenga

Indexer: Rich Carlson

For product information and technology assistance, contact us at
Cengage Learning Customer & Sales Support, 1-800-354-9706

For permission to use material from this text or product,
submit all requests online at **www.cengage.com/permissions**.
Further permissions questions can be e-mailed to
permissionrequest@cengage.com.

Library of Congress Control Number: 2010933133
ISBN-13: 978-0-538-74595-6
ISBN-10: 0-538-74595-9

Cengage Learning
20 Channel Center Street
Boston, MA 02210
USA

Cengage Learning is a leading provider of customized learning solutions with office locations around the globe, including Singapore, the United Kingdom, Australia, Mexico, Brazil and Japan. Locate your local office at: **www.cengage.com/global**

Cengage Learning products are represented in Canada by Nelson Education, Ltd.

To learn more about Course Technology, visit **www.cengage.com/coursetechnology**

To learn more about Cengage Learning, visit **www.cengage.com**

Purchase any of our products at your local college store or at our preferred online store **www.cengagebrain.com**

Printed in the United States of America
2 3 4 5 6 7 16 15 14 13 12 11

Preface

About this book

At last, here is a book about the computers that people really use, with practical tips about how to use them. *Practical Microsoft Office 2010* provides a state-of-the-art introduction to Microsoft Office software, written in an easy-to-read style. In addition to the printed book, you receive a multimedia version of the entire printed textbook that also includes videos and interactive elements such as pop-up definitions, software tutorials, and practice tests.

This book provides a focused introduction to the most important features of Microsoft Office 2010. It is designed to teach you what you really need to know about this popular software suite so that you can use it for practical tasks at school, at work, or at home.

Each chapter of this book focuses on a specific topic. The first page introduces the chapter topic and lists the chapter contents. Chapter features include the following:

- **FAQs**, or "frequently asked questions," address key questions, provide background information, and give specific tips for becoming a more proficient computer user.

- **Interactive software tutorials** guide you through each feature and task.

- **Assessment activities** include two sets of QuickCheck questions and four interactive Skill Tests designed to gauge proficiency on the concepts and software skills presented in the chapter. Scores can be saved in a Tracking file and submitted to instructors.

About the BookOnCD

Every book includes the innovative BookOnCD, which is loaded with features to enhance and reinforce learning.

 Try It! buttons produce step-by-step interactive software tutorials, which give you a chance to quickly hone your software skills.

 Interactive end-of-chapter QuickCheck questions provide instant feedback on what you've learned.

Skill Tests Skill Tests check and record your ability to perform various tasks using Microsoft Office software.

Pop-up Definitions & Glossary Clickable boldface terms display pop-up definitions. A Glossary button provides easy access to all definitions from any page.

Projects Projects located at the end of the book provide structured practice for the Microsoft Office skills presented in each chapter.

Use this book because...

You want to learn how to use Microsoft Office 2010. *Practical Microsoft Office 2010* will help you learn how to use the essential features of Microsoft Word, Excel, PowerPoint, and Access in the most efficient possible way. You won't find excess coverage of features you'll never need. Instead you'll find a focused, efficient approach to learning how to use Microsoft Office 2010 to complete real-world tasks.

You want to learn Office 2010, but don't have it on your computer. The BookOnCD includes interactive simulations to show you how to use Microsoft Office 2010 modules, even if you don't have this popular software suite installed on your computer. You only need to use Microsoft Office 2010 software if you decide to complete the projects at the end of the book.

You're looking for a product that teaches how to use Microsoft Office 2010, but that also serves as a handy reference. Your book is designed to work as both a learning environment and a quick reference. We recommend using the CD to learn new features. After you've mastered Microsoft Office 2010, keep the printed book nearby as a quick reference.

You've used previous versions of Microsoft Office and want to get up to speed with the 2010 version. *Practical Microsoft Office 2010* makes it quick and easy to get up to speed on the latest versions of Microsoft Word, Excel, PowerPoint, and Access.

You're a beginning or intermediate computer user. This book is great for beginners, but it also serves as a quick reference or refresher for intermediate users. You can skim over the features you already know and quickly learn how to use features that are new to you.

How does it work?

Practical Microsoft Office 2010 offers a unique graduated learning environment where you see it, try it, and then apply it.

1. See It

The **book** provides background information and step-by-step screen illustrations to get you oriented to a task.

2. Try It

Use the **BookOnCD** to work with hands-on, step-by-step task simulations that help you learn the basics even if Microsoft Office 2010 software is not installed on your computer.

3. Apply It

Activities in the **Projects** section challenge you to try your skills on real-world examples using Microsoft Office 2010 software.

Teaching tools

With **ExamView**, our powerful testing software package, instructors can generate printed tests, create LAN-based tests, or test over the Internet.

An **Instructor's Manual** outlines each chapter, and provides valuable teaching tips and solutions for projects.

WebTrack is a versatile tool that provides automated delivery of tracking data from any student directly to the instructor with minimal setup or administrative overhead.

Acknowledgments

When you think about how a textbook is created, you might envision a lone author who produces a manuscript that is copyedited and then sent to the printer. If that was the case, textbooks might be less expensive, but they would certainly be less effective and far less interesting.

Today, creating a textbook is more like developing a computer game than penning a novel. It is a process that requires designers, script writers, narrators, animators, videographers, photographers, photo researchers, desktop publishers, programmers, testers, indexers, editors, reviewers—and yes, somewhere in the middle of all this creative effort are the authors.

The successful launch of this textbook was possible only because of an extraordinary and diverse team of dedicated specialists who collaborate from geographically dispersed locations using the Internet. It is a team of disciplined professionals who do what it takes to meet deadlines with high-quality work and cheeriness, even after working all weekend.

We would like to acknowledge the members of our incredible team who helped to bring you this colorful, interactive textbook:

Keefe Crowley: Multi-talented Keefe produces the BookOnCD by linking together the text, photos, videos, software tours, animations, and computer-scored quizzes. He also ushers the CD through the testing process and is responsible for producing many of the photos and video sequences. Keefe keeps in shape riding his mountain bike even during snowy northern winters.

Dave Dolan: Our assistant animator, Dave, works from his office in Canada to bring you Windows and Web tours.

Chris Robbert: The voice of the Practical series, Chris records narrations from his studio in the U.S. Virgin Islands, and he is a talented musician who specializes in classical and jazz guitar.

Tensi Parsons: Our layout and desktop publishing expert, Tensi, is responsible for tracking all the elements for the printed book. Each chapter goes through at least four revisions, and Tensi's job is to keep everything straight so the final product meets the highest standards. Tensi coaches university and community rowing teams in her spare time.

Marilou Potter: Our projects and supplements maven, Marilou, updates and tests the projects, produces the content for the Instructor's Manual, and produces our test banks.

Testers, testers, testers: Kevin Lappi, Joseph Smit, Jackie Kangas, Renee Gleason, Michael Crowley, and the Course Technology Software Quality Assurance Team; they test the BookOnCD, they test the instructions, and they test the tests.

Leigh Hefferon: Our developmental editor, Leigh, helps us schedule production events and get the resources we need to complete every phase of the project.

Lisa Weidenfeld: As our content project manager, Lisa monitors the flow of chapters among the proofreader, author, and desktop publisher. She makes sure that all the final copy is clean and error-free.

Suzanne Huizenga: With today's technology, spelling errors are few and far between. But there are still a million and one grammar and style issues for the copyeditor to address, and Suzanne is a perfectionist with an eagle eye.

Ryan DeGrote: As our marketing manager, Ryan does a terrific job of explaining the product to instructors and collecting feedback that helps us improve the product with each edition.

And that's not all! We simply cannot omit the editorial staff at Course Technology who make the executive decisions and work with customers: Marie Lee, Brandi Shailer, Julia Leroux-Lindsey, and Jacqueline Lacaire. They are this product's fairy godmothers who make the pumpkin turn into a coach.

Contents

Microsoft Word

Contents

Microsoft Excel

Microsoft PowerPoint

Contents

Microsoft Access

Projects

Index

Before You Begin

You are going to enjoy using *Practical Microsoft Office 2010* and the accompanying BookOnCD. It's a snap to start the BookOnCD and use it on your computer. The answers to the FAQs (frequently asked questions) in this section will help you begin.

FAQ Will the BookOnCD work on my computer?

The easiest way to find out if the BookOnCD works on your computer is to try it! Just follow the steps below to start the CD. If it works, you're all set. Otherwise, check with your local technical support person.

To run the BookOnCD, your computer needs the Windows operating system, a CD or DVD drive, and screen resolution of 1024 x 768 or better. The CD works with Windows 7, XP, or Vista.

FAQ How do I start the BookOnCD?

The BookOnCD is easy to use and requires no installation. Follow these simple steps to get started:

1. Make sure your computer is turned on.

2. Insert the BookOnCD into your computer's CD/DVD drive. Once the CD is in the drive, you should hear the disc spinning in the drive.

3. If your computer displays an AutoPlay window similar to the one shown here, click the Run BookOnCD option.

4. When you see the screen below, the BookOnCD has started and is waiting for you to select tracking options. For information on tracking options, continue to the FAQ on the next page of your textbook.

The length of time your computer takes to start the BookOnCD depends on your security settings. If you have security set to conduct a virus check on software running from CDs, you will have to wait for that process to be completed before the digital book opens.

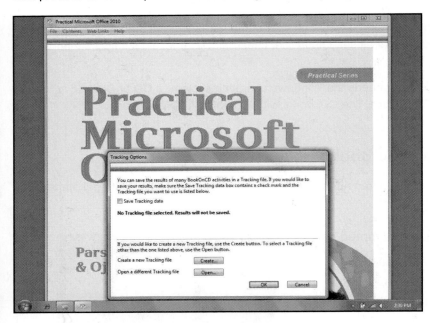

Manual Start: Follow the instructions in the figure below only if you've waited a minute or two and the Welcome screen has not appeared.

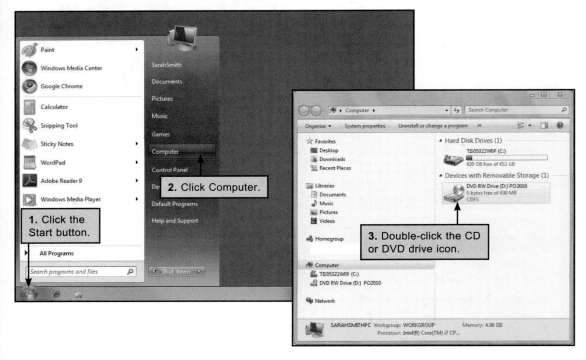

FAQ How should I set my tracking options?

When the BookOnCD starts, it displays the *Practical Microsoft Office 2010* title screen and a Tracking Options window. To proceed, you'll have to select your tracking settings.

A Tracking file records your progress by saving your scores on QuickChecks and Skill Tests at the end of each chapter. If you don't want to record your scores, simply make sure the *Save Tracking data* box is empty and then click the OK button to proceed straight to the first chapter.

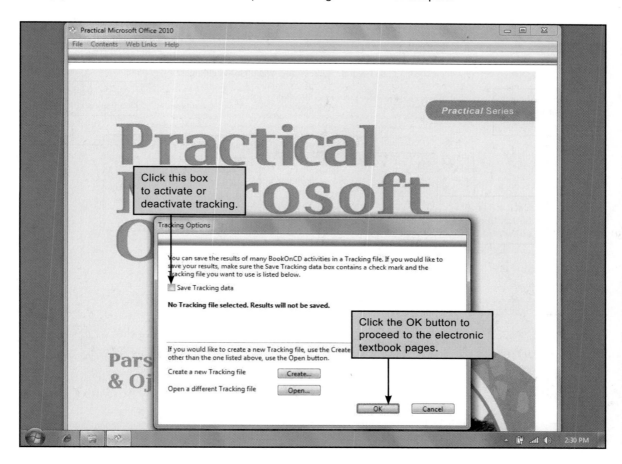

If you prefer to track your scores, then you can create a Tracking file. It's easy! Click the Create button and then follow the on-screen prompts to enter your name, student ID, and class section.

When the Save As window appears, you can select the location for your Tracking file. If you are using your own computer, the default location in the Documents folder is a great place to store your Tracking file, so just click the Save button and you're all set!

If you are working on a public computer, such as one in a school lab, be aware that data stored on the hard disk might be erased or changed by other students unless you have a protected personal storage area. When working on a public computer or when you need to transport your data from one computer to another, a USB flash drive is a better option for storing your Tracking file.

To save your Tracking file in a location other than your computer's Documents folder, click the Computer icon and then double-click a storage location to select it. Click the Save button to finalize your storage selection.

FAQ How do I navigate through the BookOnCD?

Each on-screen page exactly duplicates a page from the paper book. Tools on the menu bar help you navigate from page to page. If your computer screen does not show an entire page, use the scroll bar.

Click Contents, then click any chapter to jump to the start of the chapter.

Enter a page number here, then click the > button to jump to a specific page.

Click here to go to the previous page.

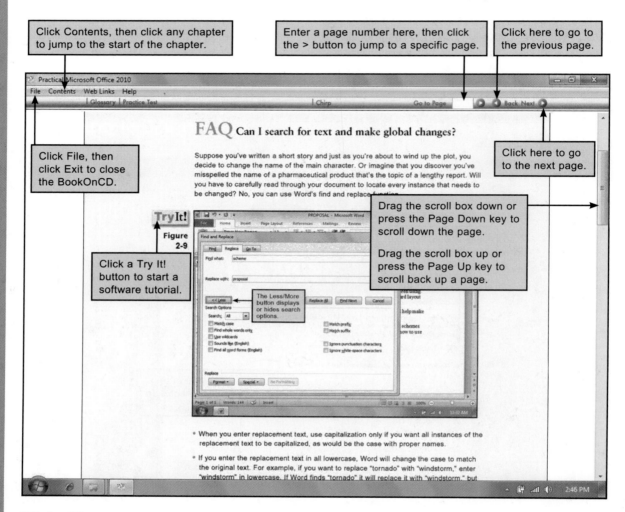

Click File, then click Exit to close the BookOnCD.

Click here to go to the next page.

Click a Try It! button to start a software tutorial.

Drag the scroll box down or press the Page Down key to scroll down the page.

Drag the scroll box up or press the Page Up key to scroll back up a page.

The Less/More button displays or hides search options.

FAQ What should I know about the Projects?

The last chapter contains projects that help you consolidate and apply the concepts presented in the chapters. All projects require the Windows 7 operating system and Microsoft Office 2010 software.

If a project requires you to send an e-mail attachment to your instructor, use your usual e-mail software, such as Thunderbird, Microsoft Outlook, Windows Live Mail, Hotmail, Eudora, Gmail, or AOL mail. First, make sure that you have saved the project file. Next, start your e-mail software. Then, follow your software's procedures for sending an e-mail attachment.

FAQ How does the interactive assessment page work?

Each chapter ends with an assessment page containing interactive activities. You can use these activities to evaluate how well you've mastered the concepts and skills covered in the chapter. If you do well on the QuickChecks and Skill Tests, then you're ready to move on to the next chapter. If you don't do well, you might want to review the material before continuing to the next chapter.

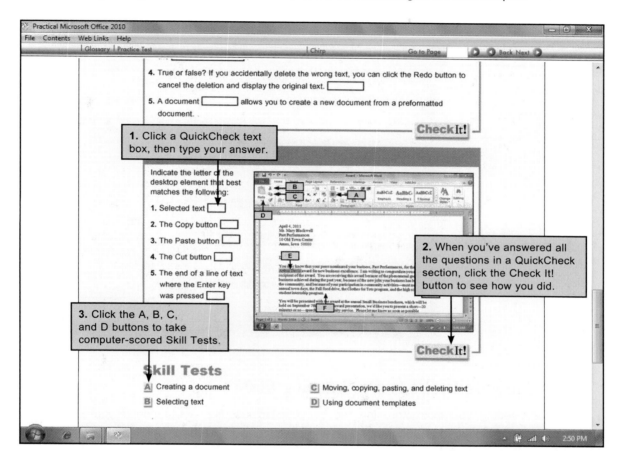

FAQ Are all my scores tracked?

Your scores on QuickChecks and Skill Tests are tracked if you have activated tracking with a checkmark in the *Save Tracking data* box.

FAQ How can I change tracking?

You can access the Tracking Options window at any time by clicking File on the menu bar and selecting Change Tracking Options. When the Tracking Options window appears, you can activate or deactivate tracking, create a new Tracking file, or select a different Tracking file.

FAQ What if the Tracking Options window shows the wrong Tracking file?

When working in a computer lab or using a computer where other students are using the BookOnCD, the Tracking Options window might show the name of a Tracking file that belongs to another person because that person was the last one to use the computer. You can use the Open button on the Tracking Options window to select a different Tracking file. Tracking files are usually stored in the Documents folder.

1. To change the Tracking file, open the Tracking Options window by clicking File, then selecting Change Tracking Options.

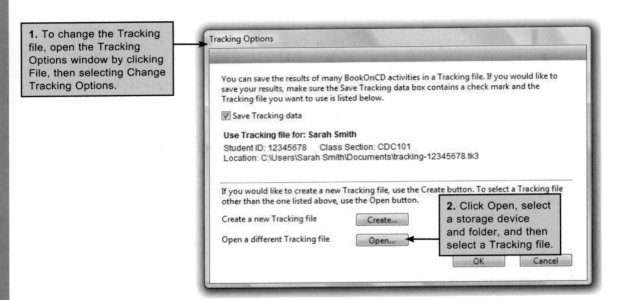

FAQ How do I submit my Tracking file?

In an academic setting, your instructor might request your Tracking file data to monitor your progress. Your instructor will tell you if you should submit your Tracking file using the WebTrack system, if you should hand in your entire Tracking file, or if you should send the Tracking file as an e-mail attachment.

FAQ How do I end a session?

You should leave the BookOnCD disc in the CD drive while you're using it, or you will encounter an error message. Before you remove the CD from the drive, you must exit the program by clicking File on the BookOnCD menu bar, then clicking Exit. You can also exit by clicking the Close button in the upper-right corner of the window.

FAQ What about sound?

If your computer is equipped for sound, you should hear narrations during the Try It! activities. If you don't hear anything, check the volume control on your computer by clicking the speaker icon in the lower-right corner of your screen. If you're working in a lab or office where sound would be disruptive, consider using headphones.

FAQ Which version of Windows do I need?

You can run the BookOnCD and use all of the tutorials if your computer runs Windows 7, XP, or Vista. Regardless of the operating system installed on your computer, however, the simulated screens you see when working with the tutorials all feature Windows 7.

FAQ What are chirps?

A chirp is a short message, similar to a Twitter-style tweet. You can use chirps to send questions about the material in the textbook to your instructor. To use chirps, click the Chirp button on the navigation bar. Make sure your instructor's WebTrack address is correct, then enter your message in the box provided. Click the Send button and your chirp will be on its way.

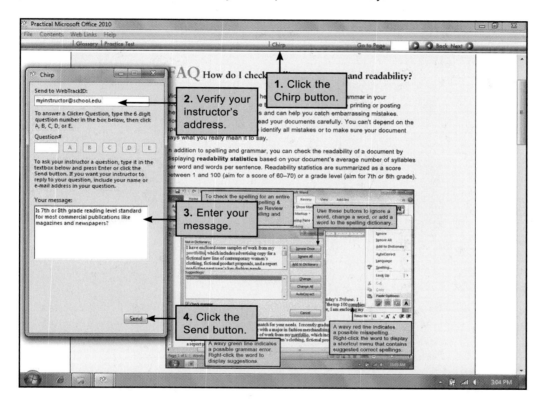

FAQ How do I get the most out of the book and the BookOnCD?

If you have your own computer, you might want to start the BookOnCD and do the reading on-screen. You'll then be able to click the Try It! buttons as you come to them and click boldface terms to see pop-up definitions. Also, you'll be able to immediately interact with QuickChecks and Skill Tests at the end of chapters.

If you do not have a computer, you should read through the chapter in the book. Later, when it is convenient, take your BookOnCD to a computer at school, home, or work and browse through the chapter, clicking each Try It! activity. After completing those activities, you can jump to the end of the chapter and do QuickChecks and Skill Tests. You can also do the projects by following the step-by-step instructions in the Project section.

Take your time. You might want to do each chapter in two sessions by first reading the FAQ (frequently asked question), Hardware, and Issues sections. Then, in a later session, you can complete the chapter QuickChecks, Skill Tests, and Projects.

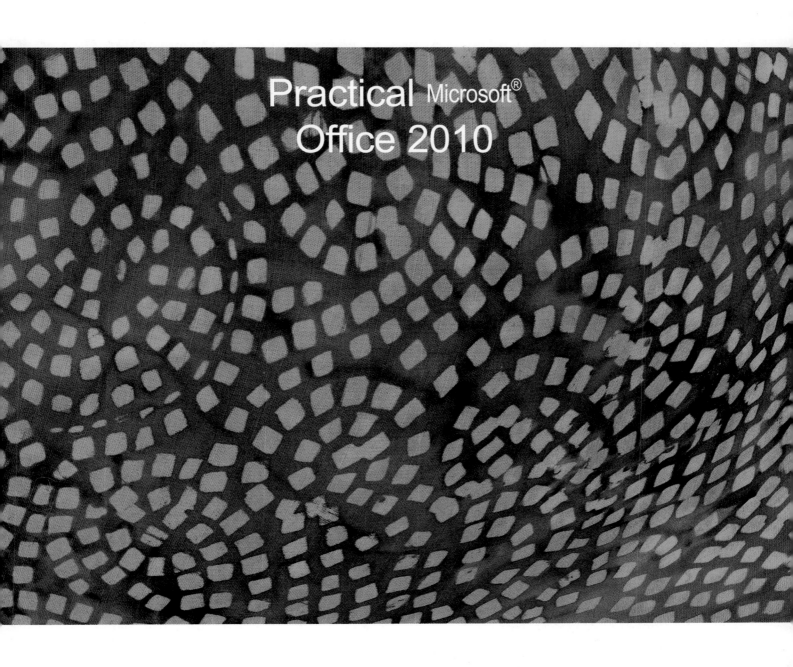

Practical Microsoft®
Office 2010

CHAPTER **1**

Getting Started with Application Software

What's Inside and on the CD?

Application software helps you use your computer to accomplish many useful tasks. Some of today's most popular software is included in the Microsoft Office suite. The suite's flagship software is Microsoft Word—a word processing application that has become a worldwide standard. Microsoft Excel is the spreadsheet software of choice for many computer owners. Microsoft PowerPoint is top-rated presentation software. Microsoft Access is among the most frequently used PC database software packages.

Understanding the features common to most Windows applications makes it easy to learn new software. In this chapter, you'll take a look at features common to many Windows applications. You can use what you learn in this chapter as a foundation for working with Word, Excel, PowerPoint, and Access in later chapters. This material also applies to working with a browser and e-mail.

● **FAQs:**

FAQ How do I start and exit Windows applications?

A software program designed for the Windows operating system is often referred to as a **Windows application**. Windows applications are sometimes referred to simply as applications or programs. This book uses the term "program" because it is consistent with Windows terminology. Before you can start a program, such as Microsoft Word, your computer should be on; and the Start button, supplied by the Windows operating system, should be displayed at the bottom of your screen. Windows provides several ways to start a program, but you'll typically use the Start button.

Windows allows you to run several programs at the same time, but it's best to close, or exit, a program when you're finished using it. Closing unused programs frees up memory and helps your computer run more efficiently. Also, remember to close all programs before you initiate the shut down procedure to turn off your computer.

Figure 1-1

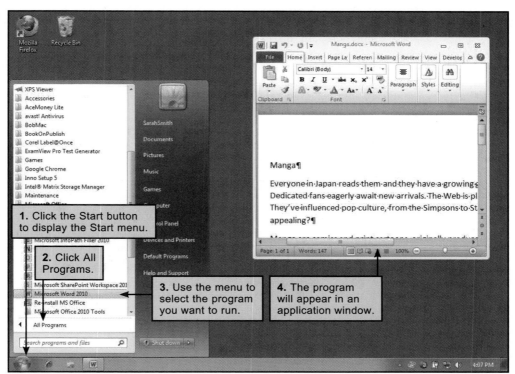

- When you install a new program on your computer, it is typically added to the All Programs menu. To start the program, click its name on the All Programs menu.

- Some menu options, indicated by a ▓ folder symbol, represent multiple programs. When you click a folder, a list of program names is displayed. Click the program you want to start from the list.

- In addition to appearing in the All Programs menu, some programs, such as Mozilla Firefox, are represented by an icon on the Windows desktop. To use one of these icons to start a program, just double-click it.

- You can also pin programs to the taskbar. To start these programs, click the program's taskbar icon.

- To close a program, click the ▓ Close button.

FAQ What are the components of an application window?

An open program is displayed in a rectangular **application window** on the Windows desktop. Application windows contain many similar elements, even when they hold very different kinds of programs.

An application window's title bar displays the name of the program, the name of the open file, and a set of sizing buttons for minimizing, maximizing, and closing the window.

The [▬] **Minimize button** hides the window, but leaves the program running. The [▢] **Maximize button** enlarges the window to fill the screen. The [✕] **Close button** closes the window and stops the application.

When a window is maximized, the Maximize button changes to a [◻] **Restore button**. Clicking the Restore button shrinks the window to the size it was just before it was maximized. You can also adjust the width and height of an application window. When a window is not maximized, you can change its height or width by dragging any edge of the window frame right, left, up, or down.

A status bar runs across the bottom of most application windows. A **status bar** contains information about the current condition of the program. Depending on the program, the status bar might display the current page number, the zoom level, or a Web page address.

A **scroll bar** on the side of the window helps you move a document or graphic up and down within the window. A horizontal scroll bar might also appear at the bottom of an application window to help you scroll wide documents and graphics from left to right.

Figure 1-2

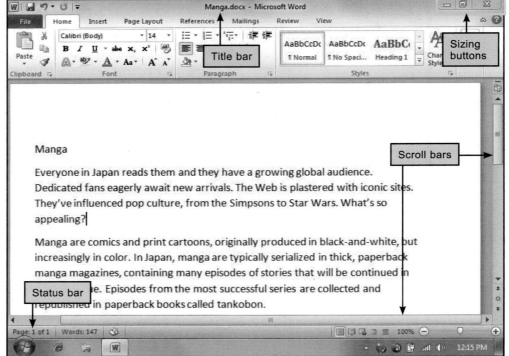

FAQ How do I switch between application windows?

You can have more than one application window open, or "running," on the desktop. This Windows feature is handy if you want to work on two projects at the same time or if you want to copy a photo from your photo editing software to a document. Open application windows are represented by buttons on the taskbar. Clicking one of these buttons brings the window to the front of the desktop. Although multiple programs can be open at the same time, only one program can be active. The active program is indicated by a distinctly colored taskbar button.

Some programs also allow several data files to be open at the same time. For example, when using Microsoft Word, you could have your to-do list open at the same time you are working on a term paper. When you have multiple data files open using the same program, such as Microsoft Word, the program's taskbar button looks like several buttons are stacked on top of each other, representing multiple files. You can customize Windows if you prefer each data file to have its own taskbar button.

Figure 1-3

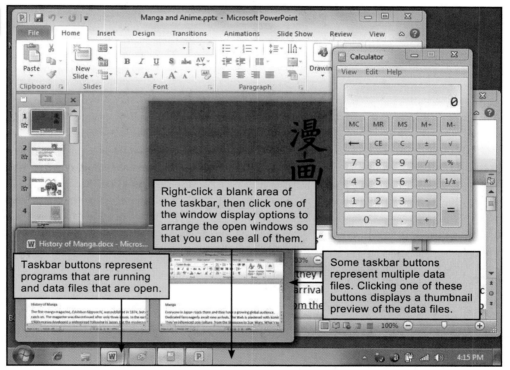

Right-click a blank area of the taskbar, then click one of the window display options to arrange the open windows so that you can see all of them.

Taskbar buttons represent programs that are running and data files that are open.

Some taskbar buttons represent multiple data files. Clicking one of these buttons displays a thumbnail preview of the data files.

- If a program window is open but hidden underneath another program window, clicking the program's button on the taskbar brings that window to the front, overlapping other windows on the desktop. You can also click any visible part of the hidden window to make it active.

- If a program window is minimized, clicking the program's button on the taskbar restores the window to its previous size and location.

- When multiple data files are open in a single program, such as Microsoft Word, you can hover the mouse pointer over the taskbar button to see a preview of the files and select the one you want.

FAQ How do menus and toolbars work?

Many application windows include a **menu bar** that provides access to commands for controlling the program. Clicking an option from the menu bar displays a menu with a list of choices. For example, clicking Edit on the menu bar displays the Edit menu. You can use this menu to accomplish several tasks. For example, the Copy option allows you to copy a selected item onto the Clipboard. If you don't remember how to access a program feature, you can browse through the menu options to find it.

Most application windows display one or more toolbars, typically located below the menu bar near the top of the window. A **toolbar** contains several buttons, sometimes called tools, that provide a single-click shortcut for the most commonly used menu options.

TryIt!

Figure 1-4

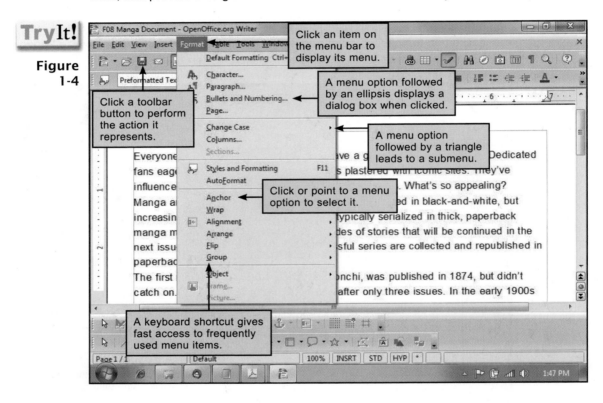

- If you open a menu and then decide you don't want to select an option after all, click the menu title again or press the Esc key to close the menu.

- You can use a **keyboard shortcut** for fast access to frequently used menu items. Hold down the Alt key and press the underlined letter to display a menu. Press the underlined letter to select an option from an open menu. As an example, for the menu item Group, the keyboard shortcut is Alt G because "G" is the underlined letter.

- Some programs have a Goto command that allows you to specify a page and jump to it. Look for this command on the menu bar or ribbon.

- Some programs hide their menu bars. To display a hidden menu bar, press the Alt key.

FAQ How does the ribbon work?

A **ribbon** offers an alternative way to access the commands for an application. Microsoft Office 2010 applications feature a ribbon instead of a menu bar and toolbars at the top of the application window. The ribbon is divided into a hierarchy consisting of tabs, groups, and commands. The tabs are divided into groups. Each group contains related commands and options for performing various actions. For example, the Home tab contains a Styles group with options for fonts to use for various levels of headings in a document.

TryIt!

Figure 1-5

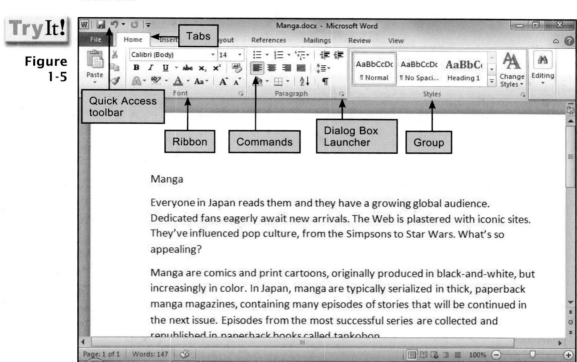

- The **Quick Access toolbar** contains commands that you use regularly. Elements of the Quick Access toolbar are completely customizable. Commands can be added by right-clicking the toolbar's down-arrow button.

- **Contextual tabs**, which contain formatting options for an object, appear when the object is selected. For example, after a table is inserted, the Table Tools tab appears. From this tab, you can change borders, insert or delete columns, and change cell properties for the table.

- Dialog boxes can be opened from the **Dialog Box Launcher** in the lower-right corner of a group. For example, in Figure 1-5, the Paragraph dialog box can be launched from the Paragraph group on the Home tab.

FAQ How do I open a file?

Data can be stored in files on your computer's hard disk and on CDs, DVDs, USB flash drives, and other storage media. Files can be referred to in different ways in different programs. For example, a file created with Microsoft Word is usually called a document, while a Microsoft PowerPoint file is usually called a presentation.

Before you can work with a file, you must open it. There are several ways to open a file. You can:

• Use an application's jump list from the Windows Start menu.

• Double-click a file shortcut icon if one exists on the Windows desktop.

• Double-click a file name from within Windows Explorer.

• Use the Open dialog box provided by an application.

When you use the Open dialog box from within an application window, you'll see a list of files and folders. The dialog box uses file extensions to filter the list of files so that it displays only those files that can be opened with the program.

TryIt!

Figure 1-6

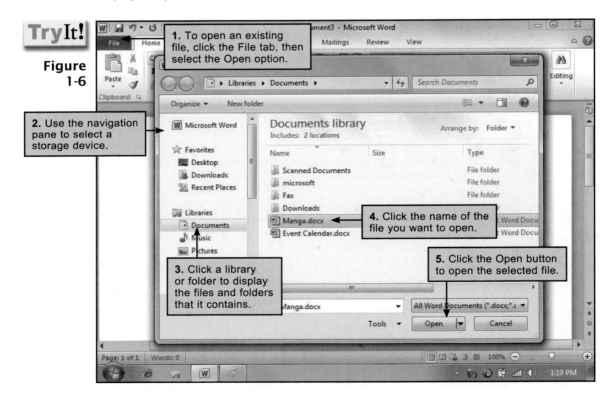

1. To open an existing file, click the File tab, then select the Open option.

2. Use the navigation pane to select a storage device.

3. Click a library or folder to display the files and folders that it contains.

4. Click the name of the file you want to open.

5. Click the Open button to open the selected file.

• Many Windows applications, including Microsoft Office, store files in your personal libraries and folders if no other drive or folder is specified. If you save a document, presentation, spreadsheet, or database and forget where it went, look in the Documents library. For photos, look in your Pictures library. For music, look in the Music library or Downloads folder.

FAQ   What if a file doesn't open?

The process of saving and opening files usually goes smoothly, but occasionally you'll encounter file problems. Here's a summary of common problems and their solutions:

- **Storage device not available.** Files can be accessed only if the device on which they are stored is connected to your computer. Before you attempt to open files from a USB flash drive, a LAN server, or Web-based online storage, make sure your computer can access the storage device. As necessary, plug in your USB drive, make sure your LAN connection is active, or make sure you have an Internet connection.

- **File not saved.** If you forgot to save a file before exiting, there's not much hope of retrieving it unless your software provides an autosave feature. **Autosave** periodically saves a file as you're working on it. Check your software's settings to find out if autosave is activated. If so, check Help to find out how to retrieve an autosaved file.

- **File stored in the wrong folder.** If you can't find a file, it might have been inadvertently saved in an unexpected location. Use your operating system's search feature to find the file by name, date, or file type.

- **File moved.** If you moved a file from one folder to another, you won't be able to access it from your software or operating system's recently used files list because those lists point to the original file location. Use your software's Open dialog box to locate and open the file.

- **File is corrupted.** The file might have been damaged—a techie would call it "corrupted"—by a transmission or disk error. You might be able to use file recovery software to repair the damage, but it is usually easier to obtain an undamaged copy of the file from its original source.

- **Incompatible file type.** Most software applications work with a limited number of file types (also referred to as file formats), corresponding to the file extension. For example, Microsoft Paint opens file types such as Windows Bitmap (.bmp), GIF (.gif), and JPEG (.jpg). If you attempt to use Paint to open a Word document (.docx) file, however, your computer will display an error message: "Paint cannot read this file." To avoid this error, be sure to use the correct application software when you open a file.

- **Wrong association.** Windows Explorer maintains a list of default programs for opening each type of file. If the association between the default program and file type is not correct, the file might not open. For example, if Paint is inadvertently set to be the default program for DOCX files, a file such as Report.docx won't open when you double-click it in Windows Explorer.

- **File has the wrong extension.** File extensions are sometimes inadvertently changed when a file is renamed. The most prevalent case is when a renamed file ends up with no extension and your computer does not know what software can open it. You can try to guess the file extension and add it. For example, if a file contains a graphic, chances are that it should have an extension such as .bmp, .gif, .jpg, .tif, or .png. If you can't guess the file type, you'll have to locate the original file with its extension intact.

- **Product or version incompatibility.** Some file formats exist in several variations, and your software might not have the capability to open a particular variation of the format. You might be able to open the file if you use different application software. For example, Photoshop might not be able to open a particular file with a .tif file extension, but Corel PaintShop Pro might open it.

FAQ How do I save a file?

When you create a file on your computer, you must save it if you want to be able to use it again in the future. Make sure you save files before you close their application windows; otherwise, you could lose the work in progress.

**Figure
1-7**

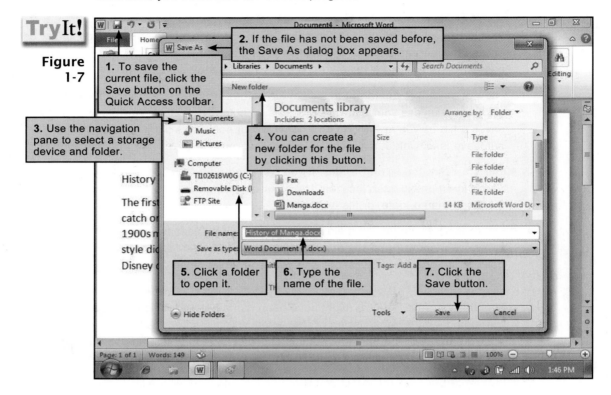

- When you first save a file, you must name it. File names can consist of letters, spaces, numbers, and certain punctuation symbols. File names cannot include the symbols / ? : = < > | and must not be longer than 255 characters. Each folder can contain only one file with a particular file name. However, different documents with the same name can be stored in different folders.

- A file extension is a set of characters that indicates the file type. A file extension is separated from the file name by a period. Windows programs add the appropriate file extension automatically, so you don't have to type it when saving a file. In Office 2010, Word documents are usually saved with .docx extensions, Excel files with .xlsx extensions, PowerPoint presentations with .pptx extensions, and Access databases with .accdb extensions.

- The dialog box produced by the Save button depends on whether or not the file was previously saved. Clicking the Save button automatically stores a file using the original name, drive, and folder where it was previously stored. If the file hasn't been saved before, clicking the Save button opens the Save As dialog box so that you can select the drive and folder where you want to save the file and enter a file name.

- If you've modified an existing file and want to save the new version under a different name, click the File tab, then click Save As to display the Save As dialog box. Enter a new name and select the drive and folder in which to store the file. The modified version of the file is saved under the new name, leaving the original version of the file unchanged under the original name.

• How do I save a file? (continued)

Many Windows programs are configured to automatically save files in the My Documents folder. Other programs are configured to save files in the same directory used for the last save operation. Regardless of the configuration, you have full control over the destination of your files. You can save to the desktop, or to any storage device connected to your computer, including the hard disk drive, CD/DVD drive, or USB flash drive. You can also save to a network or Internet server if you have access rights and permission to save files.

Each application has a default file type that it automatically uses when saving files. For example, Microsoft Word adds a .docx extension to all its files. You can, however, change the format in which a file is saved by using the *Save as type* list provided by the Save As dialog box. For example, you might want to save a document as a template (.dotx) to be used in generating a series of similar documents. You might save a document in Rich Text Format (.rtf) or as plain text (.txt) so it can be opened by other word processing software.

You can also use the *Save as type* list to save documents in a format (.doc) that can be opened by earlier versions of Microsoft Word in case a friend or colleague has not upgraded to a version of Word that stores files in a format compatible with yours.

Figure 1-8

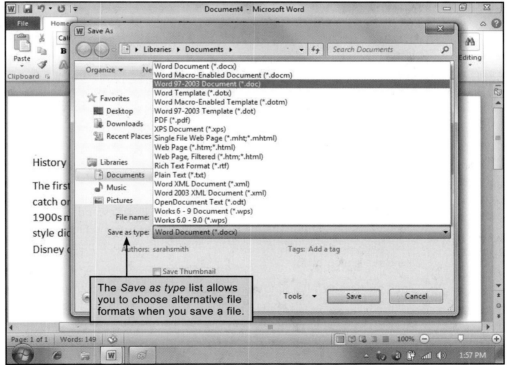

The *Save as type* list allows you to choose alternative file formats when you save a file.

After you save a file, you can close it or exit the application. Simply closing a file leaves the application open so that you can work on a different file. Closing the application, sometimes referred to as exiting, closes the file and the application.

• To close a file but leave the application open, use the File menu to select the Close option.

• To close the application, click the Close button in the upper-right corner of the application window. Or, you can use the File menu to select the Exit option.

FAQ How do I change the settings for an application?

Most application software is preconfigured with a set of **application defaults** (sometimes called preferences or default settings) that specify settings, such as where files are stored, which fonts are used to display text, how often files are autosaved, and which printer is used for output. Most software allows you to modify application defaults. Look for Options or Preferences on the File tab or on the Tools menu. Some application defaults, such as settings for autosaving, printing, and file locations, are similar across applications. Other defaults are application specific. Carefully review your application defaults and change those that will streamline your work flow.

TryIt!

Figure 1-9

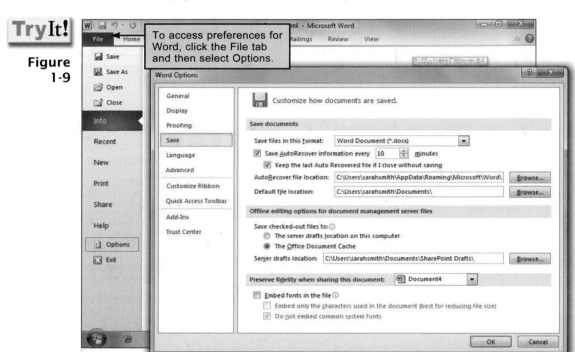

- Microsoft Office applications use your personal libraries and folders, such as Documents or Pictures, as the default location for storing files. It is a good practice to keep this default setting and simply navigate to an appropriate subdirectory when using the Save dialog box.

- Don't assume that the autosave feature is activated as your application default. Check it and make sure. Although autosave causes a slight reduction in system performance as it saves a file in the background, you'll be happy it is saving copies of your work in case of a power outage or software glitch.

- Be conservative when you change application defaults. Some applications offer hundreds of settings, but the preset defaults usually work for most tasks. When reviewing application defaults, just change a few at a time so that you can easily backtrack and reestablish the original defaults.

FAQ How do I access help for an application?

While using application software, you can access help from a variety of sources, including on-screen help, printed user manuals, Readme files on a CD, and third-party reference books. The source you turn to first depends on the type of help you need. Typically, general questions about how to use software features can be best answered by on-screen help that explains features and provides step-by-step instructions for their use.

On-screen help is probably the most frequently used help resource. Different programs offer different ways to access on-screen help. For example, Microsoft Office modules offer help through a comprehensive electronic user manual that also connects to Office Online. The help manual provides tools to scan through its Table of Contents or search by keyword.

Try It!

Figure 1-10

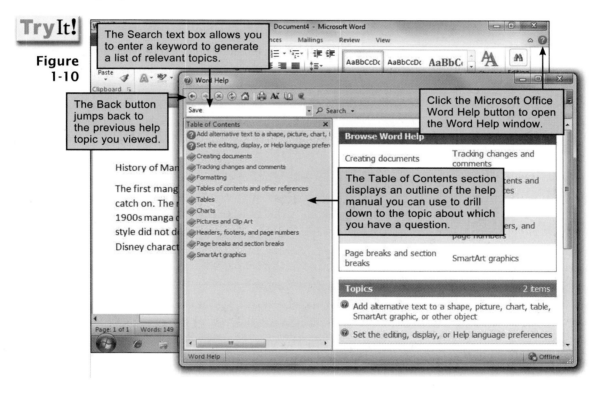

The Search text box allows you to enter a keyword to generate a list of relevant topics.

The Back button jumps back to the previous help topic you viewed.

Click the Microsoft Office Word Help button to open the Word Help window.

The Table of Contents section displays an outline of the help manual you can use to drill down to the topic about which you have a question.

- You can access the electronic user manual for Microsoft Office modules by clicking the Help button in the upper-right corner of the application window. You can also access the manual by pressing the F1 function key at the top of your keyboard.

- The Office Help window remains open on the desktop until you click its Close button. If the Help window drops back behind other windows, you can use its taskbar button to bring it to the top of the desktop.

- Microsoft Office applications automatically include online help if your computer is connected to the Internet. The Help window toolbar lets you know if you're not connected and gives you the option of going online.

• How do I access help for an application? (continued)

When on-screen help does not provide answers, you can turn to other sources of information. If you have questions about work-related procedures, your first source of information should be your organization's help desk. Sometimes, coworkers and friends are willing to answer your questions.

If a feature doesn't seem to work as explained in documentation and user manuals, consider checking online user groups or the publisher's Web site for up-to-date information. Some software publishers offer phone support to customers, but you might experience a long wait before a technician is available. You can often find answers more quickly by searching through the publisher's knowledge base or list of FAQs. These sources of information are particularly useful for troubleshooting problems and making sense of error messages. To access an online knowledge base, connect to the publisher's Web site and look for a Support link.

Another option is to use a search engine, such as Google, to get help. For example, you can type in the text of an error message to find the cause of a problem and its solution.

Figure 1-11

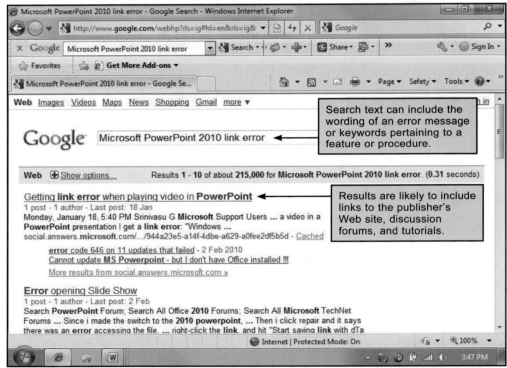

• When you use a search engine such as Google to get help, you'll get targeted results if you include the full title and version of the software you're using, along with keywords specifically related to your question.

• When seeking advice from online forums, use the advice judiciously. Some people who post advice are well-intentioned, but pose solutions that can cause more trouble than the original problem.

QuickCheck A

1. Before you close an application window, you should [_____] any work in progress.

2. Although multiple programs can be open at the same time, only one program can be [_____] .

3. True or false? When you open a file, you have to know which file name extensions the program can work with. [_____]

4. True or false? Most applications save files in the Windows folder. [_____]

5. True or false? The first time you save a file, you will use the Save As dialog box to assign the file a name and specify its location. [_____]

Check It!

QuickCheck B

Indicate the letter of the application window element that best matches the following:

1. The Save button [____]

2. The application window's taskbar button [____]

3. The Close button [____]

4. The horizontal scroll bar [____]

5. The Home tab [____]

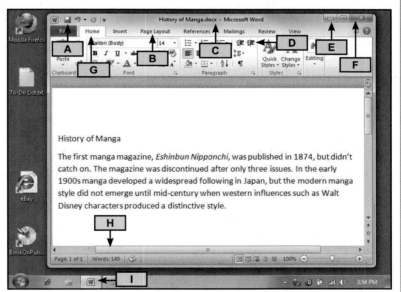

Check It!

CHAPTER 2

Creating a Document

What's Inside and on the CD?

Microsoft Word is the component of Microsoft Office best suited for creating documents such as letters and reports. As word processing software, Microsoft Word provides a set of tools for entering and revising text, adding graphical elements such as color and tables, and then formatting and printing completed documents.

Most people use Microsoft Word more frequently than any other component of Microsoft Office. Microsoft Word is an excellent tool for creating documents of all sorts—from personal letters to business proposals.

In this chapter, you'll learn how to create documents using Microsoft Word. Then you'll learn how to select and edit text, check spelling, use the electronic thesaurus, and specify print options. You'll also learn how to use document templates to quickly generate common types of documents.

FAQ What's in the Word program window?

The Word program window appears when you start Microsoft Word. To start Word, click Start, point to All Programs, click Microsoft Office, then click Microsoft Word 2010. Components of the Word program window include the title bar, Quick Access toolbar, ribbon, status bar, views, zoom control, and document workspace. You'll use these elements of the Word program window to create, edit, save, print, and format your documents.

Figure 2-1

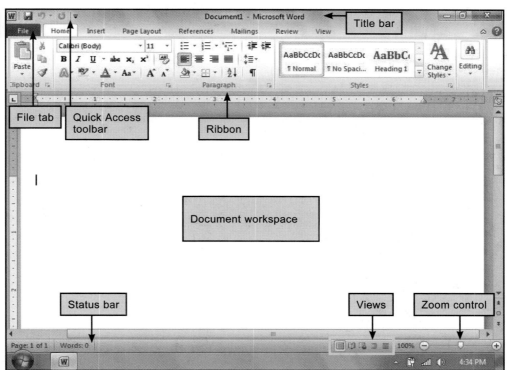

- The **document workspace** represents a blank piece of paper. Characters that you type on the keyboard appear in the document workspace. The title bar indicates the name of the current document. If the current document has never been saved, the title bar displays the generic title Document1. Word's ribbon contains commands and tools that you can use to create and edit your document.

- There are different ways to view your document. The **Draft view** allows quick text editing and formatting; headers and footers are not visible. The **Web Layout view** shows how your document would look in a Web browser. The **Print Layout view** shows how the content will look on the printed page, complete with margins, headers, and footers. The **Full Screen Reading view** displays your document with minimized toolbars at the top of the window. You can also work in **Outline view** to look at the structure of a document.

- The status bar provides information about the document displayed in the window and displays a Zoom control. The information can include page numbers and word count. If you right-click the status bar, you can customize the information displayed.

- You can increase or decrease the zoom level to view the document at various sizes by adjusting the Zoom level on the status bar.

FAQ What's in the document workspace?

The blank document workspace is bordered by scroll bars and a ruler. The scroll bars help you quickly navigate through a document. The rulers help you gauge how the spacing of your on-screen document translates to the space on a printed page. For example, if you've specified one-inch margins, the text that you enter into the workspace will be positioned to the right of the 1" mark on the ruler.

The **I-bar pointer** is equivalent to the arrow-shaped mouse pointer you see when selecting items on the Windows desktop. You move the I-bar by moving the mouse. Use the I-bar to select text and reposition the insertion point.

Figure 2-2

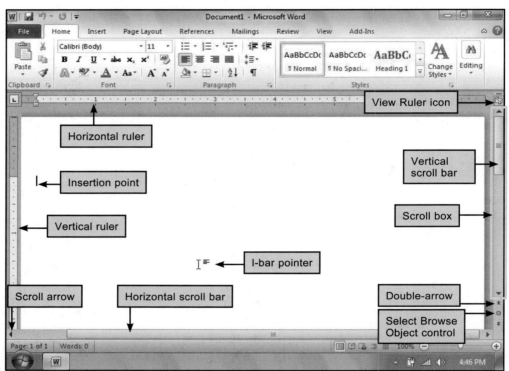

- You can set Word to display a horizontal ruler, a vertical ruler, both, or none. Use the View Ruler icon or the View tab to display or hide rulers.

- The scroll bars offer several ways to navigate a document. Drag the scroll box to smoothly scroll to any part of the document. Click the scroll arrows to move up or down one line at a time.

- When working with lengthy documents, the Select Browse Object control lets you jump to various objects, such as charts, comments, footnotes, tables, or headings.

- Double-arrows on the vertical scroll bar work in conjunction with the Select Browse Object control. If that control is set to Page, then the double-arrows take you to the previous or next page. If you have the Browse control set to Charts, the double-arrows take you to the previous or next chart.

FAQ How do I create a document?

To create a new document, just click the blank document workspace and start typing. When typing a document, don't worry too much about spelling, formatting, or arranging the document. It is very easy to edit and format a document after you've entered the text.

TryIt!

Figure 2-3

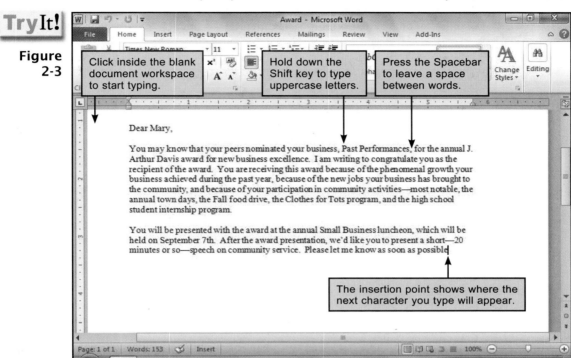

- The **insertion point** (or cursor) is a vertical bar that indicates your current location in the document. The insertion point is not the same as the I-bar. As you type, the insertion point moves to show where the next character will appear. Click anywhere in the document workspace to move the insertion point to that location.

- Through a feature known as **word wrap**, the insertion point automatically jumps down to the beginning of the next line when you reach the right margin of the current line. If the last word you type is too long for the line, it is moved down to the beginning of the next line. Press the Enter key only when you complete a paragraph.

- Press the Backspace key to delete the character to the *left* of the insertion point. You can also press the Delete key to delete the character to the *right* of the insertion point. These keys also work to erase spaces and blank lines.

- To add text in the middle of a line or word, use the mouse or arrow keys to move the insertion point to the desired location, then type the text you want to add. To make room for new text, everything to the right of the insertion point is pushed to the right and down as you type.

- Use the Insert key to toggle between Overtype and Insert mode. Overtype mode causes new characters to be typed over existing characters. Insert mode causes new characters to be inserted at the current location in the document.

- Insert special characters, such as the trademark symbol, by clicking the Insert tab, clicking the Symbol command, then clicking More Symbols. Select the symbol you want to insert, click Insert, then click Close to close the Symbols dialog box.

FAQ How do I select text for editing?

Many word processing features require you to select a section of text before you edit, change, or format it. When you **select text**, you are marking characters, words, phrases, sentences, or paragraphs to modify in some way. Selecting text doesn't do anything useful by itself; but combined with other commands, it enables you to use many of the other important features of Word. While text is selected, it is shown as highlighted with a blue background. Word provides several ways to select text.

Figure 2-4

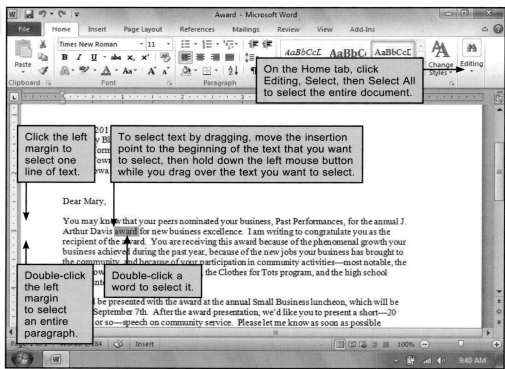

- Use the drag method to select short sections of text, such as a few characters or several words. Use one of the other selection methods when you need to select a single word, a line, a paragraph, or the entire document.

- When you point to a word, you can double-click to select only that word. You can triple-click to select the current paragraph.

- When you point to the left margin, the pointer changes to a white arrow. You can click once to select a line of text or double-click to select a paragraph.

- If you have trouble using the mouse, you can also use the keyboard to select text. Use the mouse or arrow keys to move the insertion point to the beginning of the text that you want to select. Hold the Shift key down while you use the arrow keys to select text.

- To deselect text, you should click away from the text that is currently selected. You can also press one of the arrow keys to deselect text.

- To select a section of text, such as several paragraphs, click at the beginning of the selection, then Shift-click at the end. You can also select non-contiguous text by selecting the first word or section, then using Ctrl-click to select subsequent sections.

FAQ How do I move, copy, and delete text?

As you create a document, you might want to move or copy sections of text—words, paragraphs, or even entire pages—from one part of the document to another. To copy or move text, you use the Clipboard, a special memory location that temporarily holds sections of your document.

Try It!

Figure 2-5

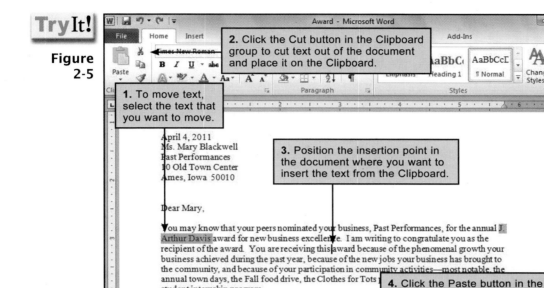

- To move a section of text from one part of your document to another, first select the text, then click the ✂ Cut button. The selected text is cut out of the document and placed on the Clipboard. To paste that text back into the document, move the insertion point to the place where you want to position the text, then click the 📋 Paste button. The text is copied from the Clipboard and placed into the document. This operation is known as **cut and paste**.

- You can also cut and paste using the drag-and-drop method. Select the text you wish to cut, and use the mouse to drag it to the new location.

- **Copy and paste** works much the same way as cut and paste, except that the text is not removed from its original location. Select the text you want to copy, then click the 📋 Copy button. The selected text is copied to the Clipboard, but the original text is not removed from the document. Move the insertion point to the place where you want to place the copy, then click the Paste button.

- After you cut or copy, the copied text remains on the Clipboard. You can use this feature when you need to put several copies of the same text into your document. Just move the insertion point to the location where you want to place the next copy and click the Paste button. You can paste as many copies of the text as you like.

- You can cut and paste text, hypertext links, graphics, tables, and other objects between different applications, such as pasting Excel worksheet data into a Word document.

FAQ Can I undo a command?

If you perform an action and then change your mind, use the 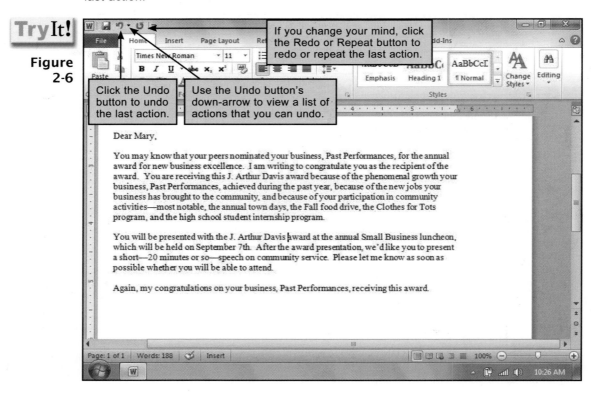 Undo button to undo the action. The Undo button has a counterpart—the Redo button—that allows you to repeat an action that you mistakenly undid. The Repeat button is used to repeat your last action.

TryIt!

Figure 2-6

- If there are no actions that can be undone or redone, the Undo and Redo buttons are disabled—they appear grayed out and nothing happens if you click them.

- The Undo button works best when undoing an editing or formatting command. Actions such as saving and printing files cannot be undone.

- If you need to undo a series of actions, click the down-arrow button on the right side of the Undo button to display a list of actions that can be undone. Drag over the list to highlight the actions you want to undo. You can also click a specific action to select it, but all the actions prior to that one will also be undone.

FAQ How do I check spelling, grammar, and readability?

Microsoft Word provides tools to help you check spelling and grammar in your documents. You should use these tools for all documents before printing or posting them—it only takes a few minutes and can help you catch embarrassing mistakes. However, you should also proofread your documents carefully. You can't depend on the spelling and grammar checker to identify all mistakes or to make sure your document says what you really mean it to say.

In addition to spelling and grammar, you can check the readability of a document by displaying **readability statistics** based on your document's average number of syllables per word and words per sentence. Readability statistics are summarized as a score between 1 and 100 (aim for a score of 60–70) or a grade level (aim for 7th or 8th grade).

TryIt!

Figure 2-7

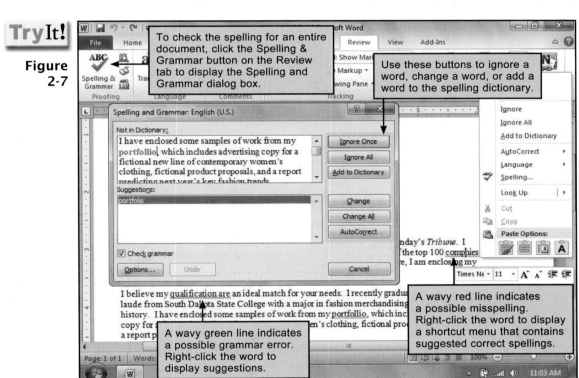

- If you don't see any wavy lines, spelling and grammar checking might be turned off. Click the File tab, click the Options button, and then click the Proofing button. Make sure there is a checkmark in the box for *Check spelling as you type*.

- You can also check the spelling and grammar of a complete document by clicking the Spelling & Grammar button on the Review tab. Words that might be misspelled are shown in red. Possible grammar mistakes are shown in green. You can click the appropriate buttons to ignore or replace each word or phrase.

- Readability statistics are shown at the end of a spelling and grammar check if the statistics feature is turned on. To turn on this feature, click the File tab, click the Options button, and then click the Proofing button. Make sure there is a checkmark in the box for *Show readability statistics*.

FAQ How do I use the thesaurus and other research tools?

A thesaurus contains synonyms for words and some common phrases. When you are composing a document and can't think of the right word, you can type the closest word that comes to mind, and then use Word's thesaurus to search for words with a similar meaning.

Try It!

Figure 2-8

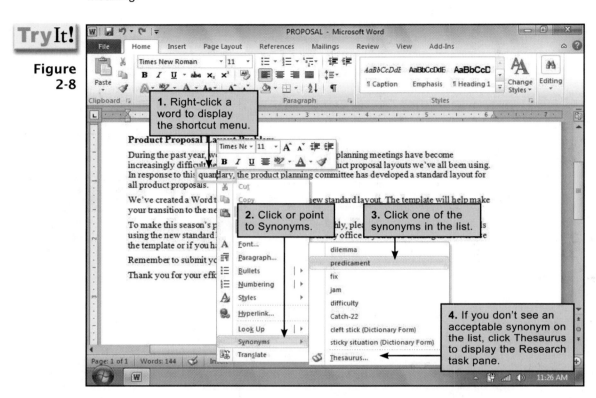

- You can also access Word's thesaurus through the Review tab. Click the Review tab, then click Thesaurus.

- To find a synonym for a phrase, select the phrase, then right-click it to display the shortcut menu. Point to Synonyms, then click Thesaurus to open the Research task pane. A list of phrases appears. Sometimes you'll find an acceptable alternate phrase, but beware—some of the phrases listed might not be appropriate substitutes.

- Microsoft Word's Review tab offers additional wordsmithing tools that are especially handy when working with multiple-language documents and when English is your second language. The Translate tool translates a word or sentence into another language. The Research button lets you search for a word or phrase in a variety of local and online sources, such as encyclopedias, atlases, and multi-language thesauri.

FAQ Can I search for text and make global changes?

Suppose you've written a short story and just as you're about to wind up the plot, you decide to change the name of the main character. Or imagine that you discover you've misspelled the name of a pharmaceutical product that's the topic of a lengthy report. Will you have to carefully read through your document to locate every instance that needs to be changed? No, you can use Word's find and replace function.

Figure 2-9

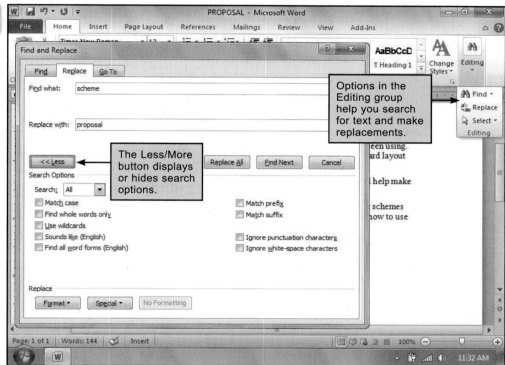

- When you enter replacement text, use capitalization only if you want all instances of the replacement text to be capitalized, as would be the case with proper names.

- If you enter the replacement text in all lowercase, Word will change the case to match the original text. For example, if you want to replace "tornado" with "windstorm," enter "windstorm" in lowercase. If Word finds "tornado" it will replace it with "windstorm," but "Tornado" will be replaced with "Windstorm."

- Word looks for your search string in any part of a word, so searching for "process" will produce matches for "microprocessor" and "processing." If you are simply looking for the word "process," use the *Find whole words only* option in the *Find and Replace* dialog box.

- The *Sounds like* option lets you find words even if you are not sure how to spell them.

- You can use wildcards, such as ? and *. For example, searching for *b?n* finds "ban" and "bin." Searching for *b*k* finds "beak," "book," "back," and so on. Refer to Word Help for more details about wildcards.

FAQ How do I use a document template?

You can create a document from scratch by entering text in the blank, new document workspace. As an alternative, you can use a **document template**, which is a preformatted document that can be used as the foundation for creating a new document. Word includes templates for many basic document types, such as letters, faxes, and resumes.

Try It!

Figure 2-10

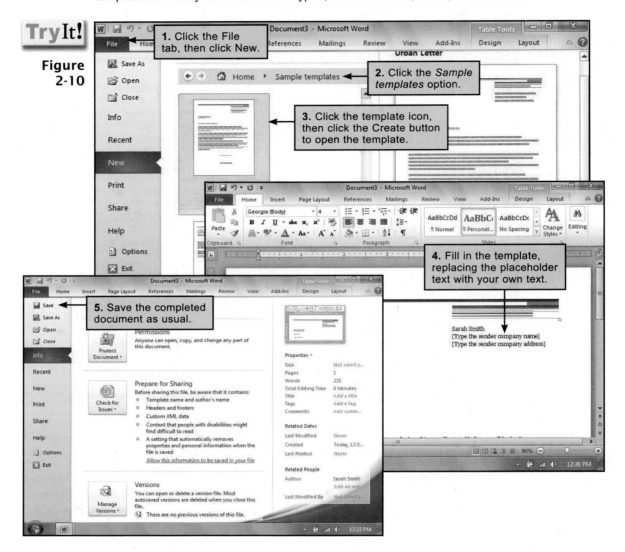

- A **placeholder** is an element in a document template into which you enter text that personalizes your document. Common placeholders provide entry areas for today's date, your name, or your fax number. To use a placeholder, click inside it and type your own text. The placeholder disappears and your text is displayed.

- Word allows you to create your own document templates. After you're more familiar with Word, you might want to explore this feature to create templates for documents that you create on a regular basis. You can find more information about creating templates in Word Help and in the program documentation.

- If you work in a large business or organization, you might be required to use templates created by managers, supervisors, or designers. Some examples of document templates used in businesses are letterheads, fax cover sheets, memos, and reports. Requiring these official templates helps businesses maintain professional standards.

FAQ How do I save a document?

After you have created a document from scratch or personalized a document template, it's important to save the document properly so that you can find and use it again. The first time you save your document, be sure to store it in the correct location with the appropriate file type.

Figure 2-11

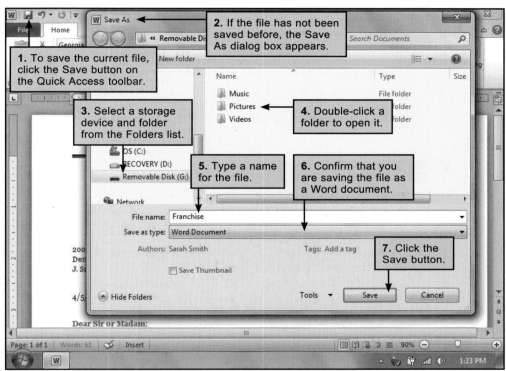

- The first time you save a document, the Save As dialog box appears. By default, Word saves your file in the My Documents folder as a Word document with a .docx extension. You can save the document in another location by selecting a different drive and folder.

- You can save your document as a different file type if you click the down-arrow button to the right of the *Save as type* text box. For instance, you might want to save the document in DOC format so it can be opened on a computer with an earlier version of Microsoft Office, such as Office 2003. You can also save a document in formats such as PDF, TXT, and RTF.

- After you save a document the first time, the next time you click the Save button, the document is automatically saved using the original file name and storage location. It's a good idea to save frequently as you work on a document to minimize the chance of losing data as a result of a power outage, software bug, or other unforeseen event.

FAQ How do I print a document?

You can print a document using the Print option available through the File tab. Before printing, you can select an alternative printer, or adjust settings to print multiple copies of a document, print selected pages, collate the printed pages, or select an alternate printer.

Figure 2-12

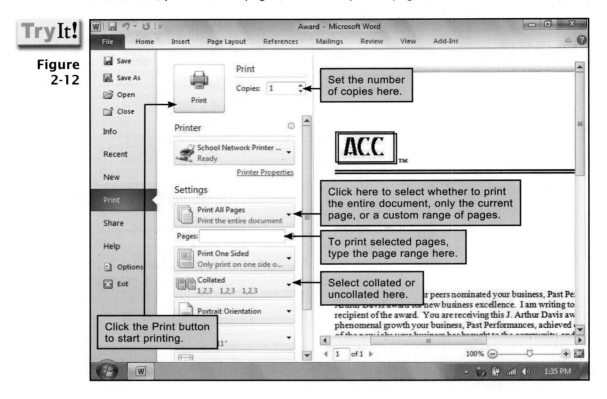

- You can select a printer by clicking the Printer button, then clicking the printer you want to use.

- To print a range of pages, enter the first page, a hyphen, then the last page in the range. For example, to print pages 13 through 28, you would enter "13–28." To print specific pages that are not in a sequence, enter the page numbers, such as "3, 7, 12," in the Pages text box, separated by commas.

- To print more than one copy of a document, use the Copies spin box.

- You can print on one side of the paper or set a duplex printer to print on both sides of the paper. You can simulate duplex printing using the *Manually Print on Both Sides* option and turning the paper when prompted to do so.

- When the Collated option is selected, each copy of a document prints in sequential page order so you don't have to collate it manually.

- In addition to providing print options, Word displays a preview showing how the printed document will look. The preview provides options for adjusting the magnification. If the print preview is acceptable, click the Print button to print the document. To return to the document without printing, click the Home tab.

FAQ How can I troubleshoot printing problems?

Suppose you try to print a document but nothing happens! Printing problems can be caused by the printer, by the software that controls the printer, or by installation glitches. Luckily, most printing problems are easily fixed. Your first step is to check the power light to make sure the printer is turned on. Also, verify that the printer is ready to print by pressing the appropriate buttons on the printer's control panel. You should also make sure the printer is loaded with the correct size and type of paper, and the ribbon, ink cartridge, or toner cartridge is properly installed.

If the printer checks out, your next step is to check the print queue. A **print queue** manages multiple documents waiting to be printed. When one document is printed, the next document in the print queue is sent to the printer. Each printer connected to your computer has a separate print queue. You can use a print queue to display information about each print job; to pause, restart, or cancel print jobs; and to move documents higher or lower in the queue. If your computer is connected to more than one printer, use the print queue to make sure you sent the document to the correct printer.

Figure 2-13

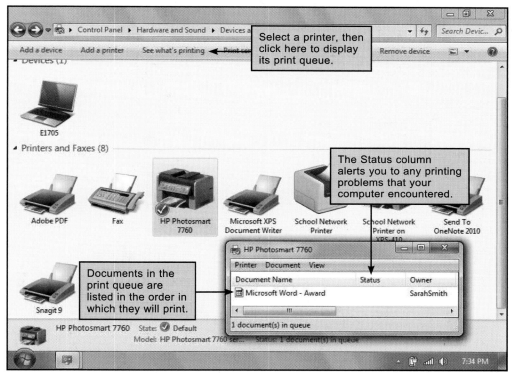

• You can view the print queue at any time by clicking the Start button, and then clicking *View devices and printers*. Select a printer, then click *See what's printing* on the toolbar to display the print queue you want to view.

• To pause, restart, or cancel a print job, click the name of the print job and choose the desired option from the Document menu.

• If the printer is shared, other people might have documents in the print queue ahead of yours. Check the print queue to see if your document is waiting to be printed.

• How can I troubleshoot printing problems? (continued)

If the Devices and Printers window contains icons for several printers, only one of those printers can be designated as the default printer. All documents are sent to the default printer unless you specify otherwise. A common printing problem occurs when you connect a different printer to your computer but forget to change the default printer. When a printing problem occurs, make sure the default printer setting is correct.

To change the default printer, click the Start button, and then click *View devices and printers*. Right-click the printer you want to set as the default printer, and choose *Set as default printer*.

The Printer Properties dialog box is another useful tool for troubleshooting printing problems. From the Devices and Printers window, right-click a printer and select Printer Properties. You can use this dialog box to change print settings, activate printer sharing, check the port used to connect your printer and computer, and even print out a test page. Printing a test page can help you determine if the printer is connected correctly.

Figure 2-14

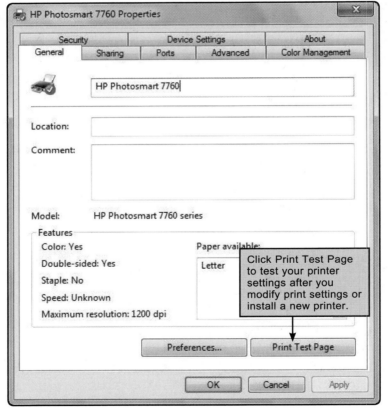

A document might not print if the page settings are not specified correctly in the Page Setup dialog box. Some printers cannot print outside of certain page boundaries, or are limited to certain page sizes. Check your printer documentation for details, and verify that the margins and page size are correct by clicking the Page Layout tab in Word, then clicking the Page Setup Dialog Box Launcher.

Another potential cause of printing problems is the printer driver software used by your computer to control the printer. If you can't find any other solution, check with your printer's manufacturer to see if an updated printer driver is available. Updated printer drivers are typically posted online and can be easily downloaded and installed.

QuickCheck A

1. True or false? In the document workspace, the insertion point is shaped like an I-bar.

[   ]

2. Press the [   ] key to delete the character to the right of the insertion point.

3. When you copy text, the selected text is copied from the original location and placed on the [   ] .

4. True or false? If you accidentally delete the wrong text, you can click the Redo button to cancel the deletion and display the original text. [   ]

5. A document [   ] allows you to create a new document from a preformatted document.

CheckIt!

QuickCheck B

Indicate the letter of the desktop element that best matches the following:

1. Selected text [   ]

2. The Copy button [   ]

3. The Paste button [   ]

4. The Cut button [   ]

5. The end of a line of text where the Enter key was pressed [   ]

CheckIt!

Skill Tests

A Creating a document

B Selecting text

C Moving, copying, pasting, and deleting text

D Using document templates

3 Formatting a Document

What's Inside and on the CD?

In this chapter, you'll learn how to format your documents using features such as bold and italic text, different fonts and font sizes, line spacing, and paragraph alignment. You'll also learn how to use tables, bullets, and numbered lists to organize and present information.

Experienced word processing software users find that it's useful to apply formatting after writing the document. The idea is to focus initially on the content of the document, while adding, deleting, and moving text as needed. After you're satisfied with the content and organization of the document, you can go back and format the document as needed.

Appropriate formatting can greatly increase the attractiveness and readability of your documents. However, it's important not to get carried away with formatting. Use different fonts, font sizes, and colors only where they add to the appearance or readability of the document. After all, you wouldn't want your documents to look like a ransom note pasted together with letters from a variety of newspaper stories!

● FAQs:

FAQ How do I select different fonts, font sizes, and text colors?

You can use the commands on the Home tab to select different text attributes for letters, words, sentences, or paragraphs. The term **font** refers to the design or typeface of each character. Don't use too many fonts—documents look more professional when limited to one or two basic fonts.

Figure 3-1

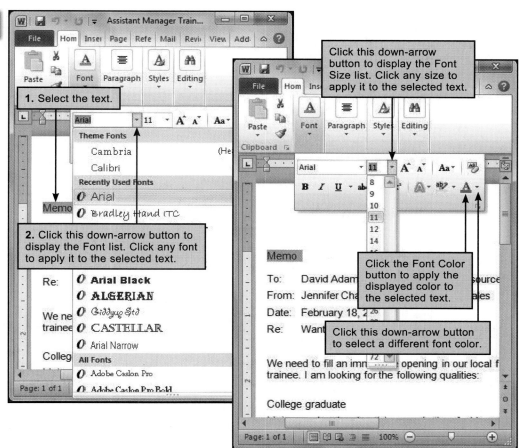

- **Text attributes** include font, font size, bold, italic, underline, and text color. Font size is normally 9–12 points, but you can select any font size up to 72 points, which is equal to one inch. You can make text even larger by typing in a number up to 1638. This feature is useful for making signs and posters.

- Once you've selected text, you can change the font, font size, and color without reselecting the text. As long as the text remains selected, you can apply additional formatting options to it. After you've formatted the text, click anywhere outside of the highlighted area to deselect it.

- **Font effects** include superscript, subscript, strikethrough, small caps, and all caps. To apply font effects, select the text, then click the Font Dialog Box Launcher in the Font group. Choose the effects you want to apply, and click OK.

- If you want to change the font or font size for an entire document, click Editing, Select, then Select All on the Home tab to select the entire document. Using Select All, you can apply any text attributes to all the text in a document, even to multiple pages.

FAQ How do I apply bold, italic, and underlining attributes?

You can use the commands in the Font group to apply text attributes such as bold, italic, and underlining to text within your document.

TryIt!

Figure 3-2

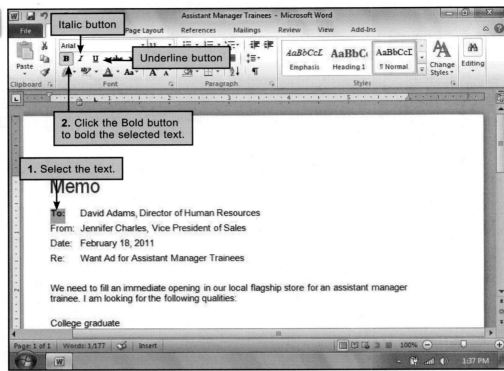

- Typically, you'll apply text attributes to text you've already typed. Just select the text, then use the desired command button in the Font group to apply the text attribute.

- You can apply the bold text attribute before typing new text. Click the Bold button, then type the text. Click the Bold button again to discontinue bold and continue typing normal text. You can use a similar procedure to enter italic or underlined text.

- Toolbar buttons both apply and remove text attributes. For instance, if you apply the bold attribute but then change your mind and want to display the text as normal, select the text and then click the Bold button again to remove the bold attribute.

- If you select a section of text that includes both normal and bold text, the first time you click the Bold button, all the selected text is displayed as bold. Click the Bold button again to display all of the selected text as normal text.

- Word automatically formats hyperlinks to Web pages such as www.facebook.com and displays them in underlined blue text. This is a special type of underlining; it is not controlled by the Underline command button. To change the format of a hyperlink, right-click it and select an option from the shortcut menu that appears.

- WordArt offers fancy font effects that you can use for the text on posters and elsewhere. To add WordArt effects to selected text, click WordArt on the Insert tab, select a style, specify a font size, and then apply any additional formatting using the Drawing Tools Format tab.

FAQ How do I use the Font dialog box?

As you've already learned, you can apply some text attributes—such as bold, italic, and underlining—using the Font group on the Home tab. But other text attribute options, such as character-spacing options, are only available from the Font dialog box.

You can also use the Font dialog box if you want to apply multiple formatting options to selected text. It's faster to use the Font dialog box to apply all the attributes in one operation than to apply the attributes one at a time using the command buttons.

Try It!

Figure 3-3

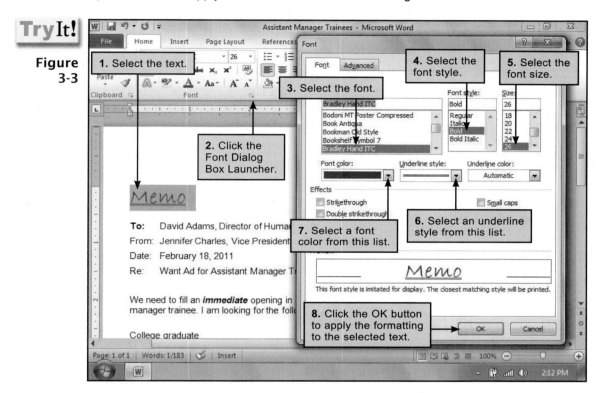

- Use the Advanced tab in the Font dialog box if you need to change the scale, spacing, vertical position, or kerning of selected text. Changing the **kerning**—the space between each letter—can be particularly useful when you need to make text fit into a limited space.

- The Preview area of the Font dialog box shows how your formatting affects the selected text. You'll see the selected font, font styles, colors, and effects before you click the OK button to accept your changes. If you don't like what you see in the Preview area, you can adjust the format settings or click the Cancel button to close the Font dialog box without applying the formatting options.

FAQ How do I center and align text?

The Paragraph group on the Home tab provides options for centering, right-aligning, left-aligning, and justifying text.

Left-aligned text is positioned straight against the left margin, but appears uneven, or "ragged," on the right margin. **Centered text** is positioned between the margins and is typically used for titles. **Justified text** has both left and right margins aligned. You might want to use justified text in the body of a formal document to give it a more professional look. **Right-aligned text** is rarely used, but can be useful for headings in a paper, for example, or for the return address in a letter.

Figure 3-4

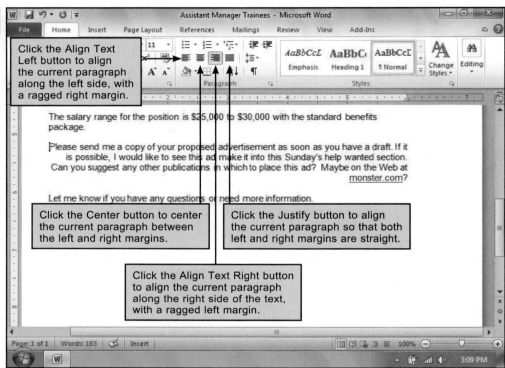

- Unlike bold, italic, and underlining, alignment options apply to an entire paragraph. You don't have to select the text to align it—just click in the paragraph you want to align, then click the appropriate alignment button.

- To center a title, press the Enter key at the end of the title so it becomes a separate paragraph. Click anywhere in the title, then click the Center button. Single lines, such as titles, are centered between the left and right margins. If the paragraph consists of multiple lines, every line in the paragraph is centered.

- To return a centered paragraph to left alignment, click in the paragraph, then click the Align Text Left button.

FAQ How do I use styles?

When formatting a document, select font and paragraph styles that fit the purpose of your document and the needs of the reader. A **style** consists of predefined formatting that you can apply to selected text. Word comes with several predefined styles. Using them will help you avoid design errors such as tight line spacing and ragged margins. Styles also allow you to be consistent in formatting text throughout a document.

In addition to predefined styles, you can create your own. If you find yourself regularly applying multiple format settings to sections of text, you can save time by defining your own style, then applying it as needed.

Figure 3-5

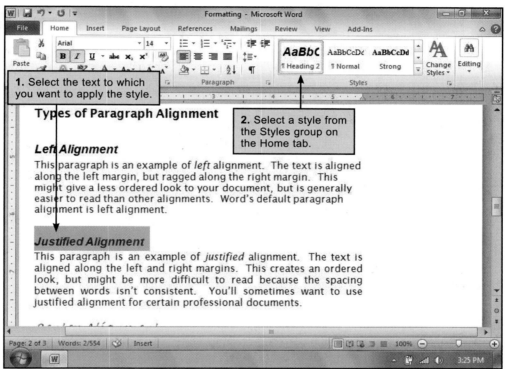

- To create a style, format a section of text using the desired font, font size, and font styles. Click the Styles Dialog Box Launcher to display the Styles dialog box. Click the New Style button to display the *Create New Style from Formatting* dialog box. Click the Name text box, then type the name for your new style. Click the OK button to close the *Create New Style from Formatting* dialog box. Click the Close button to close the Styles dialog box. Your new style is added to the Styles list. To apply the style to other text, select the text, then select your style from the Styles list.

- To remove a style from a section of text, select the text, then select the Normal style from the Styles list.

- To delete a style so that it no longer appears in the Styles list, click the Styles Dialog Box Launcher to display the Styles dialog box. Right-click the style you want to delete, then select Delete. Click Yes, then click the Close button to close the Styles dialog box.

FAQ How do I add numbering and bullets to a list?

Word's Paragraph group on the Home tab contains buttons to format a list with bullets or numbers. A **bullet** is a symbol placed before each item in a list. You can use bullets when you want to set off the items in a list but don't want to imply a specific order. A numbered list is a list with a number in front of each item on the list, which implies the items are listed in order.

Figure 3-6

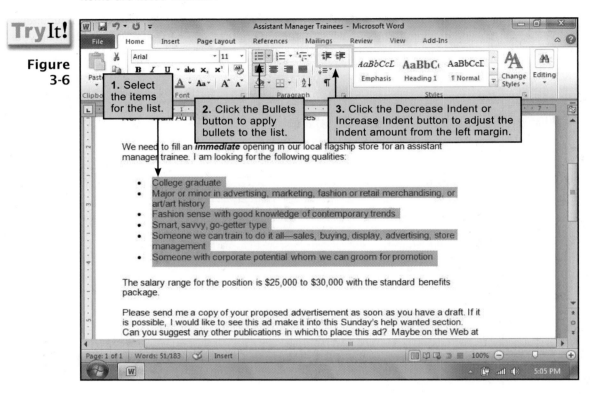

- Numbered lists work the same as bulleted lists. Select the items on the list, then click the 📋 Numbering button to add numbers to the list.

- If you haven't typed the list yet, click the Numbering or Bullets button, then type the items on the list. Each time you press the Enter key, a new number or bullet is inserted before the next list item. At the end of the list, press the Enter key and click the Numbering or Bullets button to discontinue the numbering for the next line of text.

- To remove numbering or bullets from a list, select the list, then click the Numbering or Bullets button.

- If you add, delete, or move the items in a numbered list, Word renumbers the list for you. If the numbering is incorrect, select the list, then click the Numbering button twice. This procedure removes and then reapplies the numbering, which usually corrects any problem with the numbers in the list.

- To change the numbered or bulleted list style, select the list, then right-click the list to display the shortcut menu. Point to Bullets or Numbering, then select a format.

• How do I add numbering and bullets to a list? (continued)

A multilevel list displays list items in levels and sublevels. Common uses for multilevel lists include topic outlines and legal documents. Multilevel lists can be numbered, lettered, or bulleted using a variety of predefined or customized styles.

Although you can apply bullets or numbering to a multilevel list after entering the list, the more typical procedure is to activate the Multilevel List button before you enter the list items.

Figure 3-7

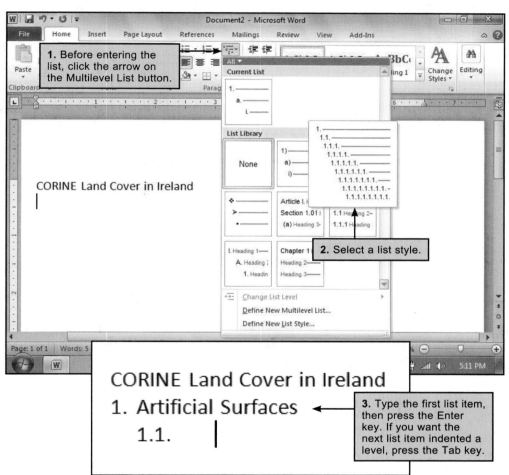

• Pressing the Enter key as you type a list automatically displays the next list number, letter, or bullet.

• Press the Tab key to change a list item to the next level down. Use Shift+Tab to move a list item up a level.

• You can define custom styles for the text, numbers, and bullets in a list by clicking the arrow next to the Multilevel List button, then selecting Define New List Style. This option is especially handy for creating a list format that you want to reuse for multiple documents.

• When entering a list, you can change a number manually by right-clicking the number and selecting Set Numbering Value from the shortcut menu. The shortcut menu contains options for starting a new list and continuing the numbering from a previous list.

FAQ How do I adjust line spacing?

Your Word document is single-spaced unless you specify another spacing option, such as double- or triple-spacing. You can apply line-spacing options to a single paragraph, to a group of paragraphs, or to the entire document. You can also adjust the space between paragraphs. Single-spacing is appropriate for letters and memos, whereas double-spacing is often used for first drafts of manuscripts and reports.

Figure 3-8

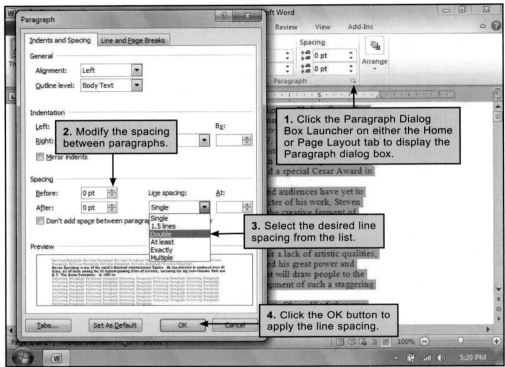

- Do not press the Enter key at the end of each line to create double-spaced text. This makes it difficult to edit your document because words won't wrap from one line to the next. The preferred way to double-space a document is to type the document as regular single-spaced text, then set the line spacing to double.

- To adjust the line spacing for one paragraph of text, position the insertion point in the paragraph, then click the Paragraph Dialog Box Launcher on the Home or Page Layout tab. Select the desired spacing from the *Line spacing* drop-down list on the *Indents and Spacing* tab. Single- and double-spacing are the most commonly used spacing settings.

- To adjust the line spacing for more than one paragraph, select the paragraphs, then adjust the line spacing as described above.

- To adjust the space between paragraphs, click the Paragraph Dialog Box Launcher on the Home or Page Layout tab. Select the desired paragraph spacing from the Before and After boxes on the *Indents and Spacing* tab.

- You can set the line spacing for the entire document before you begin typing. Click Editing, Select, then Select All on the Home tab. Click the Paragraph Dialog Box Launcher on the Home or Page Layout tab. Select the desired line spacing, then click the OK button. As you type, the text appears on the screen with the selected line spacing.

FAQ How do I use tabs?

Setting a **tab** provides an easy way to align text in columns. Word provides default tab stops at 0.5" intervals, but you can change the default tab settings and add your own tab stops. The position of a tab stop is measured from the left margin.

**Figure
3-9**

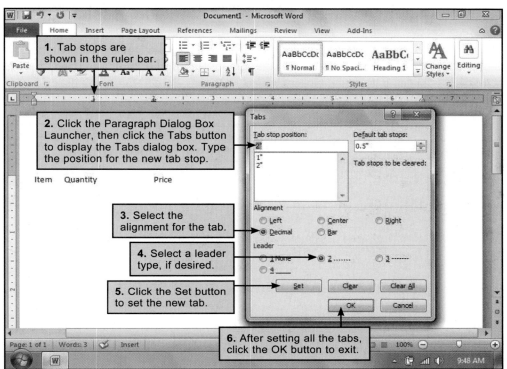

- There are many types of tab stops. A left tab stop means that text will be aligned on the left side of the tab. A right tab stop means that text will be aligned on the right side of the tab. A center tab stop centers text at that location, while a decimal tab stop aligns numbers with the decimal at the tab location. A bar tab stop places a vertical bar at the tab location.

- A **leader** is a line of punctuation characters, such as periods, that fills the area between text and a tab stop. Leaders are typically used in a table of contents to associate a page number with a chapter title or heading. To add a leader to a tab stop, click the option button to select the leader type. When you tab to that tab stop, the leader character—usually a series of periods—fills the area to the tab stop.

- To clear one tab stop, click that tab stop in the *Tab stop position* box, then click the Clear button. To clear all tab stops, click the Clear All button in the Tabs dialog box.

- On the Word ruler bar, tab stops are represented by these small icons:

L	Left tab	⊥	Center tab	I	Bar tab
⌐	Right tab	⊥	Decimal tab		

- To set tabs using the ruler, select the type of tab stop by clicking the icon at the left end of the ruler. Click a location on the ruler to set the tab stop. You can move a tab stop by selecting it, then sliding it right or left on the ruler bar.

- If the ruler bar is not displayed, click the View tab and then select the Ruler option in the Show group.

FAQ How do I indent text?

You can indent text from the left margin, from the right margin, or from both margins. You can also indent the first line of text differently from the rest of a paragraph. For example, you can indent the first line of a paragraph farther to the right than the rest of the paragraph. This **first-line indent** style is commonly used for college papers and manuscripts.

In contrast, the hanging indent style positions the first line of a paragraph farther to the left than the rest of the paragraph. **Hanging indents** are used for numbered lists, bulleted lists, and bibliographical citations. Word's Paragraph dialog box provides several options for indenting text.

Figure 3-10

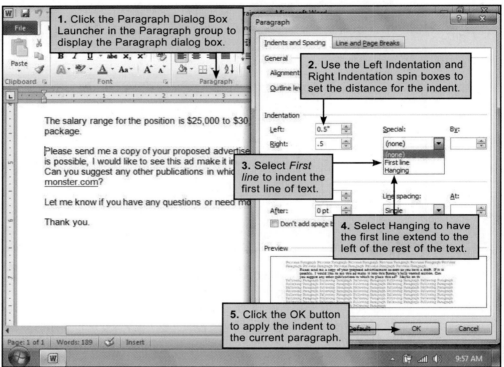

- To indent an entire paragraph from the left, click the spin box buttons in the Left Indentation box to increase or decrease the indent distance. Use the same process with the Right Indentation box to increase or decrease the right indentation.

- The Preview section shows how the paragraph will look after it is indented. As you change your selections, the Preview is updated.

- To indent the first line of text, select *First line* from the Special pull-down list. Select the amount of indentation for the first line of the paragraph from the By spin box.

- To create a hanging indent in which the first line of text extends more to the left than the rest of the text, select Hanging from the Special pull-down list. Select the amount of negative indent for the first line of the paragraph from the By spin box.

- Indent settings apply to the paragraph that contains the insertion point. To apply an indent to more than one paragraph, select the paragraphs, then use the Paragraph dialog box to set the indent.

FAQ How do I add footnotes or endnotes to a document?

Footnotes and endnotes are typically used to add comments to blocks of text or cite references to other documents. An asterisk or a superscript number appearing in the main text of a document indicates a footnote or an endnote. A **footnote** appears at the bottom of the page that contains the corresponding superscript number. An **endnote** appears at the end of a section or chapter.

Figure 3-11

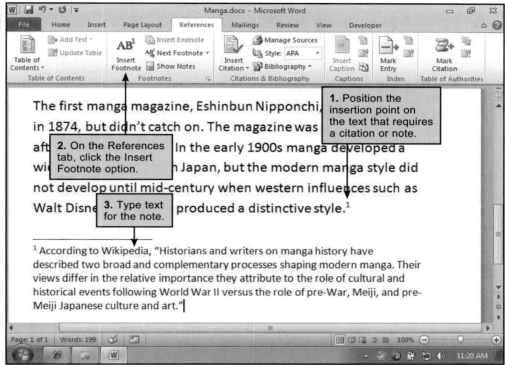

- To insert a footnote or an endnote, position the insertion point in the paragraph that contains the text needing a citation or comment. Click the References tab. Click the Insert Footnote or Insert Endnote button. A text area appears on the bottom of your screen that allows you to type the note text.

- To modify the format of a footnote or endnote, open the *Footnote and Endnote* dialog box by clicking the Footnote Dialog Box Launcher.

- To delete a footnote or an endnote, select the superscript number that corresponds to the note in the text, and press the Delete key.

- The Reference tab contains several tools for adding citations to a document. You can select a citation style, such as APA or MLA, and Word will automatically add the required formatting and punctuation to book titles and other materials you cite. Word can even produce a bibliography based on all the citations in a document.

FAQ How do I work with outlines and other document views?

Word provides several ways to view a document. You can display **format marks** to reveal hidden symbols that indicate paragraph breaks ¶, spaces ·, and tab stops →. To display hidden formatting marks, click the [¶] Show/Hide button in the Paragraph group on the Home tab.

You can also change the document view to see how it will look when printed (Print Layout view), as a Web page (Web Layout view), or as an outline (Outline view). To change the document view, click one of the view buttons in the status bar. You can also change the view by clicking the View tab, then clicking one of the views listed.

Outline view is handy for organizing the content of a document. You can assign outline levels to each title, heading, and paragraph, and view any level of the outline to get an overview or include all details. In Outline view, it is easy to rearrange sections of a document to streamline its organization. Outline view is best used to work on the structure of a document, but it is not meant to be used when you want to create a document that displays paragraph numbers or outline levels. For tools to create multilevel outlines, refer to the FAQ about bulleted and numbered lists.

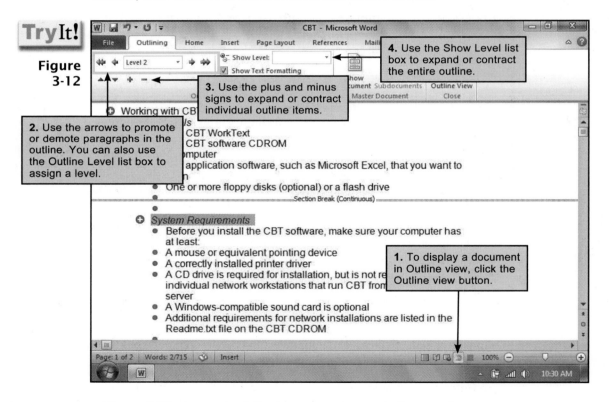

Figure 3-12

- Microsoft Word uses the following conventions to indicate outline levels:

  A plus sign ⊕ indicates a heading with subtext.

  A small solid circle ● indicates body text at the lowest level of the outline.

  A gray line under a heading indicates subordinate text that is not displayed.

  A dash ⊖ indicates a heading without subordinate text.

FAQ How do I create a table?

A **table** is a grid consisting of rows and columns. The intersection of each row and column is called a cell. Each cell can hold text, numbers, or a graphic. You can format an entire table or individual cells.

Figure 3-13

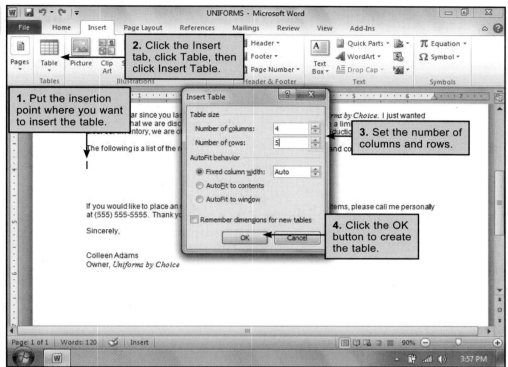

- To add text to a table, click any cell, then type text in that cell. The word wrap feature moves text down while you type and expands the size of the cell to make room for all of your text. To move to another cell, press the arrow keys, press the Tab key, or click the desired cell.

- To quickly format a table, make sure the insertion point is in the table, then click the Design tab. Select a table style from the Table Styles group. You can then modify the format to change the font or other table attributes.

- To insert a new row or column, place the insertion point in the cell closest to where you want the new row or column to appear. Click the Layout tab, then choose from among the options to specify the placement of the new row or column from the Rows & Columns group.

- To delete unused rows or columns, position the insertion point in the column or row you want to delete. Click the Layout tab, then click the Delete command in the Rows & Columns group. Select from among the options to specify what you want to delete.

- To adjust the width of a column, position the pointer over the dividing line between the columns. When the pointer changes to a ⁺‖⁺ shape, press the left mouse button and drag the column to the correct width.

- You can convert normal text into table text using the Table button on the Insert tab. When converting text into a table, use commas to separate the text for columns and use paragraph marks (Enter key) to separate the text that will become each row.

FAQ Can I format a document into columns?

There are three ways to format text into columns: tabs, tables, and columns. Tabs are most effectively used when you want to enter a single line of parallel text in each column. Tabs work well for short, multi-column lists:

Address	List Price	Days on Market
12 Main St.	$349,000	38
322 North Rd.	$149,500	36

Tables are effective when you want to enter parallel text, but some text requires multiple lines. A typical use of table-style columns is the text layout of a resume:

Work History	2008-present: Marketing & Graphics Assistant, Smith & Co., San Francisco: Created designs for consumer packaging using Adobe Illustrator and four-color processing; prepared designs for photo shoots
Education	M.F.A. Graphic Design & Marketing, 2010 San Francisco Art Institute, San Francisco, CA B.F.A. Marketing 2006 Emory University, Atlanta, GA

The third option, sometimes referred to as newspaper columns or newsletter columns, fills the left column entirely with text and then continues into the right column as shown below. Use newspaper-style columns when you want to format full paragraphs of text into columns.

Figure 3-14

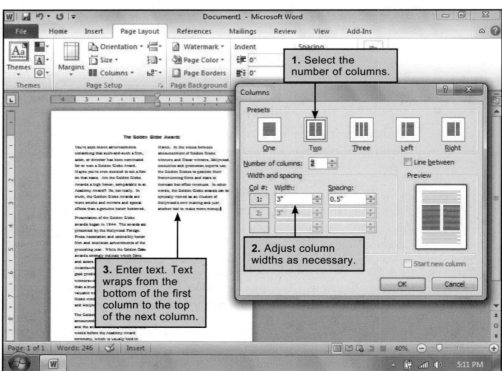

- If you want to jump to the next column before reaching the end, Ctrl Shift Enter inserts a column break into the text.

QuickCheck A

1. True or false? To create an active hyperlink in a document, select one or more words, click the Underline button, and then change the font color to blue. [＿＿＿＿]

2. Centering and alignment formats apply to an entire [＿＿＿＿＿＿＿] of text.

3. You should use the [＿＿＿＿＿＿＿] dialog box to apply multiple formatting options to text in a single operation.

4. A(n) [＿＿＿＿] is a symbol, such as a square or circle, placed before an item in a list.

5. True or false? To double-space a document, you should press the Enter key two times at the end of every line of text. [＿＿＿＿]

Check It!

QuickCheck B

Indicate the letter of the desktop element that best matches the following:

1. Underline a single word [＿＿＿]

2. Change the font size [＿＿＿]

3. Center a title [＿＿＿]

4. Create a bulleted list [＿＿＿]

5. Select a style [＿＿＿]

The salary range for the position is $25,000 to $30,000 with the standard benefits package.

Please send me a copy of your proposed advertisement as soon as you have a draft. If it is possible, I would like to see this ad make it into this Sunday's help wanted section. Can you suggest any other publications in which to place this ad? Maybe on the Web at monster.com?

Let me know if you have any questions or need more information.

Thank you.

Check It!

Skill Tests

A Using text attributes and fonts

B Centering and aligning text

C Creating lists and setting line spacing

D Setting tabs and indenting text

CHAPTER **4** # Finalizing a Document

What's Inside and on the CD?

Writing a document is only half the battle. Once the first draft is done, you'll typically want to check spelling and grammar, apply some formatting, and maybe even change a few words here and there. In this chapter, you'll learn how to add the finishing touches to prepare your document for printing or posting as a Web page.

Important features covered in this chapter include adding headers and footers, setting margins, and incorporating graphics. You'll learn how to save your document in HTML format so it can be posted as a Web page. Also, you'll find out how adding comments and tracking changes make it easy for multiple people to collaborate on a single document.

FAQ How do I create headers and footers?

A **header** is text that appears at the top of every page of a document. A **footer** is text that appears at the bottom of every page. Headers and footers typically contain information such as the title of the document, the date, the name of the author, and the current page number. Headers and footers are useful for keeping printed documents intact, for example, when a document is dropped or a part of it is misfiled.

Try It!

Figure 4-1

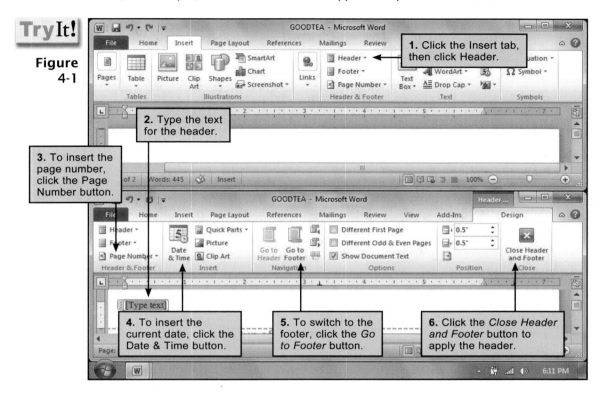

1. Click the Insert tab, then click Header.

2. Type the text for the header.

3. To insert the page number, click the Page Number button.

4. To insert the current date, click the Date & Time button.

5. To switch to the footer, click the *Go to Footer* button.

6. Click the *Close Header and Footer* button to apply the header.

- Headers and footers are displayed only in Print Layout view, in a print preview, and on printed pages.

- The header and footer have preset tabs—a center tab in the middle of the page, and a right tab near the right margin. Press the Tab key to move the insertion point to the next tab to enter text at that location.

- If you want to include text such as "Page 6" in your header or footer, click the Page Number button in the Header & Footer group, then select the desired format. Page numbers are automatically updated when page content changes during editing.

- To insert the current date and time, click the Date & Time button in the Insert group, select the desired format from the *Date and Time* dialog box, then click OK. The date and time are automatically updated each time you open the document.

- Click the *Go to Header* or *Go to Footer* button to switch between the header and footer. You can edit the header or the footer, but not both at the same time.

- You can change the font and style of page numbers just as you would change any text by using the formatting options on the Home tab.

FAQ How do I insert page breaks and section breaks?

A **page break** occurs within a document where one page ends and the next page begins. When a page is filled with text or graphics, Word automatically inserts a page break. You can also insert a manual, or "forced," page break at any point in the document. In Draft view, page breaks are shown as a horizontal dotted line. In Print Layout view, page breaks are displayed as the end of a sheet, or page, within the document.

A **section break**, displayed as a double dotted line in Draft view, divides a document into sections. You can apply different formatting to each section of a document. For example, you might define the title page of a term paper as a section, and format it as a single column with no headers. You could then define the body of the document as a separate section formatted with two columns and headers that contain page numbers.

Try It!

Figure 4-2

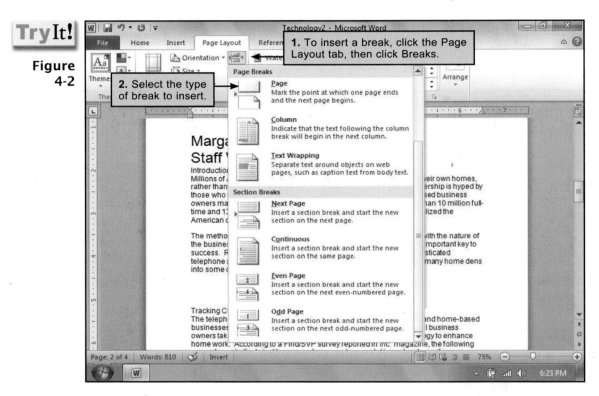

- Use sections when parts of a document require different page-based format settings for margins, borders, vertical alignment, columns, headers and footers, footnotes and endnotes, page numbering, and line numbers. Paragraph and text-based formatting options—such as line spacing, font, size, and bullets—are typically applied to selected text, rather than to sections.

- To insert a break, click the Page Layout tab, then click Breaks to open the Break dialog box. Select the type of break you want, then click OK. You can also insert a page break with the Page Break button in the Pages group on the Insert tab or by using the keyboard shortcut Ctrl Enter.

FAQ Can I insert photos into a document?

You can use two types of graphics to enhance documents created with Microsoft Word: vector graphics and bitmap graphics. Both types of graphics can be used to add pizzazz to a page, draw interest to certain text selections, or illustrate important points. Don't overuse pictures, however. Too many can cause a page to look cluttered and confusing.

A **bitmap graphic**, referred to in Word as a picture, is composed of a grid of colored dots. Digital photos and scanned images are typically stored as bitmap graphics with extensions such as .bmp, .png, .jpg, .tif, or .gif. Word does not provide a feature to create bitmap graphics, but you can insert photos and other bitmaps stored in files on your computer. Word provides a Picture Tools contextual tab to help you adjust the color, contrast, and brightness of inserted bitmap graphics. You can also use this tab to crop or rotate a picture.

Figure 4-3

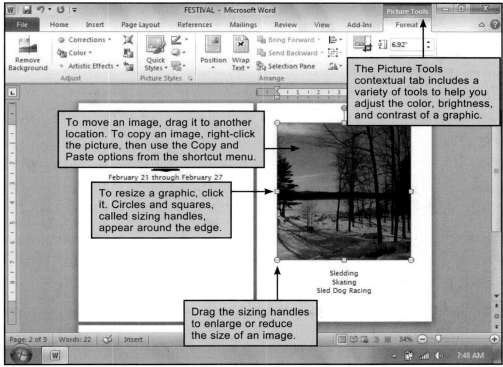

- To insert a bitmap graphic into a document, click the Insert tab, then click Picture from the Illustrations group. Use the Open dialog box to navigate to the folder that contains the picture you want to insert, and then click Insert.

- To crop a picture, select the picture, click the Crop button from the Size group, drag the edges of the picture to frame the part of the image you want to display, then click the Crop button again to finalize the crop.

- Adjust the brightness, contrast, and color of a picture by selecting the graphic and then clicking the Corrections button in the Adjust group.

- You can control the way text flows around a picture in a document. To wrap text around a picture, select the picture. From the Arrange group, click the Wrap Text button, and then select a text flow option from the list.

- To delete a picture, click it, and then press the Delete key.

FAQ Can I insert line art into a document?

A **vector graphic**, sometimes called a drawing, is created with basic shapes, such as lines, curves, and rectangles. Clip art, logos, and organizational charts are often created using vector graphics, and have extensions such as .wmf and .ai. Microsoft Office includes a clip art collection you can access by clicking the Insert tab, then clicking Clip Art in the Illustrations group.

You can use the Shapes tool to create your own simple vector graphics within a document. You can also use it to enhance vector graphics you've obtained from other sources and inserted into a document.

You can create vector drawings by combining several shapes within a rectangular area called a canvas. To open a blank canvas, click the Insert tab, click the Shapes button in the Illustrations group, then click New Drawing Canvas. When the canvas is selected, you can use the Insert Shapes group on the Drawing Tools contextual tab to add shapes to the canvas.

Try It!

Figure 4-4

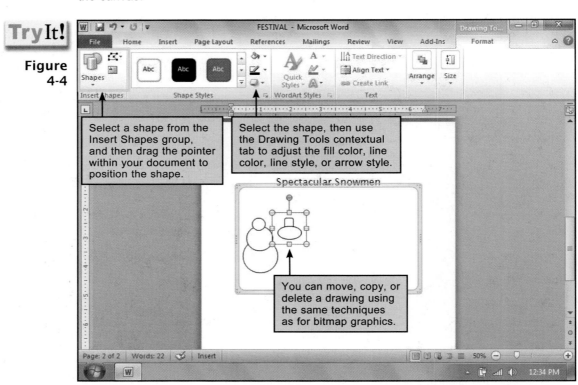

Select a shape from the Insert Shapes group, and then drag the pointer within your document to position the shape.

Select the shape, then use the Drawing Tools contextual tab to adjust the fill color, line color, line style, or arrow style.

You can move, copy, or delete a drawing using the same techniques as for bitmap graphics.

- Multiple shapes can be grouped together so that they can be moved and resized as a single unit. To group objects, hold down the Ctrl key and select the shapes you want to group. Right-click the shapes, point to Group, and then click Group. Shapes can be ungrouped using a similar procedure, but clicking Ungroup instead of Group.

- You can use layers to make shapes appear to be stacked on top of one another or to appear in front of or behind text. To move a shape from one layer to another, right-click the shape, and then click *Bring to Front* or *Send to Back*. Choose an order from the list.

- To control the way text flows around a vector graphic, click Wrap Text from the Arrange group, and then select an option from the list.

FAQ How do I set margins?

Margin settings typically apply to an entire document and are changed using the Page Setup group on the Page Layout tab.

In a Word document, the default margins are 1". Margin settings affect the amount of text that fits on a page. Small margins leave more room on a page for text than large margins.

Try It!

Figure 4-5

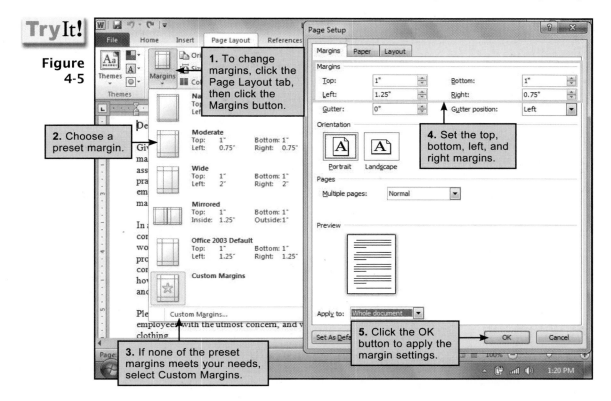

- Don't set the top and bottom margins too small if you're using headers and footers. Headers and footers do not print correctly if there isn't enough room in the top and bottom margins.

- Select Portrait orientation to print the page vertically. If you have a wide document, select Landscape orientation to print the page sideways.

- You can use the Paper tab in the Page Setup dialog box to set the paper size and control how paper feeds into your default printer. Select the appropriate paper size from the *Paper size* list. You can find more information about printing options in the printer documentation.

- The Layout tab in the Page Setup dialog box is useful for creating different headers and footers on odd and even pages. Other layout options allow you to center text vertically on the page, insert line numbers, and add graphical elements, such as borders, to the document.

- Margin settings and other page formatting options can apply to the whole document, to selected sections of the document, or to the rest of the document that follows the current location of the insertion point. You can find more information about page setup options in Word Help.

FAQ How do I perform a mail merge?

A **mail merge** allows you to create multiple documents from a starting document and a data source. The starting document can be a letter, a label template, or an envelope template. The starting document usually contains a form letter that you want to be the same for all of the document recipients. The recipient list contains the information that will be merged into the starting document. After the information is merged, the final documents can be printed or saved for future use.

Figure 4-6

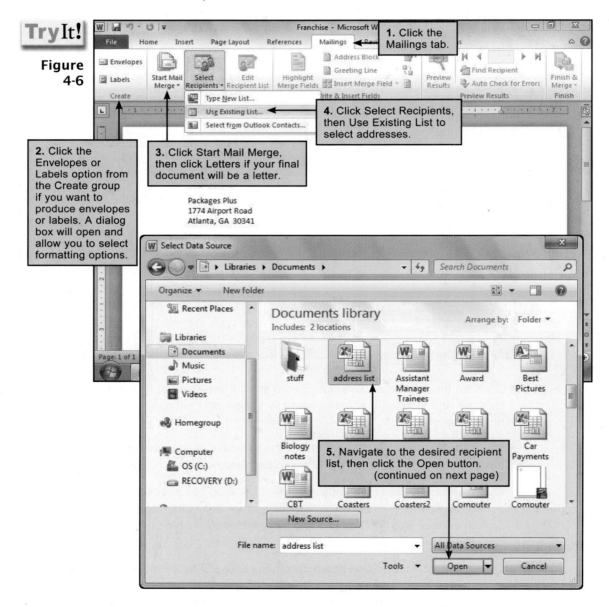

• You can compose your starting document from scratch or from a document template.

• The recipient list can come from a database file, Outlook, an Excel spreadsheet, or a Word document.

• How do I perform a mail merge? (continued)

Recipient lists contain data such as names or addresses. Each item in a recipient list is considered a field. The data from a field can be inserted into a document during a merge. The location where data is to be inserted is specified by a merge field or merge block. A **merge field**, such as <<FirstName>>, contains one item of data. A **merge block**, such as <<AddressBlock>>, can contain multiple lines of data.

Merge fields are enclosed in angle brackets to show that they will not be printed in the final document. Instead, the data represented by the merge field, such as a person's first name, is inserted and printed during the merge.

**Figure
4-7**

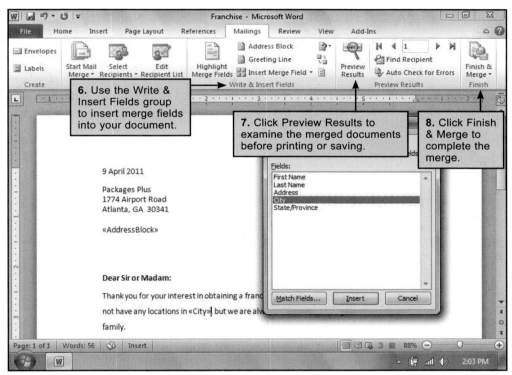

• You can insert preformatted merge field blocks or individual merge fields from the Write & Insert Fields group. Use the Match Fields button if there are any discrepancies with field names.

• Preview your final documents to make sure they are exactly what you want before saving or printing them.

FAQ How do I save a document as a Web page?

Instead of printing a document, you might want to post it on the Internet as a Web page. As with other Web pages, your document must be in HTML (Hypertext Markup Language) format to be accessible to Web browsers, such as Internet Explorer or Mozilla Firefox. You can use the Save As option accessed from the File tab to save a document in HTML format.

TryIt!

Figure 4-8

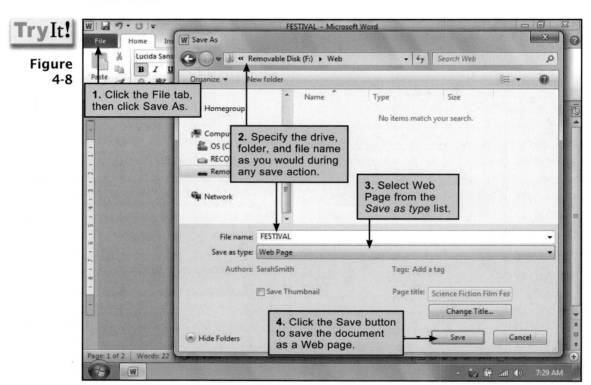

1. Click the File tab, then click Save As.

2. Specify the drive, folder, and file name as you would during any save action.

3. Select Web Page from the *Save as type* list.

4. Click the Save button to save the document as a Web page.

- Word does a fairly good job of converting a document to HTML, but several formatting options available in Word cannot be duplicated in HTML documents. If a document contains formatting that cannot be duplicated in HTML, Word displays a message during the conversion process that describes the problem areas. You then have the option of canceling or continuing with the save.

- To see how the document will look when viewed in a Web browser, locate the file with Windows Explorer, then double-click the file to open it in a Web browser.

- Documents saved as Web pages are displayed as a single long page—sort of like a papyrus scroll—even though the original Word document consisted of multiple pages. When viewing a long document in a Web browser, you can use the vertical scroll bar to move through the document.

- Contact your Internet service provider (ISP) or technical support person if you need instructions for posting your Web pages on the Internet.

FAQ How do I convert a document into a PDF?

PDF (Portable Document Format) was created by Adobe Systems and has become a universal standard for exchanging documents, spreadsheets, and other types of data files. Converting a file into a PDF ensures that when the file is viewed or printed, it retains the original layout. PDF is sometimes referred to as a fixed-layout format because once a document has been converted to a PDF, it cannot be edited.

Software for viewing PDFs is free and therefore most computers have the ability to display PDF files. You can convert Word documents into PDF files if you want to distribute them but you're not sure if the recipients have Microsoft Word.

To convert a document into a PDF file, make sure you save it first as a normal Word document. Then use the Save As command and select PDF from the *Save as type* list.

Figure 4-9

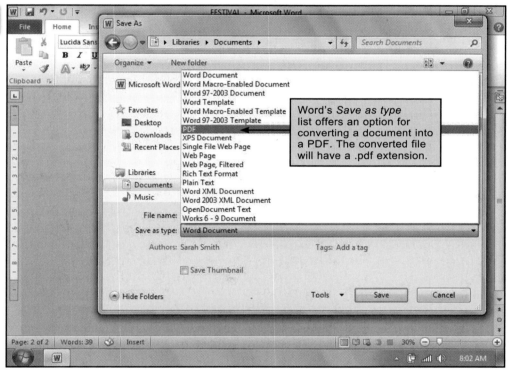

Word's *Save as type* list offers an option for converting a document into a PDF. The converted file will have a .pdf extension.

- Software for creating PDFs can be obtained in a number of ways. It is included with the Mac OS X operating system, OpenOffice, and Microsoft Office. You can download the free Adobe Reader from the Adobe Web site. Free PDF software usually allows you to create, read, and print PDF files.

- Some PDF software offers additional features. For the fullest feature set, Adobe offers Adobe Acrobat Pro. In addition to creating, viewing, and printing, Acrobat Pro allows you to annotate a PDF by inserting text, making line-out deletions, highlighting passages, and adding comments.

- **XPS** (XML Paper Specification) is a file format similar to PDF but created by Microsoft. XPS does not have the widespread popularity of PDF.

FAQ How do I work with electronic documents?

Whereas word processors were once used primarily to prepare documents for printing, today many documents remain in electronic formats that are transmitted by e-mail, sent directly to a fax machine, shared on an FTP site, or posted as Web pages and blogs.

Word has several built-in features that help you work with electronic documents. For example, the File tab's Share option can be used to attach a document to an e-mail message or send it over an Internet fax service. The *Publish as Blog Post* option is useful for creating blogs. Word even includes fax templates so you can easily create a fax cover sheet.

Figure 4-10

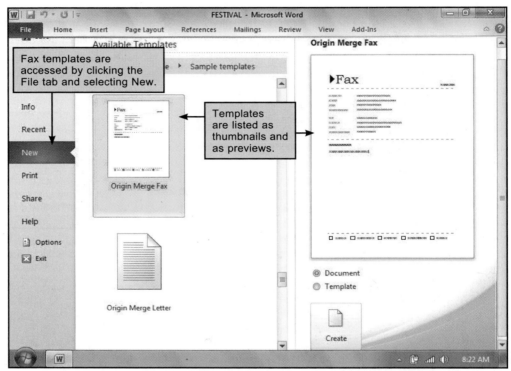

The way you plan to use a document affects the way you handle it. For most applications, you'll typically first save your document normally as a Word DOCX file. The table below contains recommendations for handling electronic documents.

E-mail attachment	Send DOCX files if you are certain the recipient has Word 2007 or 2010; otherwise, convert to DOC or PDF files. Large files might need to be zipped.
Web page	Save in HTM or HTML format. If your Web page includes graphics or links to other pages, make sure they are posted along with the document containing the primary content.
Blog	Save as a DOCX file if you are using Word's blog publishing feature.
Fax	Send any type of file that is accepted by the fax service.
FTP	Post DOCX files on the FTP site if you are certain the recipient has Word 2007 or 2010; otherwise, convert to PDF. Large files will transmit faster if they are zipped.

•How do I work with electronic documents? (continued)

When working with electronic documents, remain alert to avoid the following problems:

* **Loss of information or formatting.** When files are converted from one file type to another, some aspects of the original document might be lost. In an earlier FAQ, you learned that a Word document converted into HTML loses its pagination when all the text is incorporated into a single long Web page. Other formatting that might be lost or garbled during conversion includes columns, tabs, highlighting, comments, and graphic placement. After converting a document into a different file type, compare the two versions for significant differences.

* **Necessary software not installed.** Before e-mailing or posting a file, consider the software that's needed to view it. Not everyone has Office 2007 or 2010, so DOCX is not a universal format. PDF is more universal and might be a better choice, especially if you're not certain of the software installed on your recipient's computer.

* **Missing linked data.** Word documents and e-mail messages can contain hyperlinks to Web sites, spreadsheets can be linked to document files, and Web pages can include links to graphics and other Web pages. When e-mailing or posting documents that incorporate links, be sure to also post all the data files referenced by the links.

* **Blocked file types.** Most computers are protected against viruses and other exploits, but the protective software and hardware can inadvertently block innocent files, too. E-mail attachments with extensions such as .scr, .bat, .hlp, and .exe are especially vulnerable to being blocked, but .doc and .docx files are sometimes blocked, too. To make sure your files haven't been blocked, ask for confirmation of their arrival. Compressed files with .zip extensions tend not to get blocked, so you might consider zipping documents and other files before you send them.

* **Large files.** File size and connection speed affect upload and download times when transferring electronic documents over the Internet. You can shrink the size of a file using a process called compression or zipping.

Figure 4-11

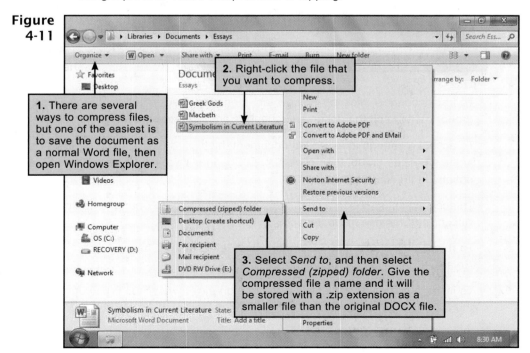

1. There are several ways to compress files, but one of the easiest is to save the document as a normal Word file, then open Windows Explorer.

2. Right-click the file that you want to compress.

3. Select *Send to*, and then select *Compressed (zipped) folder*. Give the compressed file a name and it will be stored with a .zip extension as a smaller file than the original DOCX file.

FAQ Can I track changes and insert comments in a document?

As a document is revised, you might want to maintain a record of the original wording. This capability is especially important in the development of legal documents and when multiple people collaborate on a single document. Microsoft Word provides several features for such situations.

The **Track Changes** feature maintains all deleted, changed, and inserted text for a document and displays it in a contrasting font color. You can hide or display these changes and integrate them in the document by accepting them. Word's Comment feature allows you to insert the electronic version of "sticky notes" in your document. Comments are displayed as balloons in the margins and can be displayed or hidden as needed.

Figure 4-12

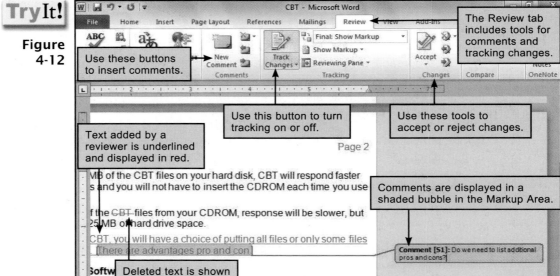

- To track changes, click the Review tab, then click Track Changes in the Tracking group. As you edit the document, changes are indicated in a contrasting font color.

- To accept a change in an edited document, highlight the changed text, click Accept in the Changes group, then click Accept Change. To reject a change, use the Reject options in the Changes group.

- To accept all changes in a document, click Accept in the Changes group, then click *Accept All Changes in Document.*

- To reject all changes in a document, click Reject in the Changes group, then click *Reject All Changes in Document.*

- To insert a comment, click New Comment on the Review tab. Type your comment in the comment bubble displayed in the Markup Area.

FAQ Is there a way to protect documents from unauthorized access?

You can protect your documents from unauthorized access in several ways. One option is to encrypt the document so that it can be opened only when a valid password is entered.

Figure 4-13

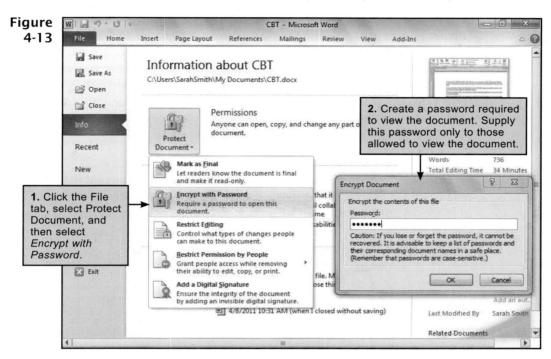

1. Click the File tab, select Protect Document, and then select *Encrypt with Password*.

2. Create a password required to view the document. Supply this password only to those allowed to view the document.

Another way to protect your documents is to allow anyone to open a document, but restrict the types of edits that can be made. You can set up these restrictions using Word's Protect group.

TryIt!

Figure 4-14

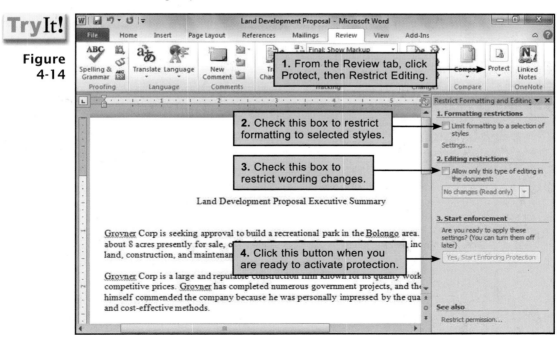

1. From the Review tab, click Protect, then Restrict Editing.

2. Check this box to restrict formatting to selected styles.

3. Check this box to restrict wording changes.

4. Click this button when you are ready to activate protection.

- If you would like to deactivate document protection, use the Protect button to access the *Restrict Formatting and Editing* task pane. Scroll to the bottom of the task pane and click the Stop Protection button.

FAQ What other features can I use to finalize my documents?

Use the following tips and tricks to create more professional-looking documents, automate document formatting, or simply spruce up your existing documents:

- Borders and shading allow you to emphasize certain sections of text or parts of a table. A **border** is a line or graphic drawn around a page or section of text. Borders can be customized by width, color, number of lines, and type of graphic. **Shading** is a grayscale or color background applied to text or table cells. Borders and shading are often used together to highlight sections of text, differentiate cells and titles in a table, or create an eye-catching page or document. To apply borders and shading to a section of a document, use options on the Borders button and the Shading button in the Paragraph group on the Home tab.

- Themes make it easy to create professional-looking documents without having to customize the style of every element in a document. A **document theme** is a predefined set of coordinated styles, colors, and text options designed to be applied to an existing document. Word includes themes such as Apex, Metro, and Office. To choose a theme for your document, click Themes on the Page Layout tab.

- **AutoFormat** allows Word to automatically format your document as you type. AutoFormat performs tasks such as replacing fractions (1/4 with ¼) and formatting Internet addresses as hyperlinks. To modify AutoFormat options, click the File tab, then click the Options button. Click the Proofing button, then click the AutoCorrect Options button.

- The **Format Painter** feature makes it easy to replicate formats from one text selection to another. Click any text that has the format you would like to replicate, click the Format Painter button in the Clipboard group on the Home tab to capture the format, then click the text where you would like the format applied. If you double-click the Format Painter button, you can copy the format to several locations. When you are finished copying the format to the desired locations, simply click the Format Painter button to stop the paste process.

Try It!

Figure 4-15

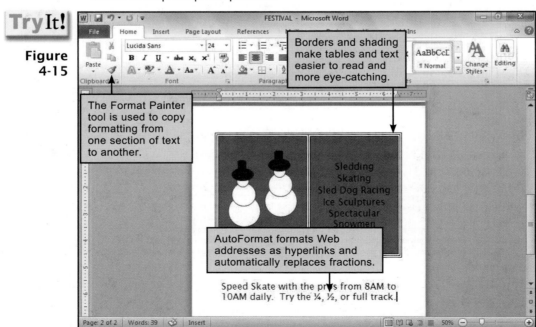

The Format Painter tool is used to copy formatting from one section of text to another.

Borders and shading make tables and text easier to read and more eye-catching.

AutoFormat formats Web addresses as hyperlinks and automatically replaces fractions.

QuickCheck A

1. If you'd like a title page formatted separately from other pages in a document, add a(n) [＿＿＿＿＿＿＿＿] break.

2. You can use the Shapes tool to create simple [＿＿＿＿＿＿＿＿] graphics, such as line drawings, arrows, and stars.

3. A(n) [＿＿＿＿＿＿＿＿] is text placed at the bottom of every page of a Word document.

4. When you save a Word document as a Web page, it is converted to [＿＿＿＿] format. (Hint: Use the acronym.)

5. You can convert a Word document into a(n) [＿＿＿＿＿＿＿] file if you are going to send it to someone who might not have Word, but is likely to have Adobe Reader.

Check It!

QuickCheck B

Indicate the letter of the desktop element that best matches the following:

1. Keep track of text inserted or deleted in a document [＿＿]

2. Text added by a reviewer [＿＿]

3. Comment added by a reviewer [＿＿]

4. Text deleted by a reviewer [＿＿]

5. Button for rejecting a suggested change [＿＿]

Check It!

Skill Tests

A Adding headers and footers

B Inserting page breaks and changing margins

C Performing mail merges

D Creating Web pages and PDF files

CHAPTER **5** # Creating a Worksheet

What's Inside and on the CD?

In this chapter, you'll learn the essentials of creating a worksheet with Microsoft Excel. **Microsoft Excel** is the component of the Microsoft Office suite best suited for working with numbers and formulas. As spreadsheet software, Microsoft Excel provides a set of tools for simple or complex calculations, such as creating a budget, estimating expenses, and creating an income and expense projection.

An electronic spreadsheet, often referred to as a worksheet, functions much like a visual calculator. You place each number needed for a calculation into a cell of the grid. You then enter formulas to add, subtract, or otherwise manipulate these numbers. The spreadsheet software automatically performs the calculations and displays the results.

FAQ What's in the Excel window?

To start Excel, click Start, point to All Programs, click Microsoft Office, then click Microsoft Excel 2010. You should notice that Excel's ribbon contains tabs, groups, and commands similar to those you learned to use in Microsoft Word. In this chapter, you will learn some of the important features of Excel that are different from the features of Word.

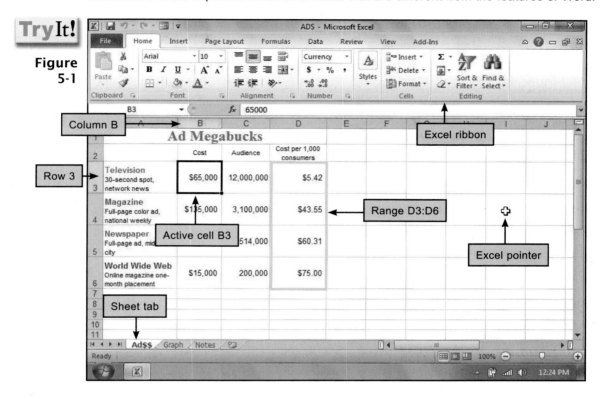

TryIt!

Figure 5-1

- A **worksheet** consists of a grid of columns and rows. The columns are typically labeled with letters, starting with A as the column farthest to the left. The rows are typically labeled with numbers, starting with 1 as the top row.

- Excel worksheets are saved in a three-dimensional **workbook**. A workbook contains one or more worksheets, each represented by a tab at the bottom of the Excel window. When you save or open a workbook, all worksheets in that workbook are automatically saved or opened. To switch to a different worksheet in the current workbook, click its sheet tab. Right-click a sheet tab to rename, insert, or delete a worksheet.

- A **worksheet cell** (or "cell" for short) is the rectangle formed by the intersection of a column and row. Each cell has a unique name consisting of the column letter and row number. For example, cell B3 is located in the second column of the third row.

- The **active cell** is the cell you can currently edit or modify, and it is marked with a black outline. You can change the active cell by clicking any other cell. You can also change the active cell by pressing the arrow keys to move the black outline up, down, left, or right.

- A **range** is a series of cells. For example, D3:D6 is a range that contains all cells from D3 through D6, inclusive. When specifying a range, use a colon to separate the first and last cells. To select a range of cells, click the cell in the upper-left corner of the range, then drag the mouse to the lower-right cell in the range.

FAQ How do I enter labels?

A **label** is any text entered into a cell of the worksheet. You can use labels for a worksheet title, to describe the numbers you've entered in other cells, and for text data, such as the names of people or cities. Any numerical data you do not intend to use in a calculation should be entered as a label. This data might be a telephone number, a Social Security number, or a street address.

Figure 5-2

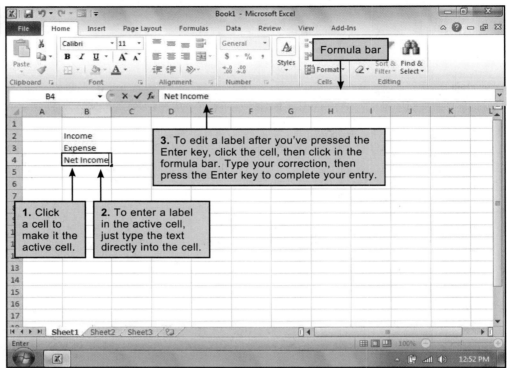

- If a label is too long to fit in the current cell, it extends into the cells to the right if they are empty. If the cells on the right are not empty, part of the label will be truncated, which means it will be hidden behind the adjacent cell's content.

- It's possible to make a long label wrap so that it is displayed in two or more lines of text inside the same cell. Select the cell or cells. From the Home tab, click the Wrap Text button in the Alignment group.

- To edit a label after you've pressed the Enter key, click the cell, then click in the **formula bar**. Use the left and right arrow keys to move the insertion point in the formula bar, and use the Backspace and Delete keys to delete characters. Press the Enter key when you finish editing the label. You can also click the ✓ Enter button on the formula bar to complete your entry. Click the ✕ Cancel button to exit the formula bar without keeping any changes.

- It's possible to edit a label inside a cell. Double-click the cell to activate it, then edit the contents using the arrow, Backspace, and Delete keys. Press the Enter key when you finish editing the label. You can clear the entire contents of a cell by clicking the cell and then pressing the Delete key on your keyboard.

FAQ How do I enter values?

A **value** is a number that you intend to use in a calculation and that is entered into a cell of a worksheet. Cells containing values can be used in formulas to calculate results. As mentioned on the previous page, numbers are meant to be used in calculations, so you should enter Social Security numbers, telephone numbers, and street addresses as labels, rather than as numbers.

Figure 5-3

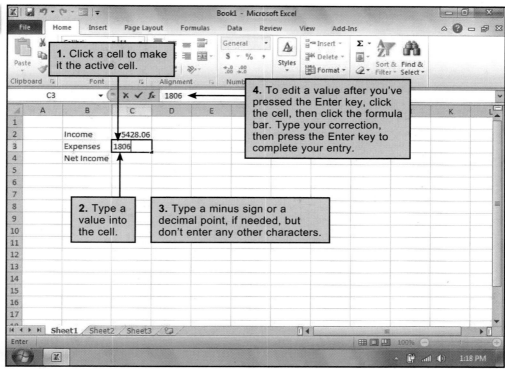

1. Click a cell to make it the active cell.

4. To edit a value after you've pressed the Enter key, click the cell, then click the formula bar. Type your correction, then press the Enter key to complete your entry.

2. Type a value into the cell.

3. Type a minus sign or a decimal point, if needed, but don't enter any other characters.

- Type a minus sign (-) before a number to enter a negative value. Although you can include the dollar sign and comma in values, it's best to just enter the unformatted number into a cell. You will learn how to format values in another chapter.

- After you've pressed the Enter key, you can edit a value just as you would edit a label—in the cell or in the formula bar.

- As you enter data, Excel tries to determine if it is a value or a label. When you want to specifically enter a number as a label, you can type an apostrophe (') before the number. For instance, type '555-1234 to enter the telephone number 555-1234 as a label.

- Values and labels can be entered automatically using the fill handle and a technique called **drag-and-fill**. Enter the first two or three items for the series to establish a pattern. Select those cells and then point to the lower-right corner of the selected area. The pointer changes to a black cross ✚ when you are in the right spot. Drag that pointer across or down several cells.

- There are several other ways to drag-and-fill data, and you can use the Fill button in the Editing group on the Home tab. You can find more information about automatically filling cells in Excel Help.

FAQ How do I enter formulas?

A **formula** specifies how to add, subtract, multiply, divide, or otherwise calculate the values in worksheet cells. A formula always begins with an = equal sign and can use cell references that point to the contents of other cells. A **cell reference** is the column and row location of a cell. In the example below, the formula =C2-C3 subtracts the contents of cell C3 from the contents of cell C2 and displays the results in cell C4.

Try It!

Figure 5-4

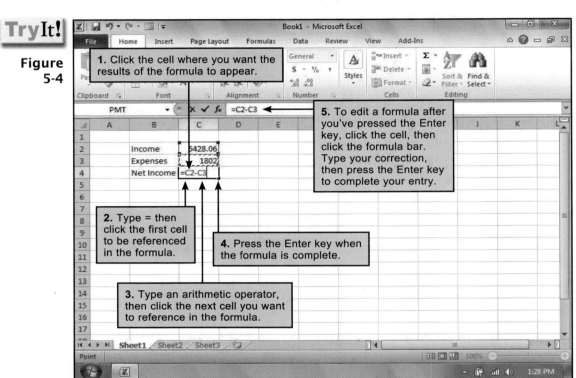

- The most common arithmetic operators are - (subtraction), + (addition), * (multiplication), / (division), % (percent), and ^ (exponent). Note that an asterisk (*) instead of the letter "X" is used for multiplication.

- The easiest way to create a formula is to use the pointer method. Basically, this method allows you to click cells instead of typing the cell reference. After you click a cell for a formula, a rectangle of dashes called a **marquee** appears around that cell. To continue creating your formula, type an arithmetic operator (+, -, *, /), then click the next cell you want to reference. Continue until the formula is complete, then press the Enter key.

- You can also type a formula directly into a cell. For example, you could type =B2*B3 and then press the Enter key to complete the formula. The problem with this method is that it's easy to make a mistake and type an incorrect cell reference.

- You can edit a formula after you've pressed the Enter key in the same way you would edit labels or values—in the cell or in the formula bar.

FAQ How do I create complex formulas?

A worksheet can be used for more than simple calculations. You can build complex formulas to calculate statistical, financial, and mathematical equations by using the usual arithmetic operators, parentheses, and a mixture of both values and cell references.

Figure 5-5

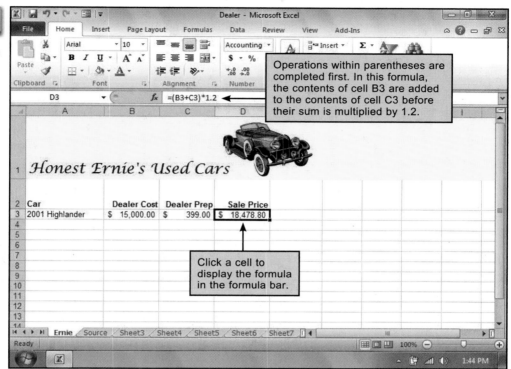

Operations within parentheses are completed first. In this formula, the contents of cell B3 are added to the contents of cell C3 before their sum is multiplied by 1.2.

Click a cell to display the formula in the formula bar.

- Use parentheses to make sure that arithmetic operations in a complex formula are executed in the correct order. If you don't use parentheses, Excel calculates the result using the standard mathematical order of operations, referred to as mathematical precedence. Multiplication and division are performed first, then addition and subtraction. For example, if you enter the formula =B3+C3*1.2, Excel first multiplies the contents of cell C3 by 1.2, then adds the result of the calculation to the value in cell B3. By using parentheses, you can specify a different order for a calculation. For example, if you would like to add the contents of B3 and C3 before multiplying by 1.2, you would enter this formula: =(B3+C3)*1.2.

- Formulas can include values, cell references, or both. For example, if the total price of an item is displayed in cell C18, you could calculate a 6% sales tax using the formula =C18*.06. Or, you could put the sales tax percentage in cell C19, then calculate the sales tax using the formula =C18*C19. The result would be the same either way.

- You should be aware that cell references in formulas can lead to unexpected results when you copy or move the formulas. You'll learn more about this topic in another chapter.

FAQ How do I use functions?

In addition to writing your own formulas, you can use predefined formulas called **functions**. Excel includes many financial functions such as payments and net present value, mathematical and trigonometric functions such as absolute value and arctangent, and statistical functions such as average and normal distribution.

Avoid common errors when using formulas and functions by verifying that your formulas and functions reference the correct cells and data. A **circular reference**—a formula that references the cell in which the formula resides—can produce erroneous results and should be avoided.

Figure 5-6

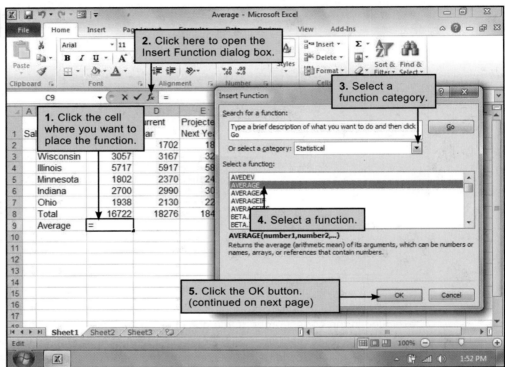

- You can use the Insert Function button to select a function from a list. Excel includes more than 250 functions from which you can choose. Commonly used functions, such as Sum, Average, Minimum, and Maximum, are located in the Statistical category.

- Another useful function is the Payment, or PMT, function, which calculates the payments for a loan. You can use the PMT function to calculate all types of loan payments, such as those for a car or for a house. Unfortunately, the PMT function is one of the more difficult functions to use, which is why it's covered in the Try It! on this page.

- Formulas can include multiple functions. For example, you could create a formula that uses both the Average and the Minimum functions to sum up a series of test scores, but first drop the lowest score.

•How do I use functions? (continued)

After you select a function, you'll specify the arguments. An **argument** consists of values or cell references used to calculate the result of the function. For example, the Average function requires an argument consisting of a series of numbers or a series of cells. When you complete the Average function, the result is calculated as an average of the values in the cells you specified.

Figure 5-7

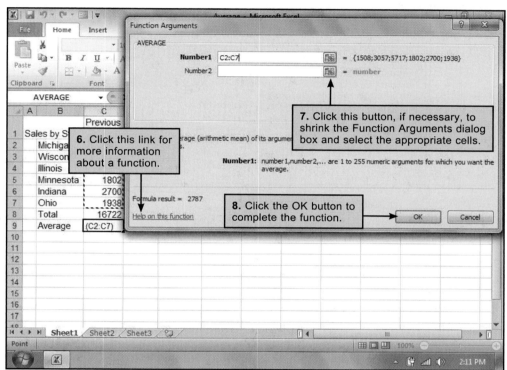

- To select a range of cells for use as arguments in a function, click the upper-left cell that contains data you want to use in the function, then drag down to the lower-right cell. When you release the mouse button, the selected range of cells is displayed in the dialog box. Click the OK button to complete the function.

- Some functions use more than one argument and those arguments can be required or optional. The Payment (or PMT) function, for example, has three required arguments (Rate, Nper, and Pv) and two optional arguments (Fv and Type).

- It can be difficult to determine how to enter the arguments for a function. For the PMT function, you have to divide the annual interest rate by 12 if you're using monthly payments. If you need help with the arguments for a function, click the *Help on this function* link.

- Be careful when using functions you don't fully understand. If you're not sure how a function works, use the Excel Help window to find out more about it. When you use a new function, you should check the results with a calculator to make sure the function is working as you expected.

FAQ How do I use the AutoSum button?

Use the AutoSum button to quickly create a function to calculate the total of a column or row of cells. Excel examines the cells to the left of and above the current cell to determine which cells should be included in the total.

Try It!

Figure 5-8

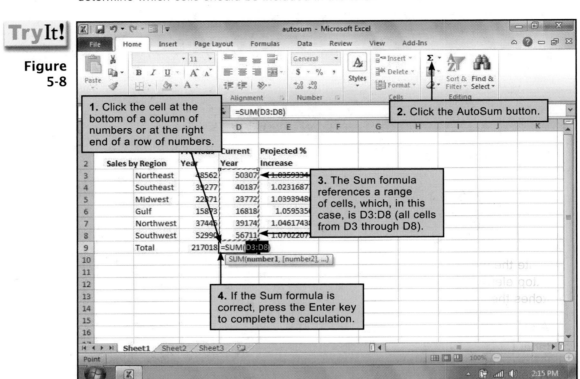

1. Click the cell at the bottom of a column of numbers or at the right end of a row of numbers.

2. Click the AutoSum button.

3. The Sum formula references a range of cells, which, in this case, is D3:D8 (all cells from D3 through D8).

4. If the Sum formula is correct, press the Enter key to complete the calculation.

- The argument for the Sum function is typically a range or a series of adjacent cells.

- The AutoSum button usually does a good job of selecting the cells to be included in the function, but a blank cell or a cell containing a label can produce an incorrect answer. AutoSum works best if every cell in the row or column of cells contains a value.

- Be careful if you use the AutoSum button to calculate the sum of a column of cells that has a number—such as 2011—as a column heading. If the heading has not been specifically formatted as a date, Excel includes it in the sum. Watch the marquee to be sure the correct range of cells is selected before you press the Enter key.

- If the AutoSum button does not automatically select the correct cells, press the Esc key to remove the function and create the Sum function manually. You can also drag across the correct range of cells, or hold down the Shift key while you use the arrow keys to select the correct range of cells. When the correct cells are selected, press the Enter key to complete the function.

QuickCheck A

1. The [_____] cell is the cell you can currently edit or modify.

2. B3:B12 is an example of a(n) [_____] of cells.

3. To edit a label, value, or formula after you've pressed the Enter key, click the cell, then click the [_____] bar.

4. The formula to subtract the contents of cell C3 from the contents of cell C2 is [_____] .

5. A(n) [_____] is a value or cell reference used to calculate the result of a function.

Check It!

QuickCheck B

Indicate the letter of the desktop element that best matches the following:

1. A cell containing a label [____]

2. A cell containing a value [____]

3. A cell containing a formula [____]

4. The AutoSum button [____]

5. The Insert Function button [____]

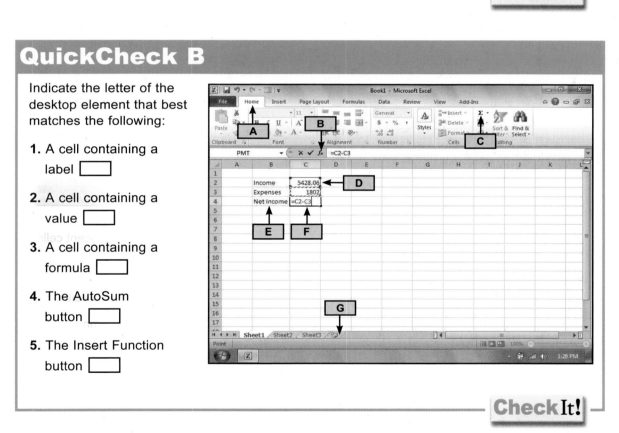

Check It!

Skill Tests

A Identifying Excel tools

B Entering labels and values

C Entering formulas

D Using functions

6

Formatting a Worksheet

What's Inside and on the CD?

In this chapter, you'll learn how to format worksheets created with Microsoft Excel. Formatting is not just for looks—an effectively formatted worksheet is more approachable and helps readers understand the meaning of values and formulas presented in the worksheet. For example, an accountant might use a red font for negative values in a large worksheet so that possible losses are easier to spot. A quarterly banking statement might use a different colored border for each month to help readers recognize which transactions were made in a particular month.

In this chapter, you will learn that each type of data has special formatting characteristics that help to identify its purpose. Rather than typing dollar signs to identify financial values, for example, you will learn to format the values as currency data.

One of the most powerful advantages of using spreadsheet software for calculations is that you can easily make changes to the data in order to see how they affect results. You will learn how to copy and move data in a worksheet, and how the new location might change formulas and produce different results. Most importantly, this chapter explains how to avoid making incorrect modifications to values in a worksheet.

● **FAQs:**

FAQ How do I add borders and background colors?

Borders and background colors define areas of a worksheet and call attention to important information. You can use the Font group on the Home tab and the Format Cells dialog box to add borders and a colored background to one or more cells.

Figure 6-1

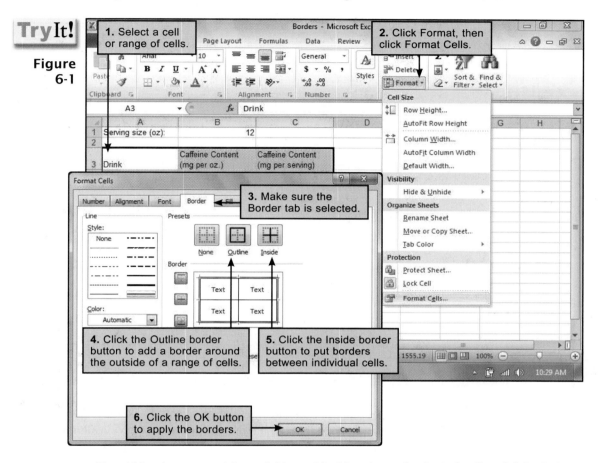

- To add borders around the outside and inside edges of selected cells, click both the Outline and Inside border buttons in the Presets section, as shown in the above figure. The Outline button puts a border around the outside edges of selected cells. The Inside button adds borders between individual cells.

- You can add and remove border lines by selecting any of the following border option buttons:

▢	Top of range	▢	Left of range
▢	Inside horizontal lines	▢	Inside vertical lines
▢	Bottom of range	▢	Right of range

- Line options allow you to select a decorative line style or to make all the border lines appear in a selected color.

- To add a colored background to the selected cell or cells, click the Fill tab. Select a color, then click the OK button to apply the background color.

- You can quickly add borders using the ▢ Borders button in the Font group on the Home tab. However, this shortcut doesn't allow you to use the options that are only available in the Format Cells dialog box.

FAQ How do I format worksheet data?

You can use buttons in the Font group on the Home tab to select different font attributes for any data in worksheet cells. Values and formula results can be formatted with the same font attributes used to enhance the appearance of labels.

Try It!

Figure 6-2

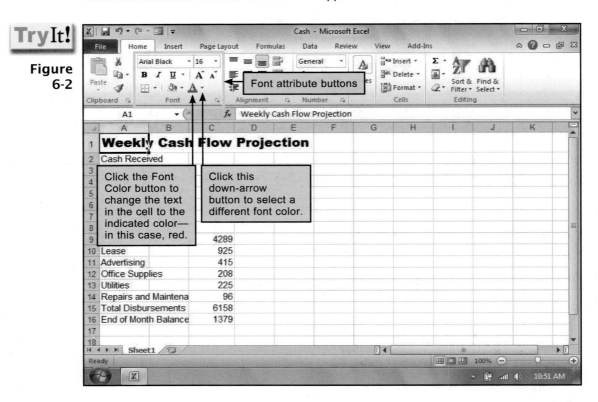

• You can apply multiple font attributes to any worksheet cell. Click the cell you want to format, then click as many font attribute buttons as you want. Click outside the cell to complete the process.

• To change the font for a range of cells, click the upper-left cell, then drag the mouse to select the cells. Release the mouse button, then apply font formatting options to the selected cells.

• Font attributes are typically applied to the entire contents of a cell, but it is possible to change the font attributes for selected text inside a cell. For example, to display one of the words in a cell in bold text, type the contents of the cell, then click the formula bar. Use the mouse or the arrow keys to select one word within the cell, then click the Bold button. You can use the same process to apply different fonts and attributes such as italic, underlining, and font sizes.

• For more formatting options, click Format, then click Format Cells from the Cells group.

• You can also use the Format Cells Dialog Box Launcher from the Font group to display the Format Cells dialog box. Click the Font tab, if necessary. Select formatting options, such as superscript or subscript, then click the OK button to apply them.

FAQ How do I use the Format Cells dialog box?

In addition to font attributes, you can also apply number formats—currency, percent, commas, and decimals—to cells that contain values. The most commonly used number formats are available as buttons in the Number group on the Home tab. In addition, the Format Cells dialog box provides some special number formatting options that can improve the readability of a worksheet.

Figure 6-3

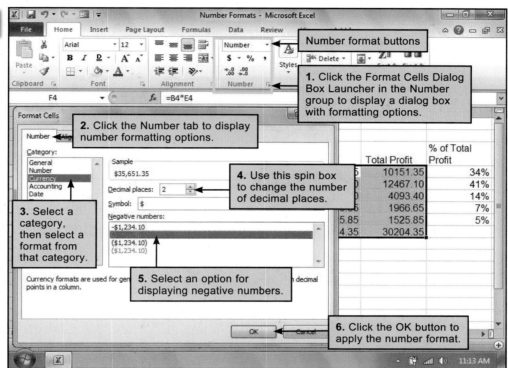

- The $ Accounting Number Format button displays cell contents in your local currency format. For example, if your copy of Windows is configured for use in the U.S., the currency option displays cell contents as dollars and cents with a leading dollar sign ($) and two digits to the right of the decimal point.

- The % Percent Style button displays cell contents as a percentage, which means .35 is displayed as 35%.

- The ' Comma Style button adds a comma to the values displayed in the cell. If your computer is configured for use in the U.S., the Comma Style button adds a comma every three digits to the left of the decimal point and displays two digits to the right of the decimal point.

- When you click the Decrease Decimal button, one fewer digit is displayed after the decimal point. When you click the Increase Decimal button, one more digit is displayed after the decimal point.

- To apply number formats to more than one cell, select a range of cells before you click any of the number format buttons or before you open the Format Cells dialog box.

FAQ How do I adjust column and row size?

If a column is too narrow, labels might be cut off and numbers are displayed as #####.
Narrow columns allow you to fit more information on the screen or on the printed page,
but you might need to adjust the width of some columns in your worksheet to make all of
your worksheet data visible.

TryIt!

Figure 6-4

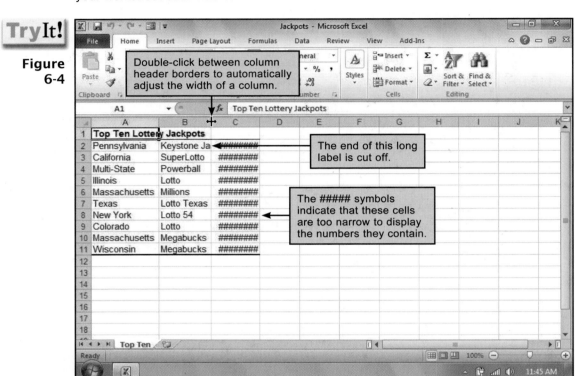

- To change the width of a cell, you must increase the width of the entire column. You can't make one cell in a column wider without affecting the other cells in that column.

- To manually adjust the width of a column, position the pointer over the vertical line between two column headings so that the pointer changes to a ✛ shape. Press and hold the left mouse button while you drag the vertical line left or right to manually adjust the width of the column.

- Excel automatically adjusts the height and width of selected cells when you use the AutoFit command located on the Home tab's Format button.

- If a label is too long to fit into a cell, it extends into the next cell on the right if that cell is empty. If the cell on the right contains data, the end of the label is cut off.

- If a value is too long to fit into a cell, Excel displays a series of # characters in the cell. This is a signal that the cell contains a value that cannot fit within the current cell width. To see the number, simply increase the column width.

FAQ How do I center and align cell contents?

By default, labels are aligned on the left edge of a cell while values and formulas are aligned on the right edge of a cell. Unfortunately, this means that a label at the top of a column of numbers is not aligned with numbers in the rest of the column. Typically, you'll want to center or right-align the headings for columns of numbers.

Figure 6-5

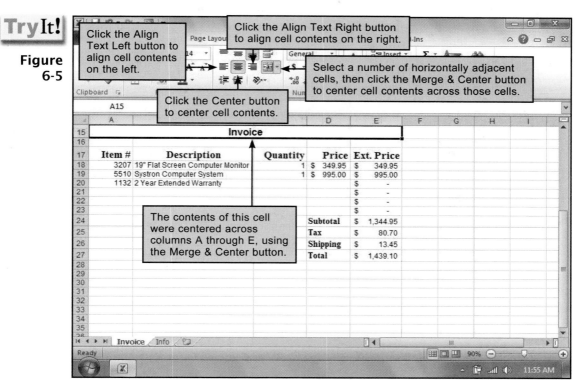

- If a cell containing label data is a column heading, select the cell and click the Align Text Right button in the Alignment group on the Home tab to move the label to the right side of the cell so that it aligns with the column of numbers.

- To change the alignment of a range of cells, select the range of cells, then click the desired alignment button from the Alignment group on the Home tab.

- To quickly select all cells in a column, click the column header at the top of the column. To select all cells in a row, click the row header on the left side of the row.

- Sometimes you'll want to center a label across a number of columns. In the figure above, the title "Invoice" is centered across columns A through E. To center text across columns, select the range of cells to be merged, then click the Merge & Center button in the Alignment group on the Home tab.

- To merge a range of cells in a column, select the range of cells, then click the Merge & Center button in the Alignment group on the Home tab. The down-arrow button next to the Merge & Center button allows you to unmerge cells as well as merge without centering.

FAQ What happens when I copy and move cells?

You can use the Cut, Copy, and Paste buttons in the Clipboard group on the Home tab to copy and move cell contents to a different worksheet location. Label data is copied or moved without changing. If you copy and paste cells that contain a formula, the copied formula is modified to work in the new location. A cell reference that changes when a formula is copied or moved is called a **relative reference**. Excel treats all cell references as relative references unless you specify otherwise.

Figure 6-6

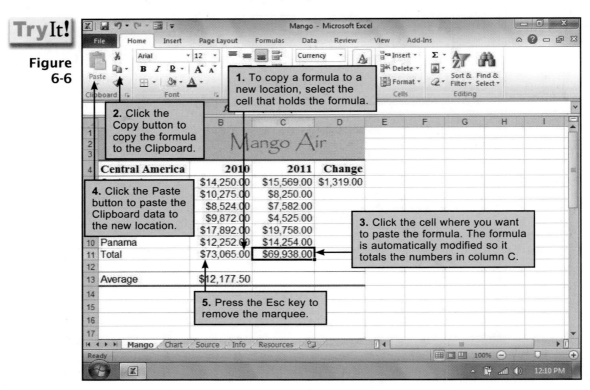

- To move the data in cells, select the cells, then click the Cut button. Click the cell where you want to paste the data, then click the Paste button. The data is moved from the original location to the new location.

- If you copy or move the data in a range of cells, the pasted data is positioned below and to the right of the active cell. In other words, click the cell in the upper-left corner of the new location before pasting the data.

- A formula that contains a relative reference changes when the formula is copied or moved. For example, assume cell B11 contains the formula =SUM(B5:B10). You then copy and paste that formula to cell C11. The formula will be changed to =SUM(C5:C10). The references B5 and B10 in the original formula were relative references. When the formula was originally located in cell B11, it actually meant "sum the numbers in the six cells above." When you copy the formula to cell C11, it still means "sum the numbers in the six cells above"—but those cells are now in column C instead of column B.

- Be careful when pasting, moving, and copying the contents of cells so that you maintain working formulas. For example, do not paste a value into a cell where a formula belongs.

FAQ When should I use absolute references?

Most of the time, you want Excel to use relative references; but in some situations, cell references should not be modified when moved to a new location. An **absolute reference** does not change, and will always refer to the same cell, even after the formula is copied or moved.

Figure 6-7

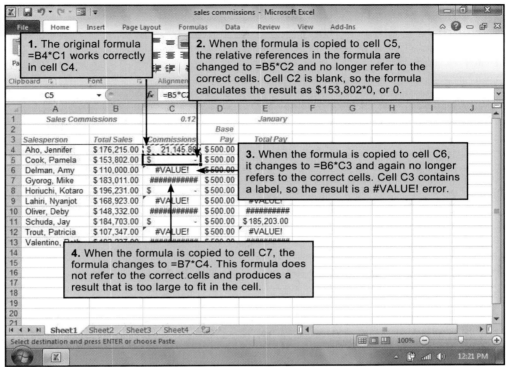

- In the example above, cell C1 contains a commission rate. When you copy the formula in cell C4 to cell C5, the original formula =B4*C1 is changed to =B5*C2. The B5 part is fine, but C2 is an empty cell. The formula should still refer to the commission rate in cell C1.

- To create an absolute reference, insert a dollar sign ($) before the column reference and another dollar sign before the row reference. In the example above, you would modify the original formula to read =B4*$C$1. Using an absolute reference, no matter where the formula moves, Excel must always refer to the contents of cell C1 for the second part of the formula. When you copy the formula =B4*$C$1 to cell C5, the formula is changed to =B5*$C$1. The absolute cell reference is protected by the $ sign and will not be modified or adjusted.

- If you want to use an absolute reference in a formula, you can start typing, then press the F4 key after you click a cell to add it to the formula. Pressing the F4 key changes a cell reference to an absolute reference.

- You can also create mixed references by combining references so that only one of the column or row references is absolute. For example, $C1 creates an absolute column and a relative row reference. C$1 creates a relative column and an absolute row reference. The absolute identifier will not change, but the relative identifier will.

FAQ How do I delete and insert rows and columns?

It is easy to delete a row or insert a blank row between rows that already contain data. You can also insert and delete columns. Excel even modifies your formulas as needed to make sure they refer to the correct cells each time you insert a new row.

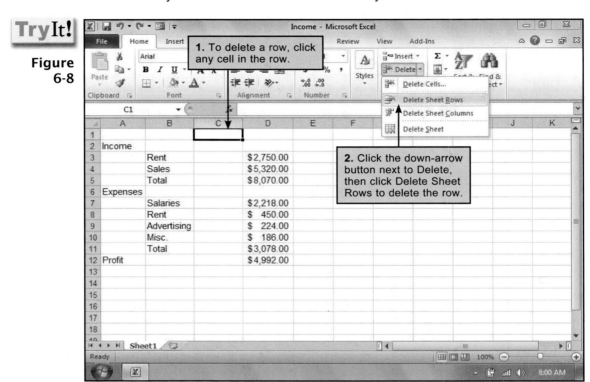

TryIt!

Figure 6-8

- To insert a row, click any cell. You can also select a row by clicking the row identifier button on the left side of the window. Click the down-arrow button next to Insert in the Cells group, then click Insert Sheet Rows. The new row is inserted above the selected row.

- To insert more than one row at a time, drag down over the number of rows you want to insert. Click the down-arrow button next to Insert in the Cells group, then click Insert Sheet Rows to insert the new rows.

- To delete more than one row at a time, drag down over the rows you want to delete. Click the down-arrow button next to Delete in the Cells group, then click Delete Sheet Rows to delete the rows.

- Use the same procedures to insert and delete columns. To insert one or more columns, select the column or columns, click the down-arrow button next to Insert in the Cells group, then click Insert Sheet Columns. To delete one or more columns, select the column or columns, click the down-arrow button next to Delete in the Cells group, then click Delete Sheet Columns.

- As you insert and delete rows and columns, Excel adjusts relative cell references in formulas to keep them accurate. For example, the formula =D3+D4 changes to =C3+C4 if the original column C is deleted. In the same way, the formula =D3+D4 changes to =D2+D3 if row 1 is deleted.

FAQ Can I use styles?

As with Microsoft Word, Excel allows you to work with styles. You can use predefined styles or create custom styles. Predefined styles are built into the software, and include formats for displaying currency, percentages, and general numbers. You can also create your own styles to enhance the appearance of your worksheet.

Figure 6-9

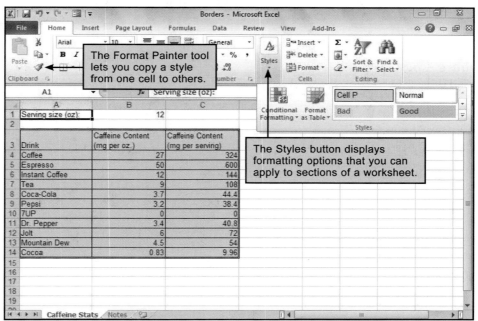

- Excel's Page Layout tab offers a variety of predefined themes that improve the appearance of your worksheets. When you select a theme, its fonts and table styles are applied immediately. Once you've selected a theme, you can then choose from a collection of color-coordinated fonts and background styles that can be applied to worksheet cells.

- The Styles group includes a variety of predefined formats designed to format sections of worksheets. To view available formats, click the Styles button in the Styles group, then select one of the styles.

- You can create your own styles for numbers or text. Click the Styles button in the Styles group, click the More button on the Styles list, then click New Cell Style. Type the new style name. If you want to modify characteristics of the new style, click the Format button to open the Format Cells dialog box. Click the OK button to accept the changes in the Format Cells dialog box, then click the OK button in the Style dialog box to create the style.

- The Format Painter button allows you to copy and paste formats from one cell to another. Click the cell containing the formats you want to copy, then click the Format Painter button in the Clipboard group. Click the cell where you want to apply the formats.

- The Hide function can be used to hide rows or columns you don't want displayed. To hide a block of rows or columns, first select the rows or columns to be hidden. Right-click the highlighted area, then select Hide.

- To display rows or columns that are hidden, select the rows or columns that border the hidden section. Right-click, then choose Unhide.

FAQ How do I manage multiple worksheets?

A workbook—sometimes called a 3D workbook—is a collection of worksheets. Workbooks allow you to group related worksheets together in one file, and easily navigate from one worksheet to another. A worksheet can access data from other worksheets in the workbook. For example, a workbook might contain a Quarterly Report worksheet, which accesses totals calculated from the January, February, and March worksheets.

Figure 6-10

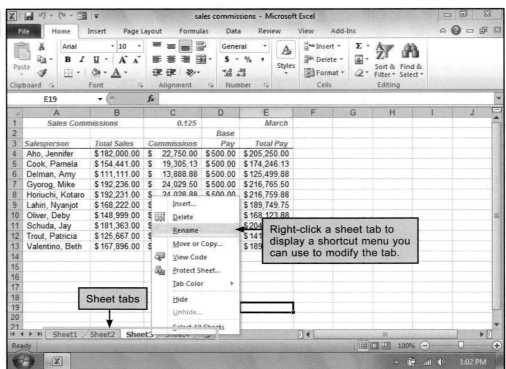

- The default workbook contains three worksheets, titled Sheet1, Sheet2, and Sheet3. Click the tabs at the bottom of the screen to navigate through the worksheets.

- You can rename worksheets, change the color of the tabs, or change the order of the worksheets by right-clicking a worksheet tab and making a selection from the shortcut menu.

- Insert a new worksheet by right-clicking the tab for the worksheet that should immediately follow the new worksheet. Select Insert from the shortcut menu, then make a selection from the Insert dialog box. You can insert a new worksheet by clicking the Insert Worksheet button after the final worksheet tab.

- Delete an existing worksheet by right-clicking the worksheet's tab and clicking Delete.

- The Move/Copy option allows you to change the order of worksheets. For example, if you want to insert a new worksheet in front of Sheet1, simply insert the sheet after any tab, then use the Move/Copy option to position it as the first worksheet.

- To reference data from other worksheets, include the tab name before the row letter and column number. For example, the reference Sheet3!A1 indicates Column A, Row 1 on the worksheet called Sheet3. You can also reference data in other worksheets by navigating to the worksheet and clicking the desired cell while entering a formula or function.

QuickCheck A

1. True or false? When the contents of a cell are displayed as #####, that cell contains a number that is too long to display in the cell. [   ]

2. To center a label across several cells, select the horizontally adjacent cells, then click the [   ] & Center button.

3. A(n) [   ] reference is a cell reference that will be modified if the formula is copied or moved to a new cell.

4. A(n) [   ] reference is a cell reference that will not be modified if the formula is copied or moved to a new cell.

5. To write the formula =B2*D6 so that it always refers to cell D6, even when moved or copied, you would change the formula to [   ] .

Check It!

QuickCheck B

Indicate the letter of the desktop element that best matches the following:

1. The Accounting Number Format button [   ]

2. The Merge & Center button [   ]

3. A cell formatted in the Currency style [   ]

4. A cell formatted in the Percent style [   ]

5. The Decrease Decimal button [   ]

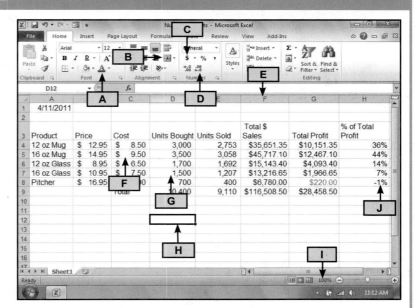

Check It!

Skill Tests

A Applying borders and background colors

B Formatting text and numbers

C Applying column width and alignments

D Copying, inserting, deleting, and hiding cells

CHAPTER 7

Finalizing a Worksheet

What's Inside and on the CD?

In this chapter, you'll learn how to finalize your worksheets by sorting data, creating charts, adding graphics, checking spelling, and testing formulas. You'll also learn how to prepare your worksheets for printing by adding page breaks, headers and footers, and gridlines. As an added bonus, you'll find out how to turn your worksheets into Web pages.

FAQ Can I sort data in a worksheet?

Excel provides tools that allow you to sort data in ascending or descending order. Data sorted in ascending order will be arranged in alphabetical order—labels that start with "A" will be positioned above those that start with "B". Data sorted in descending order will be arranged in reverse alphabetical order—labels that start with "Z" will be positioned above those that start with "Y".

Try It!

Figure 7-1

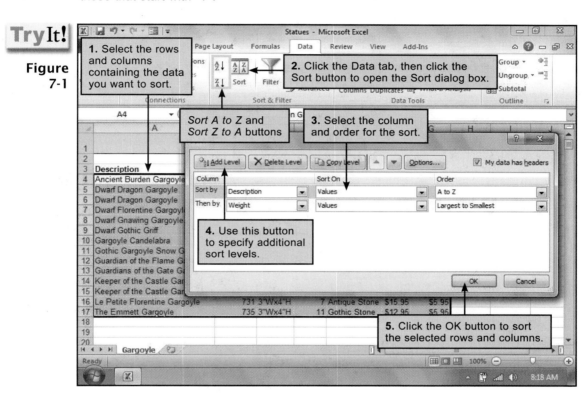

- It's a good idea to save your worksheet before performing a sort, just in case you forget to select all the necessary columns and end up scrambling your data.

- You can select the cells for a sort, or you can let Excel autoselect the cells. Either way, make sure all the related columns are selected or the data will become scrambled. For example, if the sort in Figure 7-1 is performed with only columns A through E selected, the data will become scrambled and the prices in columns F and G will no longer match the correct products.

- If data becomes scrambled as a result of a sort, click the Undo button to undo the sort. Check the data carefully to make sure each row still contains the correct data, then select all columns of data and try the sort again.

- If you simply want to sort by the data in the first column, you can use the ⍖↓ *Sort A to Z* or ⍖↓ *Sort Z to A* button in the Sort & Filter group on the Data tab.

- If you want to sort by a column other than the first column, or if you want to sort by several columns, use the procedure shown in Figure 7-1. If you need to perform a multilevel sort, add additional levels with the Add Level button and designate the columns from the *Then by* list. You can set each level of the sort for either ascending or descending order. Click the OK button to apply the sort.

FAQ How do I create a chart?

You can use the Charts group on the Insert tab to chart or graph data in your worksheet. You should pick a chart type that suits the data. A **line chart** is used to show data that changes over time. A **pie chart** illustrates the proportion of parts to a whole. A **bar chart** (sometimes called a column chart) is used to show comparisons.

Figure 7-2

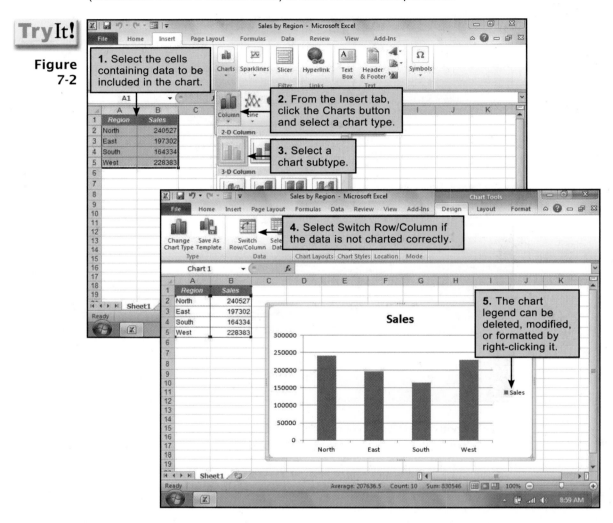

- When selecting the cells for a chart, include the cells that contain labels and they will be used to identify the lines, columns, or pie slices on the chart.

- If you are not certain which chart type to use, hover the pointer over any of the chart buttons to display a description and usage recommendation.

- By default, the chart is inserted into the current worksheet. You can move the chart with the Move Chart button on the Design tab.

- When a chart is selected, you can move it or resize it by dragging the sizing handles.

- If you change the data in a worksheet cell, Excel updates the chart immediately after you press the Enter key.

FAQ How do I modify a chart?

Excel creates a chart based on the data and labels you select from a worksheet. You can modify this basic chart by changing the chart type and adjusting the chart data.

When making changes to a chart, make sure the chart is selected so that Excel displays all of the charting tabs, including Design, Layout, and Format.

Try It!

Figure 7-3

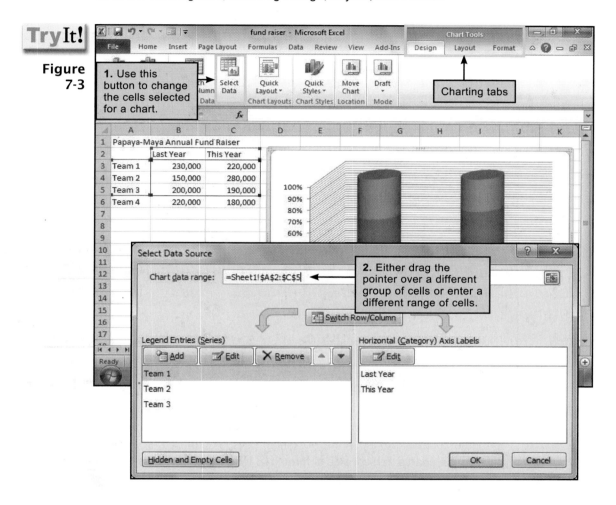

1. Use this button to change the cells selected for a chart.

Charting tabs

2. Either drag the pointer over a different group of cells or enter a different range of cells.

- As shown in Figure 7-3, you can select a different range of cells for a chart by clicking the Select Data button on the Design tab. You can then drag over the cells directly in the worksheet, or you can type a range into the *Chart data range* box.

- To select a different chart type, select the Design tab, and then click the Change Chart Type button.

- If the chart doesn't seem to make sense, make sure the chart is selected and try clicking the Switch Row/Column button in the Data group. This button swaps the data plotted on the horizontal axis with the data plotted on the vertical axis.

• How do I modify a chart? (continued)

When you're satisfied that your chart displays the right data using a meaningful chart type, you can turn your focus to improving the readability and appearance of the chart.

In general, most modifications begin by right-clicking the chart element you want to change. Excel displays a shortcut menu that contains options you can use to modify the chart element you've selected.

Figure 7-4

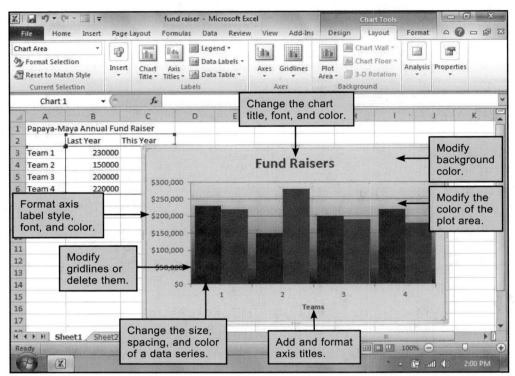

- Label formats on charts can be different from those in the worksheet cells. In Figure 7-4, data such as 150000 in the worksheet cells is unformatted, whereas corresponding data on the chart's vertical axis is formatted for currency style as $150,000.

- For readability, consider changing the units used for axis labels. In Figure 7-4, the vertical axis uses single units and displays lots of zeros. If you change the units to thousands, Excel displays $300 instead of $300,000 and adds the word "Thousands" as a vertical axis label.

- Excel includes a huge variety of colors, patterns, and gradients that can be applied to backgrounds, plot areas, gridlines, and data series. Use special effects sparingly to avoid creating charts that are distracting rather than informative.

FAQ Can I add graphics to a worksheet?

Worksheet graphics can be used to highlight important sections, add interest or pizzazz to otherwise dull pages, or graphically illustrate spreadsheet data. Vector drawings can be created using Excel's drawing tools. Photographs or clip art can be inserted from a file or imported directly from imaging devices, such as scanners and digital cameras.

Figure 7-5

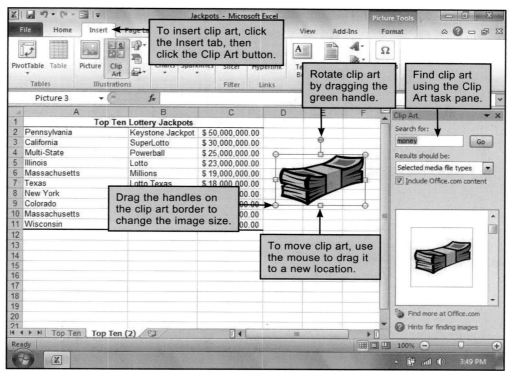

- To insert clip art, click the cell where you want to place the graphic. Click the Insert tab, then click Clip Art in the Illustrations group. When the Clip Art task pane appears, enter a keyword for the type of clip art you would like to use in the *Search for* text box, then click Go. Choose an image from the available pictures, then close the Clip Art task pane.

- Graphics can be resized using the round "handles" that appear on the edges of a selected graphic. For example, to enlarge a graphic, first select it by clicking anywhere on the graphic, then drag the handle in the lower-right corner down and to the right.

- To move a graphic, click the graphic to select it, then hold the mouse button down while dragging it to the new location.

- The round, green handle that appears at the top of a graphic allows you to rotate the graphic. To rotate a graphic, click to select it, then drag the green rotate handle right or left.

- The Shapes tools allow you to draw simple lines and shapes. To draw an arrow, click the Insert tab, then click Shapes in the Illustrations group. Select ⬉ from the Lines group. Click the worksheet cell where you would like the arrow to start, and then drag to draw the arrow.

- SmartArt is a collection of professionally designed graphics. To insert SmartArt, click the Insert SmartArt Graphic button on the Insert tab, select the shape you want to insert, and then click the OK button. You can then drag the shape to any location on the worksheet.

FAQ How do I check spelling in a worksheet?

Excel can check the spelling of all labels in a worksheet. Unlike Word, however, Excel doesn't show misspelled words with wavy red underlines. Excel also doesn't provide a grammar checker. So it is important for you to proofread your worksheets for grammar errors and spelling errors not caught by the spelling checker.

Try It!

Figure 7-6

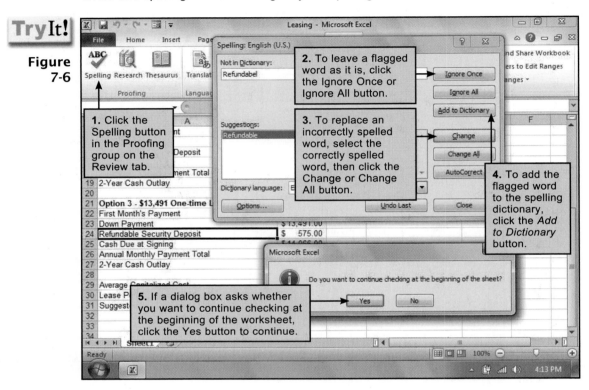

- You can begin to check the spelling with any cell selected. However, if you make cell A1 the active cell, you will avoid the question displayed in Step 5 above.

- If the correct spelling appears in the Suggestions list, click to select it, then click the Change button to correct the misspelled word.

- If no suggested spellings are displayed, click the *Not in Dictionary* text box, then type the correct word. Click the Change button to replace the misspelled word.

- If you're sure the word is spelled correctly, click the Ignore Once button to ignore this occurrence of the word. Sometimes a word—for example, a person's name—is not recognized by Excel. Click the Ignore All button if you want to ignore all other occurrences of this word throughout the entire worksheet.

- If the word is one you use frequently, click the *Add to Dictionary* button to add the current word to the spelling dictionary. For example, adding the city name "Ishpeming" to the Excel dictionary stops the spelling tool from identifying the name of this city as a misspelled word.

FAQ How do I test my worksheet?

You should always test your worksheets before relying on the results. Don't assume the result is correct just because it's generated by a computer. Your computer is almost certainly returning the correct results for the formulas and data you've entered, but it is possible you might have entered the wrong value in a cell, used the wrong cell reference in a formula, or made some other mistake in a formula.

TryIt!

Figure 7-7

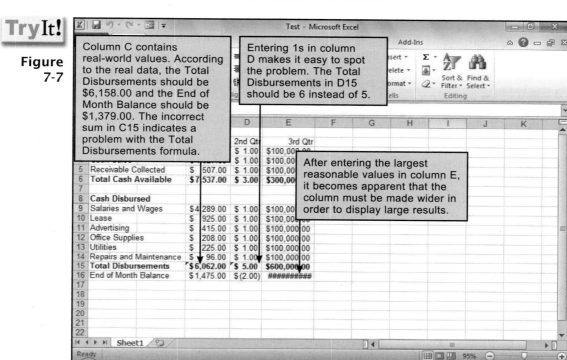

- It's a good idea to use the Save As option to rename and save an extra copy of your worksheet before testing, just in case your test significantly changes the worksheet.

- One way to test your worksheet is to enter a series of consistent and easily verified values, such as 1 or 10, into the data cells. If you enter 1s, you can quickly check the calculated results in your head and spot potential formula errors.

- Another way to test your worksheet is to enter a set of real-world values for which you already know the results. Compare the calculated result from the worksheet with the real-world result to make sure the worksheet is returning the correct results. Testing with real data also helps identify problems such as columns that are too narrow to hold calculated results.

- It is also a good idea to test your worksheet by entering the largest and smallest values that would reasonably be expected in normal use of your worksheet. Small values, including zero, can lead to errors such as division by zero. The use of large values can lead to results that do not fit into the cell where the answer is to be displayed. In such a case, you'll need to make those columns wider.

FAQ How do I control the page layout for a worksheet?

Excel's Page Layout view helps you refine the appearance of a worksheet before you print it or post it as a Web page. In Page Layout view, you can easily see how much of a worksheet will print on each page. You can adjust margins, change the page orientation, adjust page breaks, add headers and footers, and specify whether you want to view and print gridlines and headings.

To enter Page Layout view, click the View tab, then select Page Layout. Once you are in Page Layout view, the worksheet is displayed as it will appear on a printed page. Also, some of the tools on the ribbon change to give you additional layout options.

Try It!

Figure 7-8

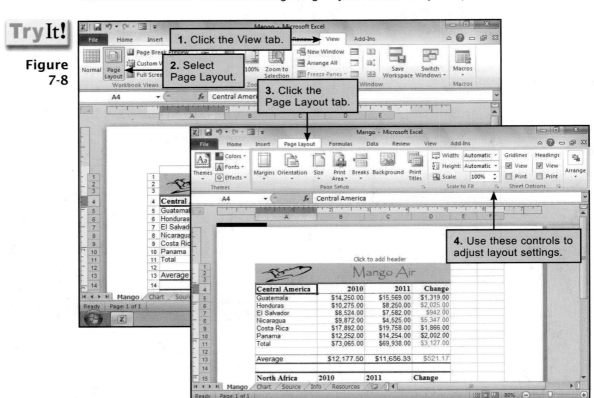

1. Click the View tab.

2. Select Page Layout.

3. Click the Page Layout tab.

4. Use these controls to adjust layout settings.

- **Gridlines** are the lines that separate one cell from another. In Page Layout view, gridlines are shown in light blue unless you turn them off by removing the checkmark from the Gridlines View box. If you do not want gridlines to print, make sure there is no checkmark in the Gridlines Print box.

- **Worksheet headings** are the column letters and row numbers. If you want headings displayed and printed, make sure there are checkmarks in the Headings View and Print boxes. Remove checks from these boxes if you don't want headings printed or if you don't want to see them on the screen.

- Orientation refers to the relative positions of the worksheet and the paper. **Portrait orientation** prints a worksheet on a vertically oriented page that is taller than it is wide. **Landscape orientation** prints a worksheet on the page sideways. Choose this option when your worksheet is wider than it is tall.

- You can select a specific area of a worksheet to print. When you use the Print Area button to select such an area, the setting is used every time you print. The Print Area button also allows you to clear the print area setting so that the entire worksheet prints.

FAQ How do I set margins?

Excel provides several ways to access margin settings, but one of the easiest ways is to drag directly in the margins while in Page Layout view. To get a good view of the entire worksheet before you change margins, you might want to reduce the zoom level to less than 100%.

**Figure
7-9**

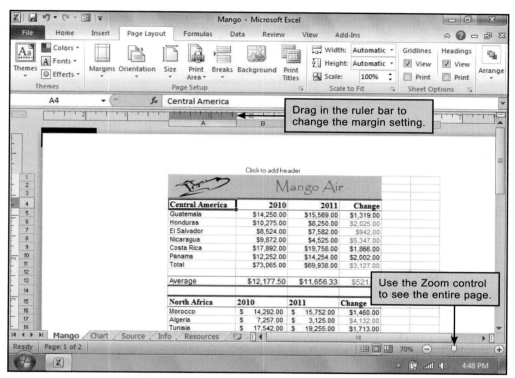

- If your worksheet contains multiple pages, the margin settings apply to all the pages.

- You can adjust column widths while in Page Layout view. Making slight adjustments to column widths can help if the worksheet is just a bit too wide to fit on one page.

- Use the Margins button if you want to select preset margins.

- Click the Margins button and then select Custom Margins if you want to control the space allocated for headers and footers or if you want to center a worksheet on the page.

- Pages that contain cells that will be printed are displayed in white; pages that will not be printed are shown grayed out.

FAQ How do I add headers and footers to a worksheet?

Like Microsoft Word documents, Excel worksheets can contain headers and footers. A header is text that appears at the top of every page. A footer is text that appears at the bottom of every page. Excel includes predefined headers and footers that contain information such as the worksheet title, current date, and page numbers. You can also create your own headers and footers.

Figure 7-10

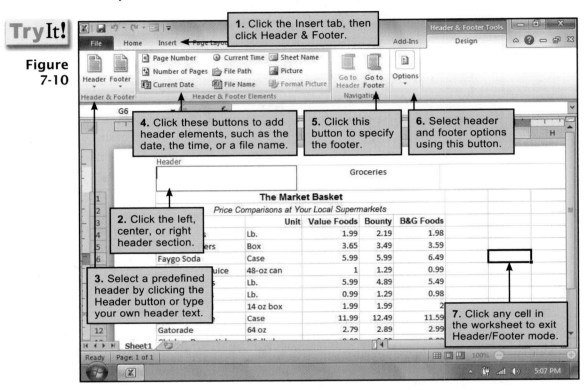

- The Options button offers several useful settings for headers and footers. Here are some suggestions on how to use them:

  Different First Page Because the worksheet title is visible on the first page, you can omit it from the page 1 header.

  Different Odd and Even Pages Specify page numbers on the left side of even numbered pages, but on the right side of odd numbered pages.

  Scale with Document Shrink headers and footers when you use the *Shrink to fit* option.

  Align with Page Margins Align the header/footer text with page margins for a clean block style.

FAQ How do I set up a multipage worksheet?

Large worksheets sometimes require additional setup so that they print correctly. Before printing a multipage worksheet, use Page Layout view to preview the information that each page will contain.

You might want to insert a manual page break if a page ends with a row that should be grouped with data on the next page. You might also consider if you would like to include row and column labels on every page to help readers identify the data presented after page 1.

Figure 7-11

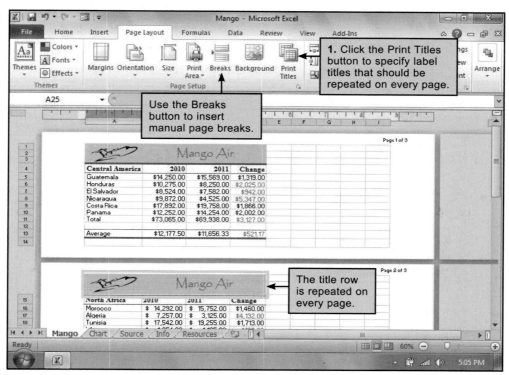

1. Click the Print Titles button to specify label titles that should be repeated on every page.

Use the Breaks button to insert manual page breaks.

The title row is repeated on every page.

- To specify the order in which pages of a multipage worksheet are printed, use the Sheet tab of the Page Setup dialog box. In the *Page order* section, choose *Down, then over* or *Over, then down*.

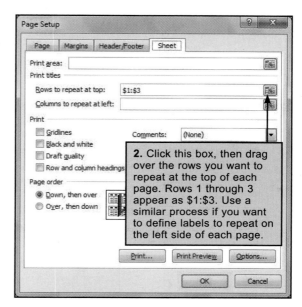

2. Click this box, then drag over the rows you want to repeat at the top of each page. Rows 1 through 3 appear as $1:$3. Use a similar process if you want to define labels to repeat on the left side of each page.

FAQ How do I print a worksheet?

Use the File tab's Print option to print a single copy of the current worksheet, to print multiple copies, to designate selected pages, or to use advanced print options. For example, you can print all the worksheets that make up a workbook. The default setting prints only the current worksheet.

Figure 7-12

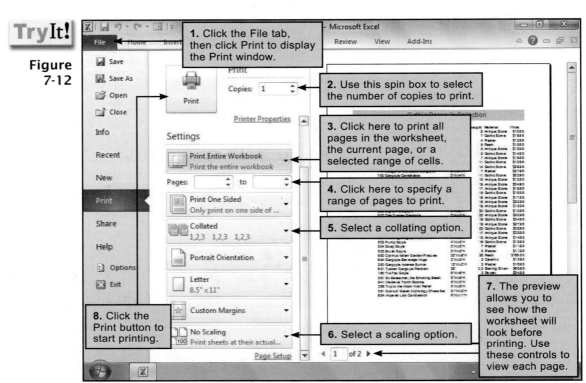

- Determine what you want to print before opening the Print window. By default, Excel prints the entire active worksheet. If you want to print only a section of the worksheet, select the range of cells before you click the File tab and select Print. You can then change Print Entire Workbook to Print Selection.

- To print only the current worksheet, select the Print Active Sheets option instead of the Print Entire Workbook option.

- To print all worksheets in the current workbook, select the Print Entire Workbook option in the Settings section of the window.

- The scaling option is handy if you want to shrink the entire worksheet so that it fits on one page. Be aware, however, that scaling can produce a worksheet in tiny print. Check the print preview so you don't waste paper printing a worksheet that is unreadable.

- If your worksheet doesn't print, verify that the printer is online, and make sure you have specified the correct printer in the Print window.

FAQ How do I save a worksheet as a Web page?

You can save your worksheet as a Web page that you can post on the Internet. This Excel feature provides an easy way to make your worksheet data accessible to a large number of people without having to send each person a printed copy of the worksheet.

**Figure
7-13**

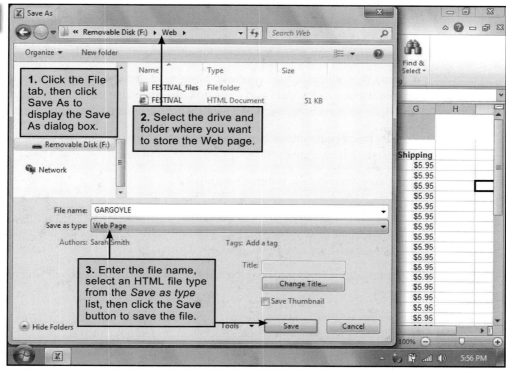

- Before you save a worksheet as a Web page, it's a good idea to save it in normal Excel .xlsx format.

- Tables are a valuable formatting tool for creating Web pages. You can use Excel to create a table for this purpose. First, select the range of cells you want to include in the table, then follow the same steps to save as a Web page. In the Save As dialog box, click the Selection option, choose an HTML file type, name your file, and click Save.

- Some formatting options available in Excel cannot be duplicated in a Web page. If a worksheet contains formatting that isn't available in HTML, you'll be notified of the problem areas and will have the option of canceling or continuing with the save.

- Not all worksheets convert successfully to Web pages, so you should preview your worksheet in a Web browser to make sure the conversion is acceptable before you post your worksheet Web pages on the Internet.

FAQ What makes a good worksheet?

Well-organized and well-formatted worksheets present data accurately, concisely, and in a format that is easy to understand. Consider the following recommendations for creating effective worksheets and avoiding common design errors:

- When deciding whether to put your data into rows or columns, structure your data so that the longest data sets go down the screen. For example, if you have 100 years of climate data for each of 12 months, put the labels for the years down the left side of the worksheet, and place the labels for each month across the top.

- Arrange the information on your worksheet so it reads from left to right and top to bottom. Organize the data into rows and columns. Use cells outside of the main data area to hold constants, such as sales tax rate, that are referenced by multiple formulas.

- Provide meaningful labels for all data. Labels should be spelled correctly and use consistent capitalization.

- Make sure your data is entered accurately.

- Enter formulas and functions carefully and test them for accuracy.

- Avoid the mistake of incorporating cells that contain labels into mathematical formulas, as sometimes happens when you copy formulas or fill a series of cells with a formula.

- Avoid circular references in which a formula references the cell in which the formula is entered.

- Make sure you understand the rules of mathematical precedence (i.e., multiplication and division are performed before addition and subtraction) so that formulas produce the results you intended; use parentheses to indicate the parts of formulas to be calculated first.

- Use absolute and relative references appropriately. In formulas, refer to cells that hold the data, rather than entering the data itself. For example, suppose cell B12 holds the total price of merchandise in a buyer's shopping cart. When calculating sales tax for a purchase, instead of using the tax rate directly in a formula like =.04*B12, place the sales tax rate into a cell such as D3. The formula to calculate sales tax becomes =D3*B12.

- Avoid using too many fonts, font sizes, and colors in a worksheet, but do use font attributes to highlight the most important data on your worksheet, typically totals and other summary data. By convention, red is the color used for negative values, overdrafts, and deficits.

- Format numbers for easy reading. For example, use commas in numbers and currency symbols for cells that hold numbers pertaining to money.

- Use consistent formats for similar data. For example, format all currency using the same number of decimal places and comma placement.

- Format cells so that data fits into them rather than spilling into neighboring cells. The exception to this rule is for worksheet titles that can be allowed to stretch over several cells.

- Add documentation as necessary, especially if other people will be entering data or modifying the worksheet.

QuickCheck A

1. True or false? Excel displays a wavy red underline under words that might be misspelled.

2. If the labels "apple", "banana", and "peach" are sorted in descending order, which label would be at the top of the sorted list?

3. True or false? Spreadsheet software always calculates correctly, so it's not necessary to test your worksheets before using them.

4. Use a(n) _____ chart to show proportions of a part to a whole.

5. True or false? Excel includes a feature that fits a worksheet onto a single page of paper when printed.

Check It!

QuickCheck B

Indicate the letter of the desktop element that best matches the following:

1. The Spelling button

2. The sort ascending button

3. The Clip Art button

4. The button used to add page numbers

5. A column that is good for testing data because it contains easily verified values

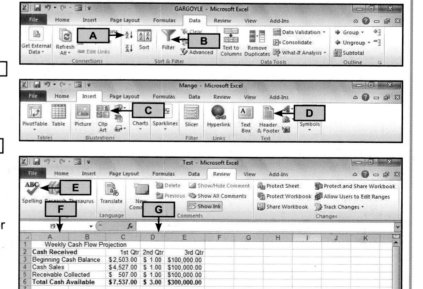

Check It!

Skill Tests

A Sorting data and creating charts

B Checking spelling and testing worksheets

C Adding headers and footers

D Printing worksheets and saving as Web pages

8 Creating a Presentation

What's Inside and on the CD?

Microsoft PowerPoint is the component of Microsoft Office best suited for creating visual backdrops for speeches and oral presentations. As presentation software, Microsoft PowerPoint provides a set of tools to help you script, organize, and display a presentation.

Good graphic design makes presentations visually compelling and easy to understand. A few simple bullets can be used to list key concepts. Numbered lists can present the steps in a process. Tables, charts, and graphics can simplify complex ideas and present numerical or statistical data creatively. To design effective presentations, avoid clutter and unnecessary graphical elements. Put common elements, such as the title of the presentation or the name of the author, on each slide to create consistency and tie the presentation together.

FAQ What's in the PowerPoint window?

A **PowerPoint presentation** consists of several slides. Each **presentation slide** contains objects such as titles, bulleted lists, graphics, and charts. Slides can even contain multimedia elements, such as video clips and sound bytes. Typically, slides are presented with a computer and a projection device. PowerPoint presentations can also be printed on transparent sheets for use with an overhead projector, printed on paper for handouts, or converted to movies that can be displayed on the Web.

To start PowerPoint, click Start, point to All Programs, click Microsoft Office, then click Microsoft PowerPoint 2010. The PowerPoint window includes several work areas, called panes, in addition to controls on the ribbon, scroll bars, and status bar.

Figure 8-1

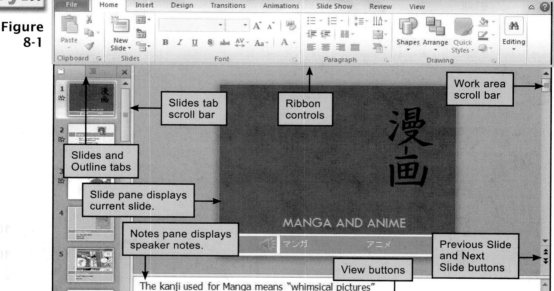

- When a presentation is open in Normal view, the current slide is displayed in the Slide pane of the PowerPoint window, the Slides and Outline tabs are shown in the left pane, and the Notes pane near the bottom of the window provides a place to type speaker notes.

- Use the scroll bar or the ⬆ Previous Slide and ⬇ Next Slide buttons to move from one slide to another in Normal view.

- You can also navigate through a presentation using the scroll bar on the Slides tab and by clicking any slide that you want to view.

FAQ How do I create a presentation?

When PowerPoint opens, it displays a blank presentation and a slide that you can use as the title slide. Before you add more slides to your presentation, you can select a theme.

A **presentation theme** is a collection of professionally selected slide color schemes, fonts, graphic accents, and background colors. All the slides in a presentation should have a similar look, or design. Once you select a theme, PowerPoint automatically applies it to every slide in your presentation.

Figure 8-2

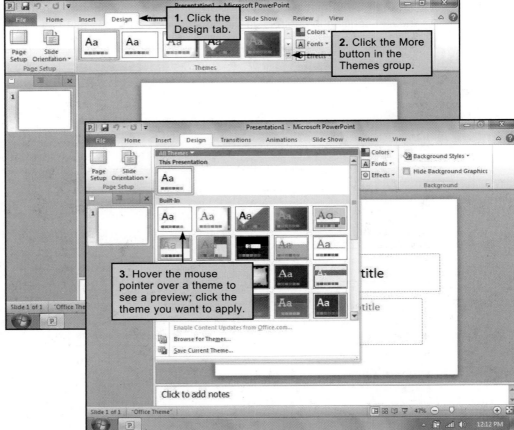

- It's a good idea to save your presentation as soon as you have created the first slide and selected a theme. PowerPoint presentations are saved with a .pptx extension. As you are building the presentation, you should save frequently. When you save a presentation, all slides in the presentation are saved in the same file.

- If you change your mind about the theme you selected for a presentation, you can change it by clicking the Design tab. Click any theme from the Themes group to apply the new theme to all slides in the presentation. You can also apply a theme to just one slide or to a group of slides by selecting the slide(s), right-clicking a theme in the Themes group, then selecting *Apply to Selected Slides*. All formatting applied before you change the theme is replaced with the new design.

- Change the background color of a slide by clicking the Design tab, selecting Background Styles from the Background group, then selecting a style from the drop-down list. Additional background formatting is available from the Format Background option in the drop-down list.

FAQ How do I add a slide?

The New Slide button adds a slide to your presentation. When you add a slide, PowerPoint gives you a choice of slide layouts. Most slide layouts include at least one placeholder, in which you can enter text or graphics. You'll typically use the Title Slide layout for the first slide in your presentation, but you might want to also use the Title layout to define sections of your presentation. Other slide layouts are set up for arranging bulleted lists, graphics, charts, tables, clip art, and videos.

TryIt!

Figure 8-3

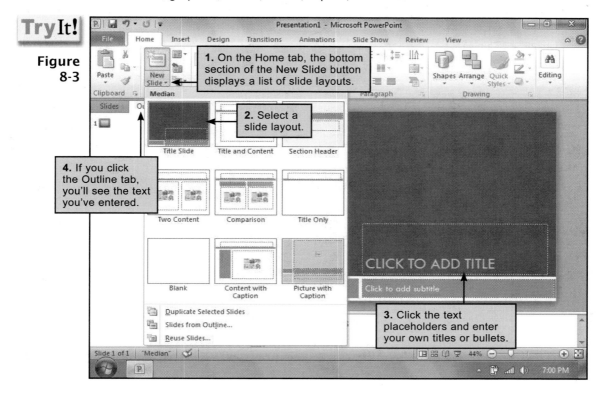

- If you don't like the predefined slide layouts, you can use the Blank layout and then use commands on the Insert tab to add placeholders for text boxes, pictures, clip art, photos, shapes, or charts. For example, click the 🖼 Text Box button in the Text group, then drag across a section of the slide to create a text placeholder. Click inside the placeholder, then type your text.

- You can resize any placeholder or any slide object by using its sizing handles—the small circles and squares that appear on the object's borders.

- In addition to entering text into placeholders, you can enter text for slides in the Outline tab entry area whenever the slide show is displayed in Normal view. You can edit this text, much like working with a word processor, using the editing keys. You can also rearrange items by dragging them to new locations in the outline.

FAQ How do I add a bulleted list?

When you want to present a list of bulleted or numbered points, use one of PowerPoint's title and content layouts, such as Title and Content, Two Content, or Comparison. Bulleted lists focus the audience's attention on each point you are making. Each bullet should be a brief summary of what you are saying. Numbered lists help the audience to focus on sequences, priorities, and rankings.

Figure 8-4

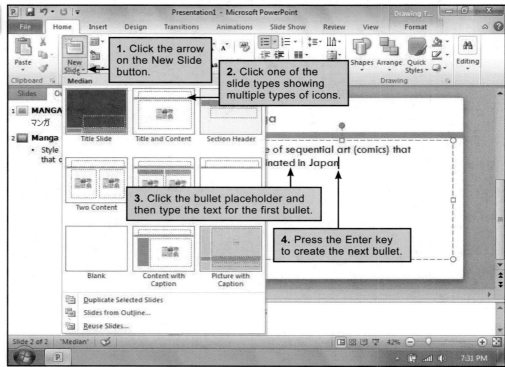

- If you would like the list numbered, use the ⊞ Numbering button, located in the Paragraph group.

- Press the Enter key after typing each item in a list. Each time you press the Enter key, PowerPoint generates a new bullet or number. After you type the last item in the list, press the Enter key. Click the Bullets button in the Paragraph group to stop generating bullets. Or, click the Numbering button to stop generating numbers.

- You can press the Backspace key to remove a bullet or number.

- If you decide that you do not want bullet symbols in front of each list item, you can click the ⊞ Bullets button in the Paragraph group on the Home tab to remove them.

- To create sub-bullets, use the ⊞ Increase List Level button in the Paragraph group on the Home tab.

- You can add animation effects to a bulleted list to make the bulleted items appear one by one. You'll learn how to do this in the next chapter.

- Bullets effectively present an overview or summary of information, but you should limit their use to a maximum of five to seven per slide.

FAQ How do I add a graphic?

You can add visual interest to your slides with graphics. The easiest way to add a slide with a graphic is to select a slide layout that includes media icons. After adding the slide, you'll replace the Picture, Clip Art, or SmartArt placeholder with the graphic you want to use.

Figure 8-5

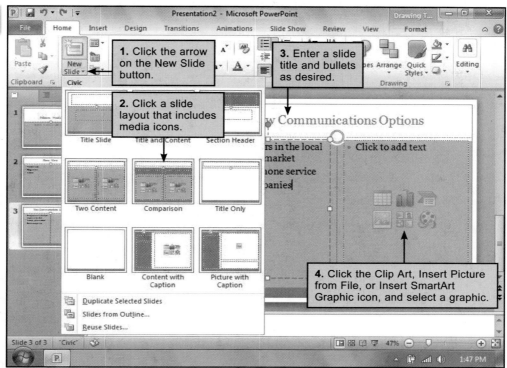

- To add clip art, click the Clip Art icon. The Clip Art task pane opens. Click any graphic to select it. The graphic is inserted in the slide, replacing the placeholder.

- The Clip Art task pane includes a search tool to look for clip art. Enter a search specification in the *Search for* text box, then click the Go button.

- To add a photo or scanned image instead of clip art, click the *Insert Picture from File* icon displayed in the slide's placeholder. When the Insert Picture dialog box appears, use it to specify the picture's device, folder, and file name.

- SmartArt is a collection of graphical templates that can be used to depict organizational charts and processes. It can also provide a visually interesting backdrop for slide text and offer a modern alternative to the use of bullets. Clicking the Insert SmartArt Graphic icon displays PowerPoint's roster of SmartArt designs.

- Click any picture, clip art, or SmartArt to select it and display sizing handles. Use the sizing handles to change the position or size of any graphical element.

- To delete a graphic, select it, then press the Delete key.

- You can insert pictures, clip art, or SmartArt into any slide layout, even if it doesn't contain a graphic placeholder. Click the Insert tab; click Picture, Clip Art, or SmartArt; then select a graphic. Use the sizing handles to position and size the graphic.

FAQ How do I add a chart?

PowerPoint provides several slide layouts containing chart placeholders. You can use the ▮▮ Insert Chart icon to add a bar chart, line chart, or pie chart. The chart comes complete with sample data in a datasheet, which you'll change to reflect the data you want to display on your chart. Some slide layouts provide an area for a large chart, while others are designed to accommodate a smaller chart plus bullets or other text.

Try It!

Figure 8-6

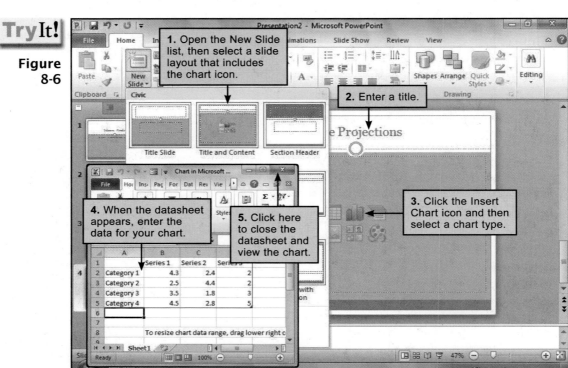

- You'll need to change the table of sample data by entering your own column headings, row labels, and data values. Click each cell containing sample data and replace it with your own labels or numbers.

- If you want to delete sample data in the datasheet's columns or rows, select the cells, then press the Delete key.

- Use the scroll bars to view additional rows and columns.

- If you want to move data, select the cells, then right-click to display the shortcut menu. Click Cut, then right-click the cell where you want to move the data. Click Paste on the shortcut menu.

- To insert a row, right-click the cell where you want the row inserted. Click Insert on the shortcut menu, then select Table Rows Above. The steps to insert a column are similar to the steps to insert a row. The steps to delete a row or column are similar to the steps to insert them, except you use the Delete option on the shortcut menu.

FAQ How do I add a table?

You can add a table to a slide if you want to display text or graphics arranged in columns and rows. Select the Insert Table icon on any new slide layout to specify the number of columns and rows for your table. A blank table is displayed, and you can enter data into each cell.

Figure 8-7

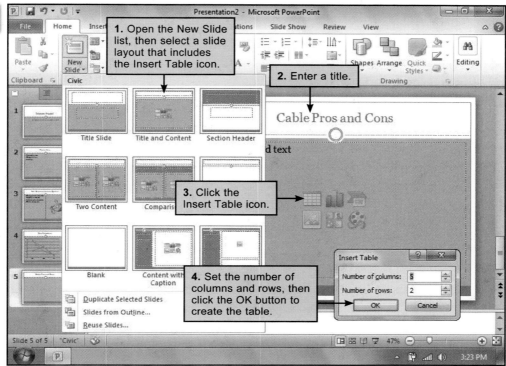

- When a table is inserted into a slide, the Table Tools Design and Layout contextual tabs appear. Using the buttons on these tabs, you can format table borders, add color shading to cells, and adjust the alignment of text in cells.

- To add text to a cell, click inside the cell, then type the text. You can edit and format text inside a table the same way as other slide text. You will learn more about formatting text in the next chapter.

- To add a graphic to a cell, click the cell, then click the Insert tab. Select Picture or Clip Art from the Images group, depending on the type of graphic you want to insert.

- To adjust the height or width of cells, position the pointer over one of the dividing lines between cells. When the pointer changes to a ✛ or ✛ shape, drag the dividing line to the correct position.

- To insert rows, click the cell where you want to insert a row, then click either Insert Above or Insert Below from the Rows & Columns group on the Table Tools Layout contextual tab. The steps to insert a column are similar to the steps to insert a row, except you click either Insert Left or Insert Right. The steps to delete a row or column are similar to the steps to insert them, except you use the Delete option from the Rows & Columns group on the Table Tools Layout contextual tab.

FAQ How do I work with multimedia elements such as videos?

You can launch an audio clip or video segment from a PowerPoint slide. Audio clips are most frequently added to slides as sound effects, a process covered in the next chapter. You can easily insert videos stored in Flash Video, ASF, AVI, MPEG, and WMV formats. PowerPoint does not support clips from video DVDs, such as commercial films. MOV files can be played if Apple's QuickTime Player is installed. Refer to PowerPoint Help for details.

Figure 8-8

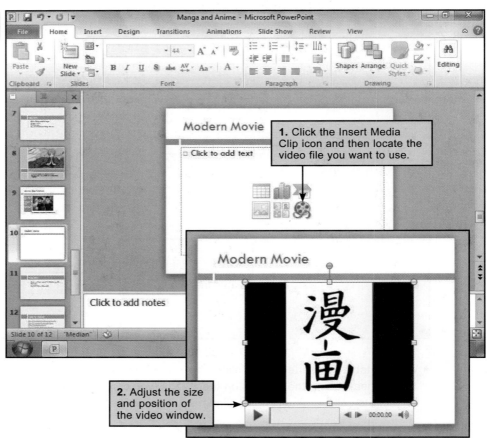

- To stop a movie during a presentation, simply click the movie window.

- PowerPoint offers a set of Video Tools for adjusting the way movies appear on slides and play during presentations. To access Video Tools, click the movie window and then select the Format or Playback tab.

- Movies play within the movie window displayed on the slide. You can change the size of the movie window by dragging its sizing handles.

- You can configure a movie to fill the screen when it plays, regardless of its size on the slide. Select the Play Full Screen box on the Playback tab.

- You can hide the movie window so it does not appear on a slide during the presentation, but the movie still plays automatically when you reach the slide. Use the Playback tab to select Hide While Not Playing and Play Full Screen.

- Additional settings on the Playback tab allow you to set a movie to loop until you stop it or rewind after it is played.

FAQ Can slides include Web links?

PowerPoint slides can display several types of links, including links to Web sites. If you want to link live to a Web site during a presentation, simply add the Web site's URL to create a hyperlink on a slide. Clicking the hyperlink automatically opens a browser and displays the specified Web page. Just make sure the computer at your presentation site has an Internet connection.

You can create more sophisticated links using the Hyperlink button on the Insert tab. The Insert Hyperlink dialog box lets you specify link text that appears on the slide instead of the actual URL, as shown in Figure 8-9.

Figure 8-9

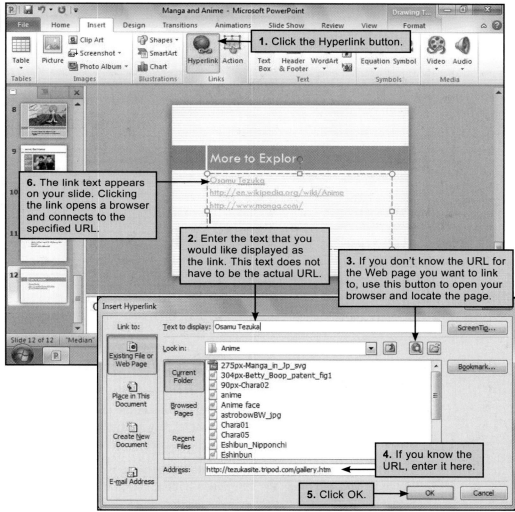

- When the Insert Hyperlink dialog box is open, you can click the ⊞ *Browse the Web* button to find a Web page and insert its URL. Using this method, you don't have to type lengthy URLs.

- Test hyperlinks before giving your presentation to make sure they work correctly.

- In addition to Web links, you can use the Hyperlink button to create links to other slides in your presentation so that you can quickly skip ahead or backtrack. You can also create links to slides in different presentations, to e-mail addresses, or to various files.

FAQ How do I view a slide show?

When you build a presentation, your screen contains the ribbon and other objects that should not be displayed when you deliver your presentation to an audience. In this chapter, you have seen how to create and modify a presentation in the Normal view. When you are ready to see how your slides will look to your audience, switch to the **Slide Show view**, which maximizes the slide pane so it fills the screen.

Figure 8-10

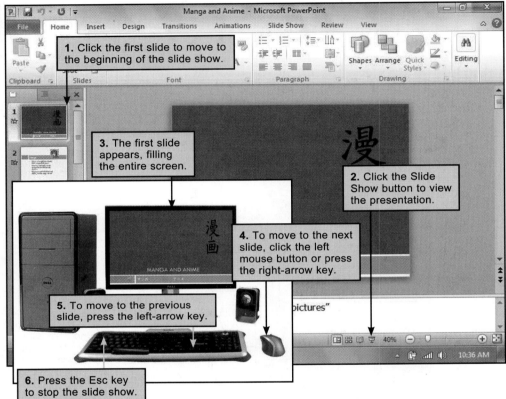

- The slide show starts with the current slide, so it's important to move to the first slide before starting your presentation.

- During a presentation, you can use the buttons in the lower-left corner of the slide to navigate through the slides, write on the slide with the PowerPoint pen or highlighter, or switch to another program.

- During a presentation, you can navigate through the slides in several ways. For instance, you can press the left mouse button, click the right-arrow key, or press the N key to display the next slide. Press the left-arrow key or the P key to move to the previous slide.

- Right-click a slide to display a shortcut menu that allows you to select a specific slide to display. Click Previous on the shortcut menu to go back one slide.

- Press the Esc key to end the slide show and return to the PowerPoint application.

- Before presenting to an audience, be sure to familiarize yourself with the content of each slide. Then, practice the timing of your presentation.

QuickCheck A

1. Microsoft PowerPoint is an example of [   ] software.

2. After adding a slide, you click the title text [   ] to replace it with your own title.

3. To add a new bullet to a bulleted list, press the [   ] key at the end of the previous bullet.

4. When you add a(n) [   ] to a presentation, you specify the number of rows and columns that will be displayed on the slide.

5. Before displaying a presentation, you should move to the [   ] slide in the presentation.

CheckIt!

QuickCheck B

Indicate the letter of the desktop element that best matches the following:

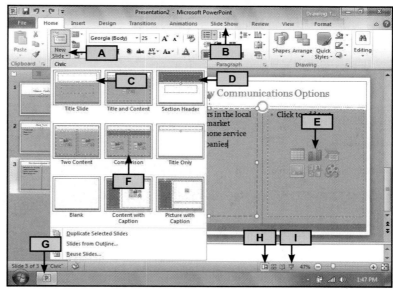

1. The New Slide button [   ]

2. The Title Slide layout [   ]

3. The Normal view button [   ]

4. The Slide Show button [   ]

5. The Insert Chart button [   ]

CheckIt!

Skill Tests

A Creating presentations

B Adding titles and bulleted lists

C Adding graphics and charts

D Adding tables and viewing presentations

Finalizing a Presentation

What's Inside and on the CD?

In this chapter, you'll learn how to use the different views offered by Microsoft PowerPoint. In addition, you'll learn formatting techniques, as well as how to add animation and other visual effects to your slides. To finalize presentations, you'll learn how to print your presentation script, create handouts for your audience, save your presentation as a movie, and use an overhead projector if a computer projection device is not available.

FAQ How do I use the Normal view?

Microsoft PowerPoint provides different views you can use to build, modify, and display your presentation. Most of the time, you will work in **Normal view**.

**Figure
9-1**

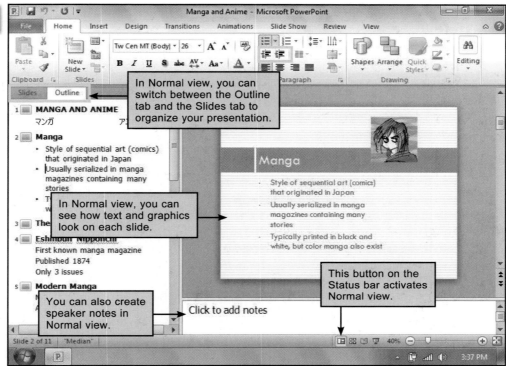

- In  Normal view, you can work in any of the three panes—the Slide pane, the Notes pane, or the Outline/Slides tab pane. Normal view is convenient for building the basic structure of your presentation and for adding speaker notes.

- For an overview of the text on all of your slides, use the Outline tab. After you create most of the slides in a presentation, the Outline tab is useful for revising and rearranging the contents of your presentation. Use the Increase List Level button to indent a bullet, or use the Decrease List Level button to return a bullet to its previous level.

- When you are satisfied with the order of the content in your presentation, use the Slides tab to add graphics and visual effects to one slide at a time. You can navigate to and work on other slides by clicking the slide icons in the Slides tab or by using the scroll bar on the right side of the PowerPoint window.

FAQ How do I use the Slide Sorter view?

Slide Sorter view allows you to view miniaturized versions of all the slides in a presentation. In this view, it is easy to delete slides, hide slides, and duplicate them, but Slide Sorter view is especially useful for rearranging slides.

Try It!

Figure 9-2

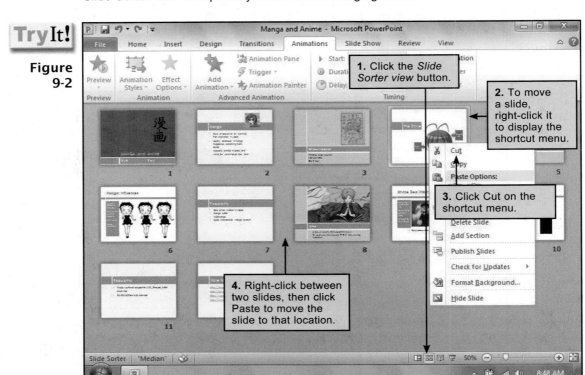

- You can use the drag-and-drop method to move a slide. Select the slide, then drag it to a new location. PowerPoint displays a vertical line between slides to indicate the proposed slide position before you release the mouse button.

- To delete a slide, right-click the slide to display the shortcut menu, then click Delete Slide. You can also select a slide, then press the Delete key on your keyboard.

- You can duplicate a slide in several ways. You can use the Copy and Paste buttons on the Home tab. You can right-click a slide and use the shortcut menu's Copy and Paste options. You can also click the down-arrow on the New Slide button on the Home tab, then select Duplicate Selected Slides. Before using any of these methods, click the slide you want to duplicate.

- You can hide a slide so that it won't appear when you show the presentation. While in Slide Sorter or Normal view, right-click the slide, and then click Hide Slide on the shortcut menu. Repeat this procedure when you want to make the slide visible again. Hiding slides can be handy when you would like to give a shortened version of your presentation. Rather than showing slides without commenting on them, you can just hide the slides you won't have time to discuss.

FAQ How do I add transitions?

A **slide transition** is an effect that specifies how a slide replaces the previous slide during a presentation. Transitions include fades, wipes, and other effects. You can also select sound effects to go along with each transition. If you do not specify a transition, a new slide replaces the entire current slide all at once. Carefully selected transitions can make a presentation more interesting and help the audience pay attention, but overuse of transitions can become irritating and distract attention from the content of your presentation.

Figure 9-3

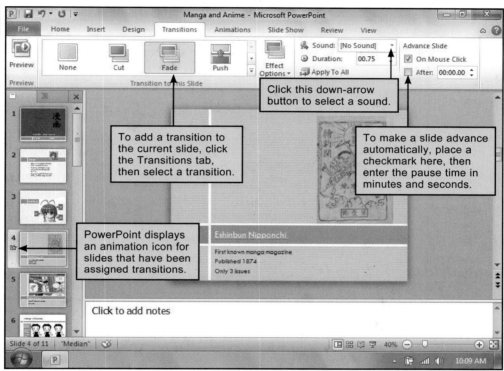

- After you apply a transition, it is indicated by a  Play Animation icon. You can see the icon on the Slides tab (Normal view) or in Slide Sorter view. While developing your slide show, you can click the icon any time you want to see how the transition looks.

- You can change a transition by selecting a slide, clicking the Transitions tab, then selecting a different transition from the *Transition to This Slide* group.

- In Slide Show view, a presentation advances from one slide to the next when you click the mouse or press a key. If you want a slide to advance automatically after a specified period of time, click the After checkbox in the Timing group on the Transitions tab. Use the spin box to set the display time. The time is displayed as mm:ss.ss, where the first two digits represent the number of minutes and the last four digits represent the number of seconds. To force the slide to advance after 1 minute and 30 seconds, for example, enter 01:30.00 in the After spin box.

FAQ How do I format text on a slide?

PowerPoint includes themes preformatted with fonts and font sizes specially selected to complement the background design. In most cases, these fonts work well; but sometimes you'll find it necessary to modify font attributes.

Try It!

Figure 9-4

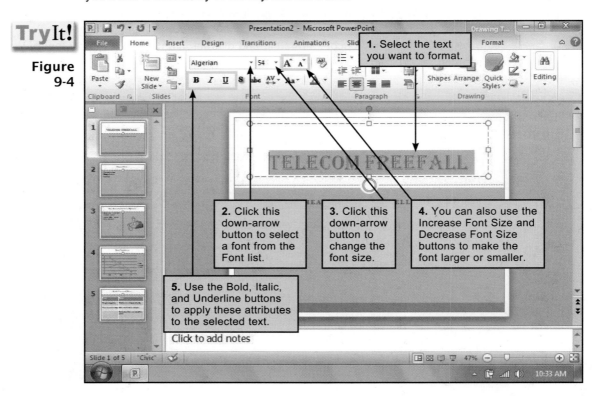

1. Select the text you want to format.

2. Click this down-arrow button to select a font from the Font list.

3. Click this down-arrow button to change the font size.

4. You can also use the Increase Font Size and Decrease Font Size buttons to make the font larger or smaller.

5. Use the Bold, Italic, and Underline buttons to apply these attributes to the selected text.

• For more font options, select the text, then click the Font Dialog Box Launcher in the Font group. Select the desired font, font style, size, color, and effect, then click the OK button to apply the font changes.

• When you select font sizes, you should consider the size of your presentation venue and use fonts that are visible from the back of the room. When using a large font, you might have to use fewer words on each slide.

• You also should consider the lighting in the room in which your presentation will be given. In a brightly lit room, slides are easier to read if you use a dark font color on a light background. In a dark room, you should use a dark background with light font colors. You can experiment with font colors to find the combination that works best in the room in which you will deliver the presentation.

• You can change the font attributes for all the slides in your presentation at the same time by using the slide master. The **slide master** is a template you can modify to create a consistent look for your presentation. Click the View tab, then click Slide Master from the Master Views group. Select the text styles you want to modify, then change the font attributes using the Font dialog box. To close the slide master, click Close Master View on the Slide Master tab. Use Slide Sorter view to verify that the new font attributes are applied to the text on all of the slides in your presentation.

FAQ How do I add animation effects to a bulleted list?

The Animations tab provides options for adding animation effects and sounds to items on a slide. **Animation effects** are typically used to draw attention to bullets as they appear on the slide during a presentation. For example, each bulleted item can "fly" in from the side when you click the mouse button. Animation effects can also be accompanied by sound effects to draw attention to each new bullet. You can use the Animation pane to add effects to bullets.

**Figure
9-5**

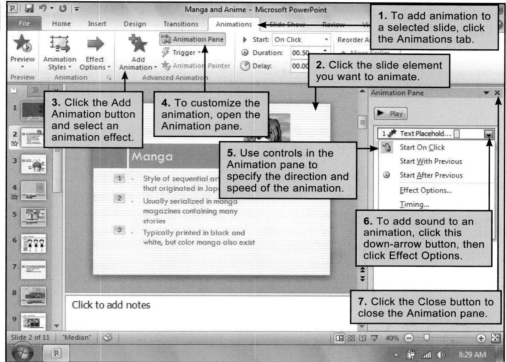

- You can apply animation effects to any slide element, including text, graphics, charts, and tables. After you apply an animation effect, you can test it by clicking the 🌠 Play Animations icon next to the slide in the Slides pane. You can also select the slide and then switch to Slide Show view.

- After selecting Effect Options, you can use the *After animation* option to indicate whether the object should change to a different color or disappear after the animation. For example, you can change a bullet to a light font color just before the next bullet appears. The new bullet in a darker font will then become the focus.

- Use sounds sparingly—a sound effect can be humorous and effective the first time it's used, but it can become less amusing after 10 or 20 slides. If you use sounds for a presentation, make sure your presentation equipment includes a sound system with adequate volume for your audience.

FAQ How do I check spelling in a presentation?

PowerPoint's spelling checker is very similar to the one you use in Word. It provides an inline spelling checker that automatically indicates possible spelling errors with wavy red lines. As with Word, simply right-click a word marked with a wavy red line to view a list of correctly spelled alternatives. You can also use the Spelling button on the Review tab to manually initiate a spelling check of the entire presentation.

Figure 9-6

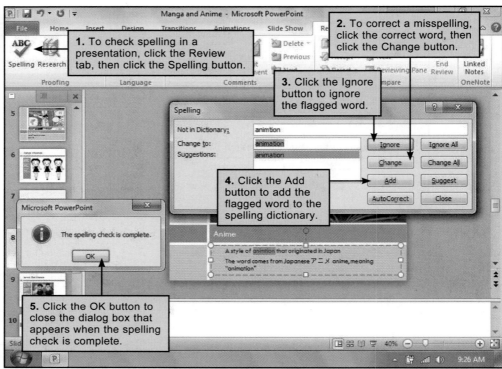

- Don't worry—the wavy red lines do not appear in Slide Show view when you display a presentation.

- You should always check spelling in a presentation before you save the final version. Misspellings can make your audience doubt the accuracy and validity of your statements.

- PowerPoint does not include a grammar checker, so make sure you proofread your presentation to eliminate grammar errors. Bulleted items are usually sentence fragments, but sometimes complete sentences are more appropriate. You should try to be consistent on each slide, using either complete sentences or only phrases.

- PowerPoint's AutoCorrect feature can automatically correct common typing errors as you work. Click the File tab, the Options button, the Proofing tab, and then the AutoCorrect Options button. In the AutoCorrect dialog box, select any options that are useful to you. Options include automatically capitalizing the first word in a sentence and the names of days, changing two capital letters at the beginning of a word to a single capital letter followed by a lowercase letter, and correcting capitalization errors caused by accidental use of the Caps Lock key.

FAQ How do I work with speaker notes?

You can prepare **speaker notes** that remind you what to say about each slide. Speaker notes can be printed or they can be viewed on the computer you use at the lectern while the presentation without speaker notes is projected for the audience.

Figure 9-7

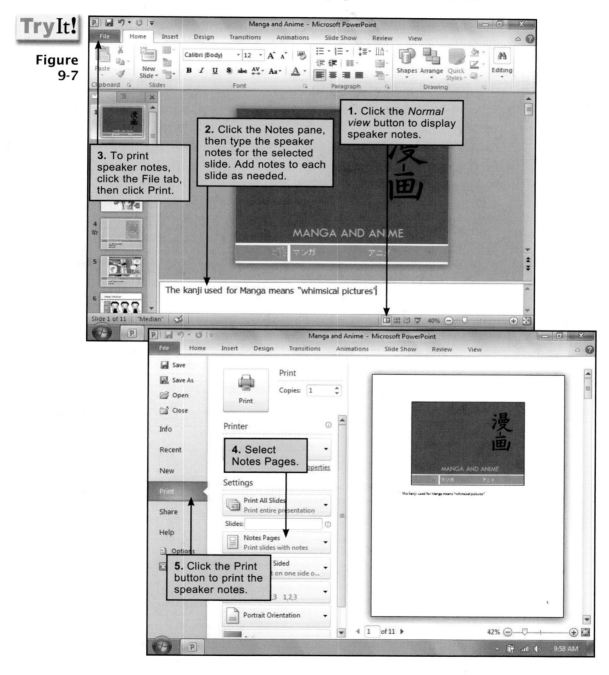

- Speaker notes shouldn't include the exact text that appears on the slide. Use speaker notes for any additional comments you want to make.

- To print speaker notes, click the File tab, then click Print. Select Notes Pages in the Settings section. Click the Print button to print the speaker notes.

• How do I work with speaker notes? (continued)

PowerPoint offers **Presenter View** for showing your speaker notes on the computer screen you use at the lectern, but displaying the notes-free slides on the projected image that's seen by the audience. To use this handy feature, Windows has to be configured to support two monitors. The signal for one monitor is sent to the projector. The signal for the display with speaker notes remains on the computer that's running the slide show. Additional settings are required from within the presentation software.

Figure 9-8

PowerPoint displays speaker notes on the computer you use at the lectern.

PowerPoint projects the image without notes for the audience.

Setting up Presenter View requires just a few steps, but give yourself time to configure and test your setup before your presentation begins.

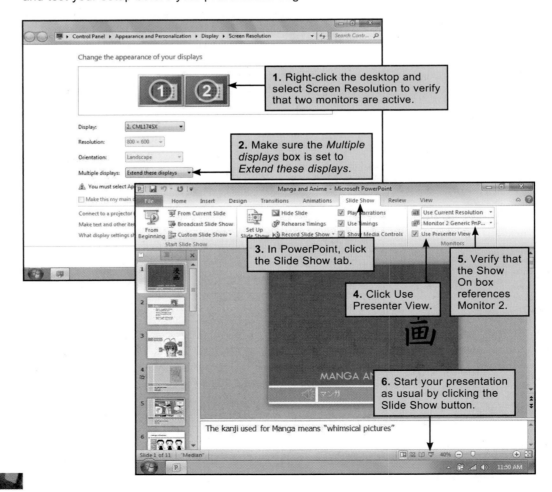

1. Right-click the desktop and select Screen Resolution to verify that two monitors are active.

2. Make sure the *Multiple displays* box is set to *Extend these displays*.

3. In PowerPoint, click the Slide Show tab.

4. Click Use Presenter View.

5. Verify that the Show On box references Monitor 2.

6. Start your presentation as usual by clicking the Slide Show button.

FAQ How do I print handouts?

Handouts help your audience remember the content of your presentation. Microsoft PowerPoint offers several print layouts for handouts. Choose the one that best fits the content and number of slides in your presentation.

TryIt!

Figure 9-9

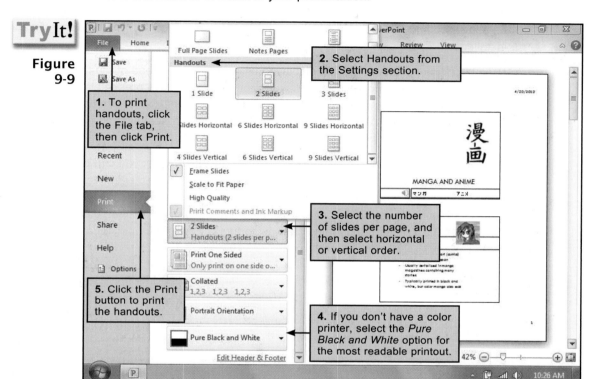

- If your presentation is brief, you can print two or three slides per page for handouts. The two-slide layout prints each slide on one-half of the page. It is appropriate to use this layout when the graphics and bullets on the slides include most of the details of your presentation content. The three-slide layout prints blank lines to the right of each slide. It is appropriate to use this layout when you expect your audience to write notes about each slide.

- You can save paper by printing four to nine slides per page. You can select either horizontal or vertical order for all of these print layouts. Horizontal order prints multiple slides (in order) across the page; vertical order prints the slides (in order) down the page.

- The biggest advantage of using a PowerPoint presentation is the variety of colors and graphics you can use to enhance your slides. Your handouts can be printed in black and white, or in color, depending on your printer. Select the *Pure Black and White* option to convert the colors in your slides to the most readable grayscales for a black and white printer.

- The Frame Slides option gives your handouts a professional look by drawing a thin black line around each slide.

- You can print a text-only version of your presentation by selecting Outline View in the Settings section. This handout is useful for very long presentations that include a number of bulleted items. Graphics do not print in the Outline View version.

FAQ How can I distribute my presentations?

As an alternative to delivering a presentation to a live audience, you can distribute your presentation in several other ways. For example, you can output your slides as overhead transparencies by simply printing the presentation on transparency film. You can print your slides on paper and distribute them as handouts. PowerPoint presentations can also be converted into PDF format, which can be viewed on any computer with Adobe Reader installed.

PowerPoint presentations can be displayed using a viewer instead of the full presentation software product. A program called PowerPoint Viewer displays presentations on computers on which PowerPoint is not installed. PowerPoint Viewer can be downloaded free from the Microsoft Web site. You can package your presentation on a CD along with PowerPoint Viewer for people who cannot attend your live presentation.

Some presentation software converts slides to HTML pages that you can post on the Web, but these pages typically do not incorporate transitions and animations. With PowerPoint 2010, however, you can save the presentation as a video that includes transitions, animations, and sounds. These PowerPoint videos can be posted on the Web. Click the Try It! button to find out how to turn a PowerPoint presentation into a video.

Figure 9-10

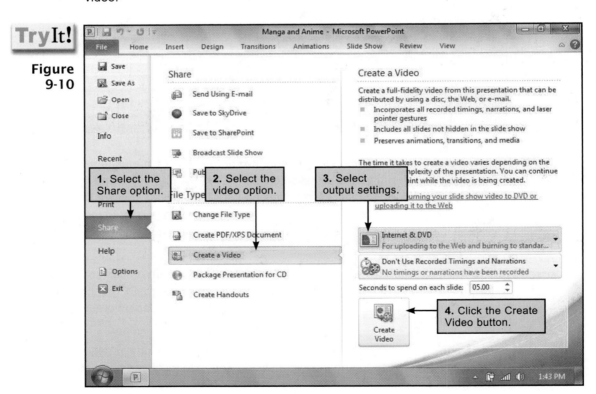

QuickCheck A

1. [_____] notes help you remember what to say when each slide is displayed during a presentation.

2. A(n) [_____] effect can make bullets "fly" onto the screen one at a time.

3. A slide [_____] controls the way a slide replaces the previous slide during a presentation.

4. True or false? PowerPoint viewer packages slides into printed handouts or PDF outlines. [_____]

5. True or false? To package a presentation, including animations and sound, for display on the Web, simply convert the slides to HTML format. [_____]

CheckIt!

QuickCheck B

Indicate the letter of the desktop element that best matches the following:

1. The Slide Sorter view button [____]

2. Settings for displaying speaker notes at the lectern [____]

3. A slide with a transition [____]

4. The *Slide Show view* button [____]

5. The *Normal view* button [____]

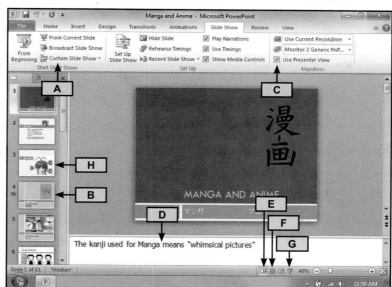

CheckIt!

Skill Tests

A Sorting slides and changing fonts

B Adding transitions and spell checking

C Adding animation and sound to bullets

D Adding speaker notes

Creating a Database

Microsoft Access is the component of the Microsoft Office suite best suited for working with large collections of data called databases. As database software, Microsoft Access provides a powerful set of tools for entering and updating information, deleting information, sorting data, searching for specific data, and creating reports.

FAQ How is data organized in a database?

Because it is useful for organizing many types of data, database software, such as Microsoft Access, can be complex. A few simple concepts, however, should provide you with the background necessary to start working with this important data management tool.

Microsoft Access is designed for creating and accessing relational databases. A **relational database** is very flexible because it can store data for several different but related categories. For example, a relational database could be used to store information about films and actors. Each category of data is stored in a **database table**. An Academy Awards database could have a table with information about Best Picture winners and another table containing biographical information about actors.

A table is composed of records and fields. A record contains information about a single entity in the database—a person, place, event, or thing. A field contains a single unit of information, such as the title of a film that won the Best Picture award.

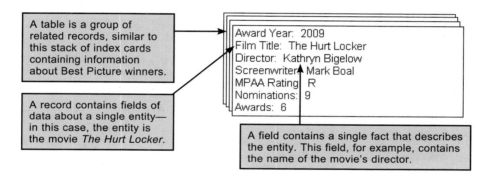

A table is a group of related records, similar to this stack of index cards containing information about Best Picture winners.

A record contains fields of data about a single entity—in this case, the entity is the movie *The Hurt Locker*.

Award Year: 2009
Film Title: The Hurt Locker
Director: Kathryn Bigelow
Screenwriter Mark Boal
MPAA Rating R
Nominations: 9
Awards: 6

A field contains a single fact that describes the entity. This field, for example, contains the name of the movie's director.

The data in a table can be displayed in different ways. Most of the time, you'll work with the data arranged in rows and columns, such as in the figure shown below. Each row contains one record. Each cell in a row contains the data for one field.

Try It!

Figure 10-1

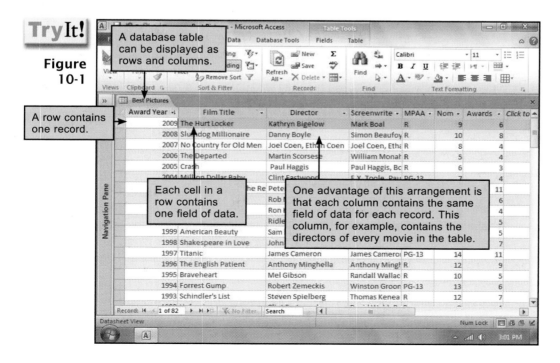

A database table can be displayed as rows and columns.

A row contains one record.

Each cell in a row contains one field of data.

One advantage of this arrangement is that each column contains the same field of data for each record. This column, for example, contains the directors of every movie in the table.

FAQ What's in the Access window?

To start Access, click Start, point to All Programs, click Microsoft Office, then click Microsoft Access 2010. Unlike other Microsoft Office applications, Access doesn't automatically display an empty workspace when you start the program. When you start Access, the File tab appears. You can use this tab to connect to Microsoft Office Online, search for an existing file, create a new database, or open an existing database.

Figure 10-2

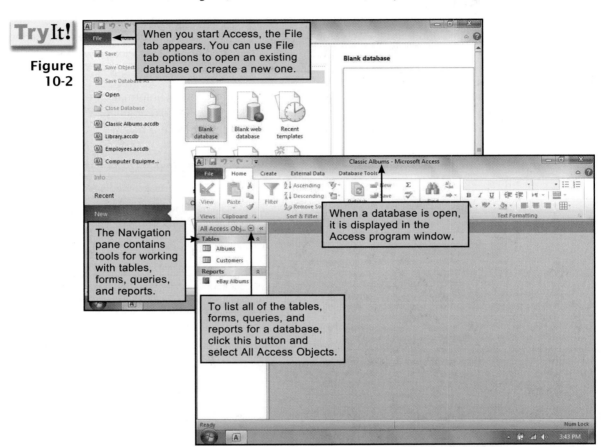

When you start Access, the File tab appears. You can use File tab options to open an existing database or create a new one.

Blank database

When a database is open, it is displayed in the Access program window.

The Navigation pane contains tools for working with tables, forms, queries, and reports.

To list all of the tables, forms, queries, and reports for a database, click this button and select All Access Objects.

- When working with Access, you typically will not create a new database each time you use the program. Instead, you'll open an existing database in order to add to or edit the data it contains.

- As you've learned in previous chapters, documents and spreadsheets appear on-screen similar to the way they will look when printed. Databases are different—their data can be displayed and manipulated in many different ways.

- Access provides several tools you can use to create, modify, and display data in the database. These tools are contained in the Navigation pane on the left side of the database window. In this chapter, you'll learn how to use these tools to create tables and simple queries. In the next chapter, you'll learn how to use additional tools to create simple forms and reports.

- Access also offers many ways to use each of the tools. You should remember that Access is complex software. In order to simplify your introduction to Access, you will learn some basic ways to use the most common tools.

FAQ How do I create a new database or open an existing database?

Creating a database is different from creating a document, worksheet, or presentation. With Word, for example, you typically enter text into a new document before you save it. With Access, first you save an empty database, then you create the elements that make up the database. These elements include tables, reports, forms, and queries.

Try It!

Figure 10-3

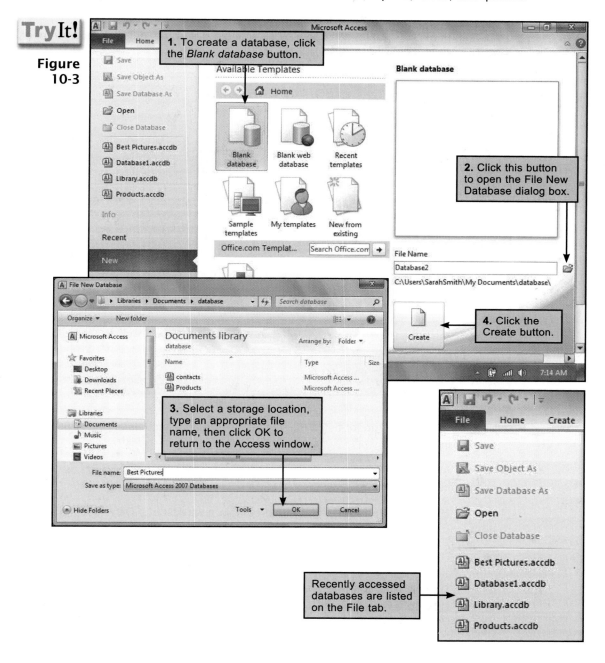

- To open an existing database, you can use the recent databases list, the Recent button, or the Open button on the Access File tab.

FAQ How do I create tables?

Before you can enter data in a database, you must specify the structure of the tables, records, and fields in your database. A table contains records. Each record consists of one or more fields, and each field contains a particular type of data, such as a name or date. When you create a new database, Access creates an empty table called Table1. You can create additional tables by clicking the Create tab and selecting the Table tool.

To define a field for a table, you begin by selecting a **data type**, such as Text, Number, or Memo. You can then select a name for the field.

Figure 10-4

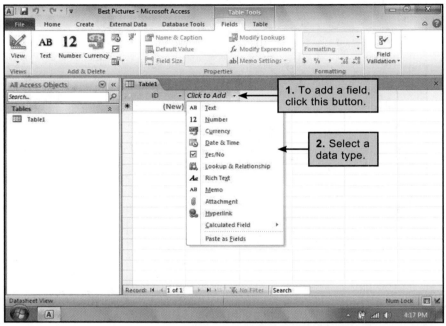

- Use the **Text data type** for fields that contain words and symbols of up to 255 characters in length.

- Use the **Memo data type** for fields that contain variable length data, such as comments, notes, and reviews.

- Use the **Number data type** for fields that contain numeric data. Don't use the Number data type for data consisting of numerals that will not be used in calculations. For example, the data type for telephone numbers should be defined as Text rather than Number.

- Use the **Date & Time data type** for dates and times. This special data type makes it much easier, for example, to determine if one date occurs before or after another date.

- When you allow Access to define the primary key, the ID field is created using the **AutoNumber data type**. A unique number is automatically entered in this field as you enter each new record.

- The **Yes/No data type** can be useful for fields designed to hold simple Yes/No or True/False data. For example, you might use a Yes/No data type for the field "Subtitled?"

• How do I create tables? (continued)

After you select a data type, Access waits for you to enter a field name. Simply type the field name and then press the Enter key.

Figure 10-5

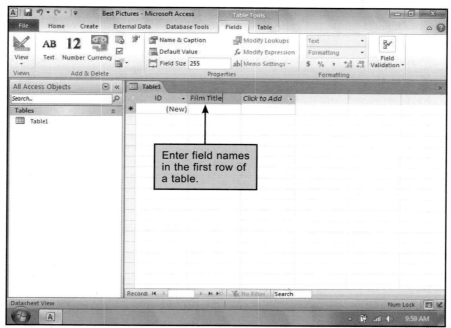

Enter field names in the first row of a table.

• Field names can contain spaces, so "Film Title" is acceptable. To make documentation easier, some database designers prefer not to use spaces in field names, in which case the field name would be "FilmTitle". Whichever style you use for field names, try to use consistent spacing and capitalization for all fields.

• The maximum length for a field name is 64 characters, but in most cases try to limit the size of a field name to 20 characters or less.

• You can change the name of a field at any time, even after you've entered data into a table.

• How do I create tables? (continued)

The empty table contains an ID field designed to be used as the primary key. A **primary key** is a field that uniquely identifies each record. It's very important that no two records are ever assigned the same value for this unique field.

The ID field's data type is AutoNumber, which means that Access automatically assigns a unique value to each record, beginning with 1 for the first record. Because the primary key field must be unique for each record, there is a checkmark in the Field Validation group's Unique box.

You can modify the ID field to accommodate primary keys, such as SKUs, Social Security numbers, or telephone numbers, by changing the field name and data type as necessary. For example, in the Best Pictures database, only one movie receives the award each year, so the year can be used as the primary key.

Figure 10-6

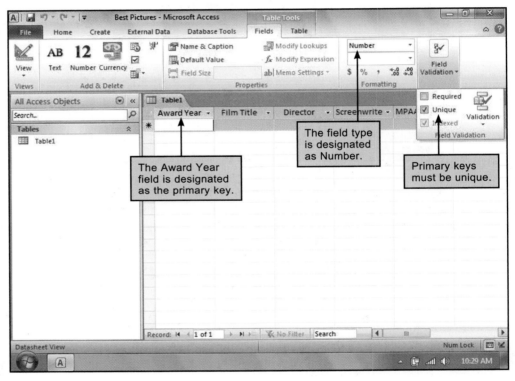

• When the Unique box contains a checkmark, Access will make sure that the contents of the field are unique for each record. For example, if the table contains a Best Picture winner for 1964 and you mistakenly enter "1964" when adding a new record, Access will not save the new record until you correct the date.

FAQ How do I save tables?

You can save a table at any time as you are defining the fields or entering data. After saving a table, you can continue to edit it, so the save process is simply a way of saving work in progress as a precaution against power outages or hardware glitches.

The quickest way to save a table is to click the Save icon on the Quick Access toolbar. You'll be asked to supply a name for the table; and once the save is complete, the table name will appear in the Tables list and on the Table tab.

Figure 10-7

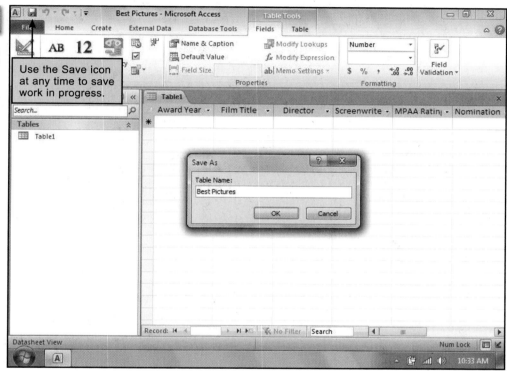

- To create additional tables, click the Create tab and then select Table.

- Give each table a unique and descriptive name so that you can identify it easily.

- A table can have the same name as the database, but that is not a requirement. For example, a database called Contacts.accdb might have tables called Contacts, Meetings, and so on.

- All tables in the database are stored in the same database file.

- If you are saving on a CD, DVD, or USB flash drive, do not remove it from the computer until the Access window closes. If you remove it too soon, your database file might become corrupted and some of your data could be lost.

- To open a table the next time you start Access, open the database and then double-click the table name in the Navigation pane.

FAQ How do I enter and edit data in a table?

Once you've defined the fields for a table, you can enter data. If you have just created a table, the table is open. If the table is not open, double-click the name of the table in the Navigation pane. Access displays an empty record into which you can begin to enter data.

Figure 10-8

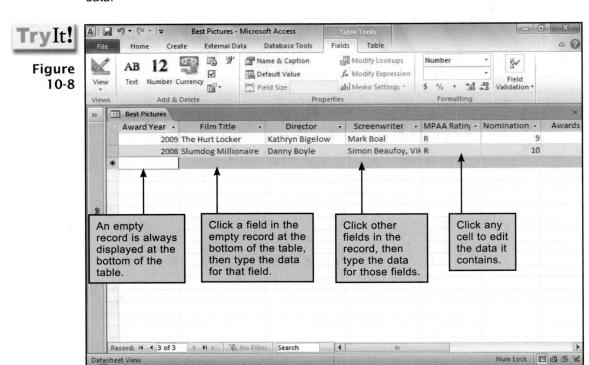

An empty record is always displayed at the bottom of the table.

Click a field in the empty record at the bottom of the table, then type the data for that field.

Click other fields in the record, then type the data for those fields.

Click any cell to edit the data it contains.

• When entering data, you can use the Tab key to move from one field to the next without having to move your hand to the mouse.

• Be careful to enter data in a consistent manner. Do not, for example, enter PG-13 in the MPAA field for some records, but enter PG 13 without the hyphen in other records. Without consistent entries, the search term "PG-13" won't find all of the films containing material that might be inappropriate for children younger than 13.

• To edit data, click the cell containing the data. Use the left-arrow and right-arrow keys to move the insertion point within the field. Use the Backspace and Delete keys to delete text to the left or to the right of the insertion point, respectively.

• To delete an entire record, right-click the row header containing the record. Click Delete Record on the shortcut menu, then click the Yes button.

• Access saves each record as you enter it; it is not necessary to click the Save button to record changes to the data as you complete the entry for each one.

FAQ Can I import data into a database?

As an alternative to typing data into a database table, you can import data from files created with other software, including worksheets created with Excel, databases created with older versions of Access, and e-mail address books created with Outlook. You can also import comma-delimited files created with a word processor or exported from other software.

A **comma-delimited file**, sometimes referred to as a **CSV file** (comma-separated values), is simply data separated by commas similar to the following:

Stray Cat Blues,The Rolling Stones,4:37,Classic Rock
Buenos Aires,Madonna,4:09,Soundtrack
Over the Rainbow,Jason Castro,3:30,Folk

Many software applications offer an export option that creates a comma-delimited file. You can use the export option to create a file that can then be imported into Access. Import options are listed on Access's External Data tab.

Suppose you have a list of classic albums that you're planning to sell on eBay. The list has become so large that you want to manage it in Access. To import the list, begin by selecting *Import text file* from the External Data tab and then select the file that currently holds the music list.

TryIt!

Figure 10-9

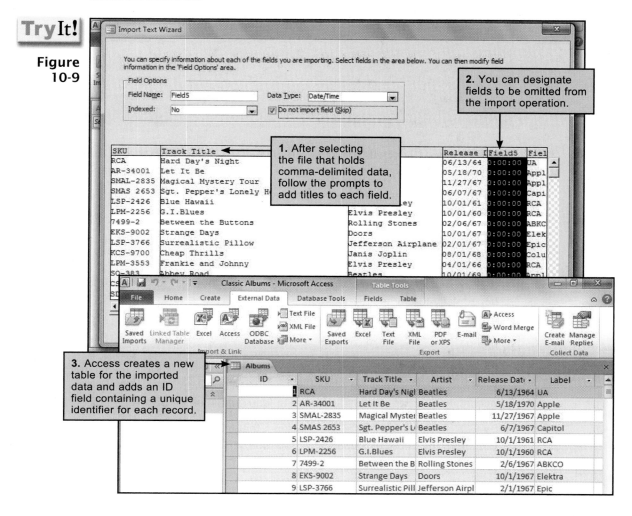

FAQ How do I work with tables?

Working with the data in an Access table has similarities to working with data in an Excel worksheet. You can add, delete, move, and sort data, as well as search for specific data items. Controls for these operations are on the ribbon, but they can also be accessed by right-clicking the column or row you want to work with.

Figure 10-10

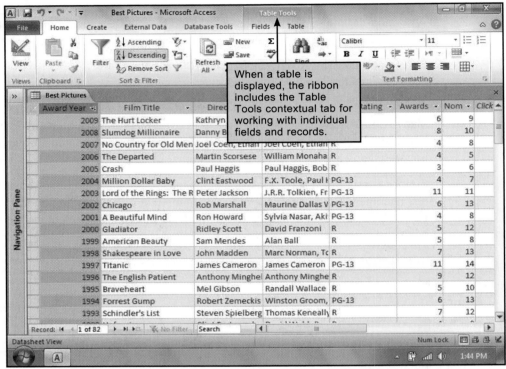

When a table is displayed, the ribbon includes the Table Tools contextual tab for working with individual fields and records.

- **Modify data.** Click the field you'd like to modify. Use the Backspace, Delete, and typing keys to change the data. Press the Enter key to complete the modification.

- **Insert a record.** Click the New (blank) record button at the bottom of the database window. New records are always added at the end of the table.

- **Delete a record.** Right-click the light-blue box on the left side of the record you want to delete. Select Delete Record from the shortcut menu.

- **Move a field.** Select the column or columns that you want to move. Drag the column horizontally to the desired location.

- **Hide a field.** Right-click the column title and select Hide Columns from the shortcut menu.

- **Sort records.** Right-click the column that holds data you want to use as the sort key; for example, click the MPAA Rating field if you would like all the records sorted according to rating. From the shortcut menu, select either *Sort A to Z* or *Sort Z to A*.

- **Search.** Right-click the title of the column that is likely to hold the data you seek. Select Find from the shortcut menu. Enter the data you seek in the *Find and Replace* dialog box. Click the Find Next button.

FAQ How do I create a query using a wizard?

After you have organized your data into one or more tables, you can manipulate the data in many ways. For example, you can search a company database for all customers in a specific state or search the Best Pictures database for winners from the years 1929–1945.

You can create a **query** to search your database for records that contain particular data. A query contains criteria that specify what you would like to find. You can also use a query to display data for only selected fields. The Query Wizard offers a quick way to create simple queries and use them to locate data.

Figure 10-11

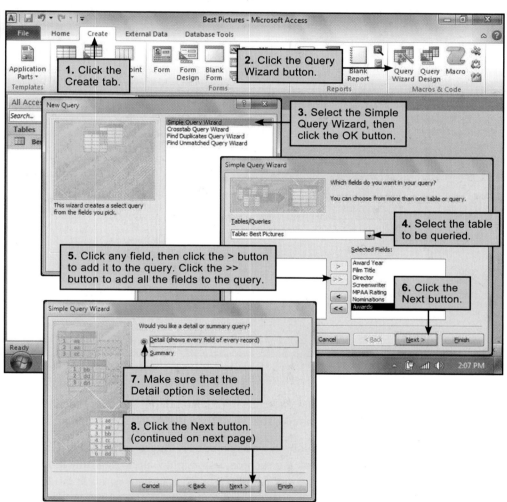

Simple Query Wizard - Which fields do you want in your query?

- The fields you select in this step will be included in the query results. Click a field, then click the > button to add an individual field. Click the >> button to add all fields. Click the < button to remove a field from the query. Click the << button to remove all fields.

Simple Query Wizard - Would you like a detail or summary query?

- Selecting the Detail option shows all of the specified fields for the records, whereas selecting the Summary option only displays the number of records that match your criteria.

• How do I create a query using a wizard? (continued)

**Figure
10-12**

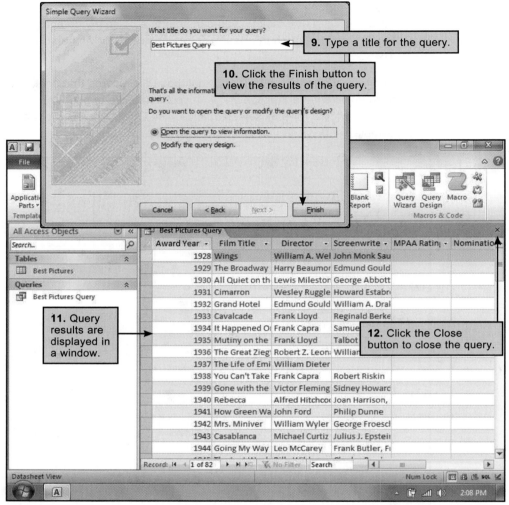

Simple Query Wizard - What title do you want for your query?

- After you enter a title and click the Finish button, the query results appear in a new window. In this example, results show data for the four fields specified by the query.

- To further refine a search, you can specify **query criteria**. For example, instead of a query that returns all the records, you might want to see only those records for films after 1995. To add query criteria, right-click the query tab at the top of the window, then click Design View on the shortcut menu. Type >1995 in the criteria row under the Award Year field. Click the [?] Run button in the Results group on the Query Tools Design contextual tab to display the query results. Records that match the criteria are displayed in the query results window.

- When you close the query window after modifying a query, you'll see a message asking *Do you want to save changes to the design of query 'Query Name'?* Click Yes if you would like to use the same criteria every time you use this query.

- After a query is saved, you can run it repeatedly to display all the records—including new and updated data—that match the criteria you've specified.

QuickCheck A

1. True or false? A relational database contains information that is organized into tables containing columns and rows. [＿＿＿＿＿]

2. A(n) [＿＿＿＿＿＿＿＿＿] contains a single piece of information, such as a name or zip code.

3. A(n) [＿＿＿＿＿＿＿＿＿] contains fields of information about a single entity in the database, such as a person, event, or thing.

4. True or false? Each time you enter new data into a record, you must save the table. [＿＿＿＿＿]

5. A(n) [＿＿＿＿＿] contains criteria that specify the data you want to find in a database.

Check It!

QuickCheck B

Indicate the letter of the desktop element that best matches the following:

1. A text field [＿＿＿]

2. A date field [＿＿＿]

3. A primary key field [＿＿＿]

4. A currency field [＿＿＿]

5. A blank field in a new record [＿＿＿]

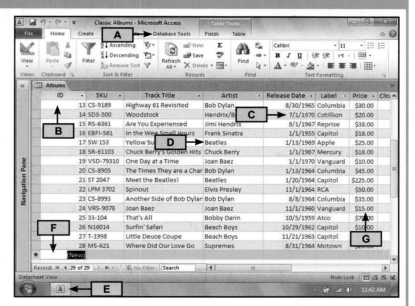

Check It!

Skill Tests

A｜ Creating database files

B｜ Creating tables

C｜ Entering data

D｜ Creating queries

Finalizing a Database

FAQ How do I create a form using a wizard?

You can organize your data into rows and columns using a table, which is the best way to view the data contained in a large number of records. Another way to display your data is with a form.

A **database form** allows you to view your data one record at a time, with the fields of each record arranged on your computer screen as they might be arranged on a printed form. Forms allow you to customize the way Access displays records by selecting particular fields, specifying the field order, and adding descriptive field labels. On-screen forms can be designed to resemble printed forms and simplify the data entry process. The Form Wizard helps you design an on-screen form in which you can enter and manipulate data for each record of a database.

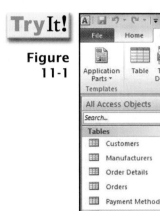

Figure 11-1

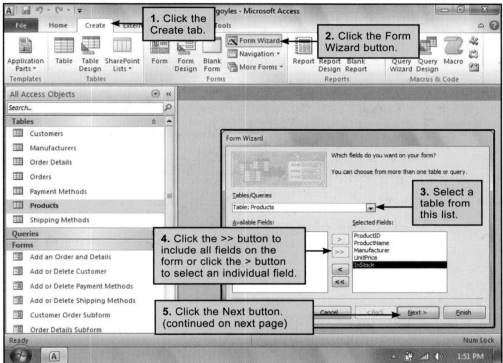

Form Wizard - Which fields do you want on your form?

- Most of the time, you'll want to include all fields on the form. To do so, click the >> button.

- As an alternative, you can select individual fields. For example, if you are going to enter specific data, such as today's purchases, you might use a form that shows only ID, FirstName, and LastName, along with a field for the purchase amount. You don't need to see the contact's address information while you are entering purchase data. To select a specific field, click it, then click the > button. Repeat these steps for each field you want to include on the form.

- You can remove an individual field from the Selected Fields list by clicking the < button.

•How do I create a form using a wizard? (continued)

Figure 11-2

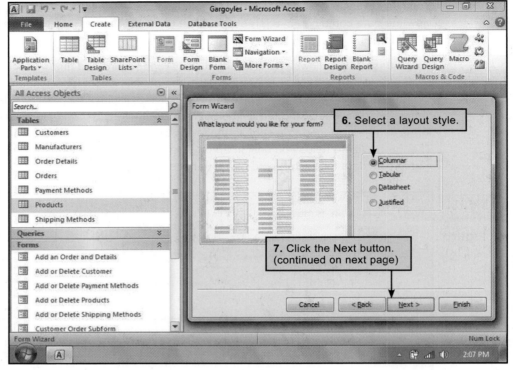

Form Wizard - What layout would you like for your form?

• The Columnar layout places labels next to fields, and lists the fields in columns. If you want your on-screen form to resemble a printed form, select the Columnar layout.

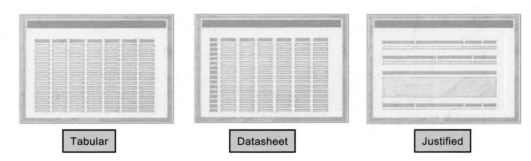

| Tabular | Datasheet | Justified |

• You can experiment with other layouts to see how they work for different types of data. The Tabular layout places field labels at the top of a column, which makes it appear like a table. The Datasheet layout resembles a spreadsheet, with cells for entering data. The Justified layout displays fields across the screen in rows, with a label above each field.

• How do I create a form using a wizard? (continued)

Figure 11-3

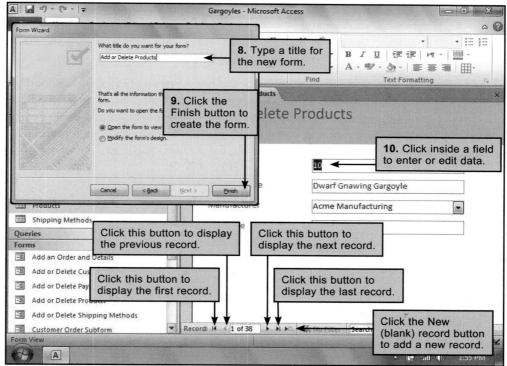

Form Wizard - What title do you want for your form?

- Forms that you create are automatically saved in the database file, so you don't have to save a form separately.

- When you use a form to add or change the data in a record, you have to use the Refresh All button on the Home tab to update the corresponding table.

- You can modify the design of any form by right-clicking the tab at the top of the form and selecting Design View.

- Click any label to edit it. To move a label and the associated data field, click to select the object, move the pointer over the edge of the object until the pointer changes to a ✛ shape, then drag the label and data field to a new location. To delete a label and data field from the form, right-click the label, then click Cut on the shortcut menu.

- You can change the form layout by right-clicking the form's tab, selecting Layout View, and using the buttons in the Table group on the Arrange tab.

- As you become more familiar with Access, you might eventually want to create forms using Design View rather than the Form Wizard. Start with a blank form, then add labels and controls. Design View provides maximum flexibility for designing a form, but requires more time on your part.

FAQ How do I create a report using a wizard?

When you want to create a polished printout of some or all of the data in your Access database, you can create a report. A **database report** is typically a printed document containing data selected from a database. Like a query, a report can be based on criteria that determine which data is included in the report.

To create a report, simply specify the fields you want to include. Reports often include totals and subtotals as well as detailed information. For example, you might create a report that lists inventory items sorted by manufacturer and item name. You could configure the report to simply display totals or you can create a report that calculates the total value of the inventory. The Report Wizard simplifies the process of creating a report.

TryIt!

Figure 11-4

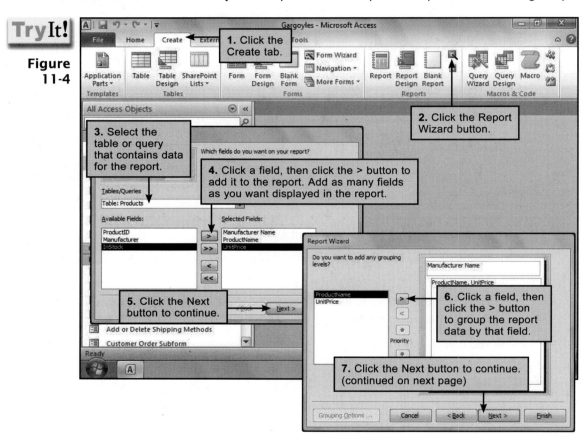

Report Wizard - Which fields do you want on your report?

- To add individual fields to the report, click a field, then click the > button. Click the >> button to add all available fields to the report.

Report Wizard - Do you want to add any grouping levels?

- When you add a grouping level, records are sorted according to entries in the group field. You can add several grouping levels to a report. For example, you might group a list of products by the manufacturer, then group them by item name. Grouping also helps arrange data when you want to produce a report containing subtotals.

• How do I create a report using a wizard? (continued)

**Figure
11-5**

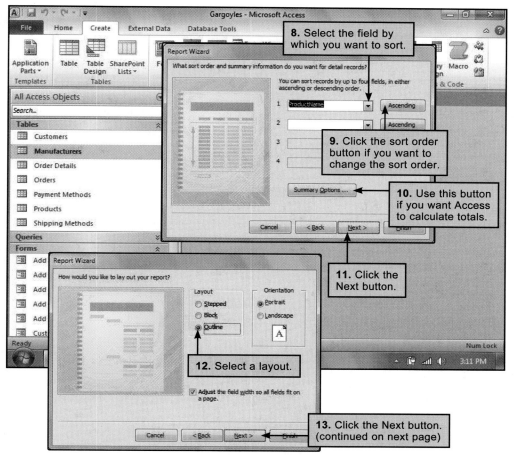

Report Wizard - What sort order and summary information do you want for detail records?

- To sort records within a group, click the down-arrow button and select the field by which you want to sort.

- Click the Ascending button to sort from A to Z (from low to high). Click the Descending button to sort from Z to A (high to low).

- The Summary Options button can be used to display totals, averages, minimums, or maximums for fields containing numeric data.

Report Wizard - How would you like to lay out your report?

- Select an option button in the Layout section. The preview area helps you visualize the layout of the completed report.

• How do I create a report using a wizard? (continued)

**Figure
11-6**

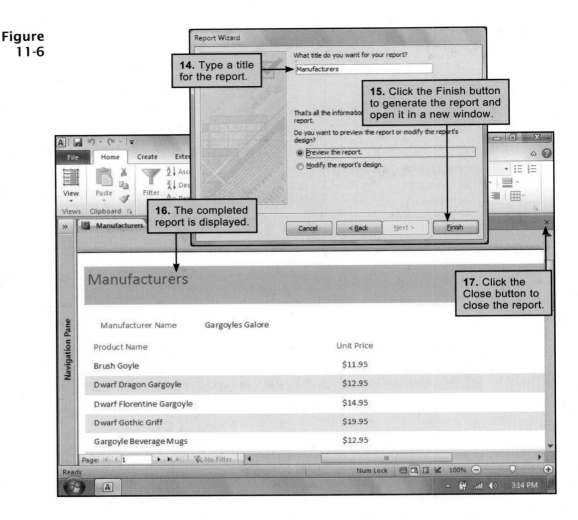

14. Type a title for the report.

15. Click the Finish button to generate the report and open it in a new window.

16. The completed report is displayed.

17. Click the Close button to close the report.

Report Wizard - What title do you want for your report?

- Type a report name, which is used to identify the report so that you can open it in the future. The report layout is automatically saved in the database file along with the tables, queries, and forms that you have already created.

- When you click the Finish button, the report is displayed. Use the vertical and horizontal scroll bars to view parts of the report that are not initially visible.

- You can modify the report layout at any time. Right-click the report name in the Navigation pane. Click Design View from the shortcut menu. You can use the options on the Report Design Tools tabs to modify the report. Select an object on the report, then use the sizing handles to adjust their size. To move an object, click the object to select it, move the pointer over the edge of the object until the pointer changes to a ✛ shape, then drag the object to a new location.

FAQ How do I print a report?

Each time you display or print a report, the contents of the report are automatically updated to reflect the current data stored in the database. For example, suppose that you print a report today. Over the next week, you add and change data in the database. If you display or print the report next week, it will include all of the updated data.

TryIt!

Figure 11-7

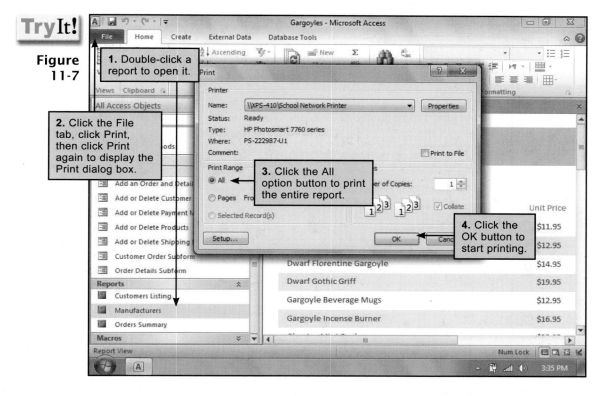

- The data in a printed report is a "snapshot" that shows the status of your database at a particular point in time. When you edit or add data to the database, your report includes new and revised data. It is a good idea to include the date the report was printed on all pages to help readers determine if the data is current.

- To add the date or time as a report header, right-click the report name in the Navigation pane, then click Design View on the shortcut menu. Click the *Date and Time* button in the Design tab. Select the date and time formats, then click the OK button. You can move the date and time fields to any location on the report. Select both fields by holding down the Shift key while you click each field. Move the pointer over the edge of the fields until the pointer changes to a ⊹ shape, then drag the fields to the desired location in the report.

Figure 11-8

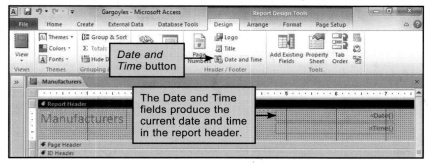

FAQ How do I save a report as a Web page?

Once you've created a report, you can print it or post it on the Web. As with other Web pages, your report must be in HTML format to be accessible to Web browsers.

Try It!

Figure 11-9

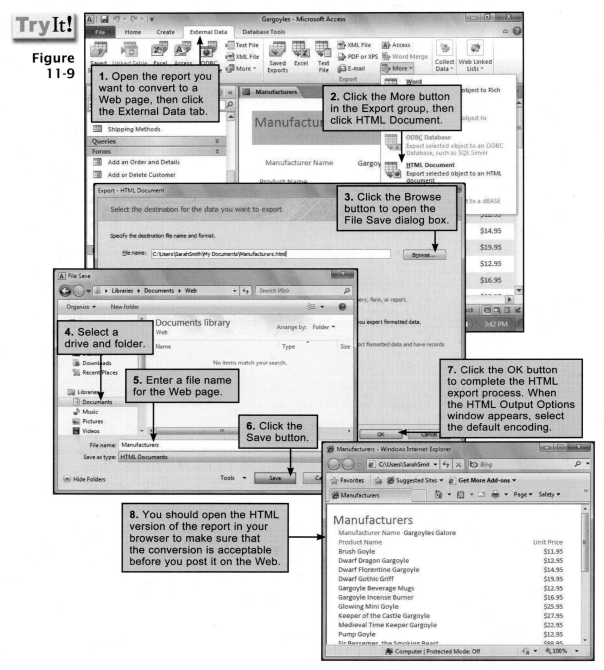

1. Open the report you want to convert to a Web page, then click the External Data tab.

2. Click the More button in the Export group, then click HTML Document.

3. Click the Browse button to open the File Save dialog box.

4. Select a drive and folder.

5. Enter a file name for the Web page.

6. Click the Save button.

7. Click the OK button to complete the HTML export process. When the HTML Output Options window appears, select the default encoding.

8. You should open the HTML version of the report in your browser to make sure that the conversion is acceptable before you post it on the Web.

- Use a Web browser to preview the report as a Web page. Microsoft Access usually does a fairly good job when converting reports to Web pages, but you should check to make sure that the report layout and data appear to be correct.

- As the data in your database changes, the Web page version of the report will become increasingly out of date. Periodically, you should open the report and export it again as a Web page. This action ensures that all new data is included in the Web-based version of the report.

FAQ Do I need to specify relationships?

In a relational database, tables can be related to each other and you can use that feature to make data management more efficient. For example, suppose that you operate a small eBay store selling gargoyle merchandise. You maintain an Access database to keep track of your merchandise. You also would like to keep track of orders.

You quickly realize that it doesn't make sense to add fields for customer names and addresses to your table of merchandise. You also realize that because a customer can order more than one item at a time, you need some way to include several items on an order. To handle orders, you can create two additional tables: one table with information about who placed the order, and one table for the items on each order. You can create links between the data in the three tables to view the data as a single order form showing all the details about the customer and ordered items.

In database terminology, a link between two tables is called a **relationship**. There are several types of relationships. In a **one-to-many relationship**, one record from a table is related to many records in another table, as when one order contains many items purchased by a customer.

In a **many-to-many relationship**, a record in one table can be related to several records in another table and vice versa. This complex relationship exists between movies and actors. One movie can have many actors, but any of those actors can also have roles in many other movies. A **one-to-one relationship** means that a record in one table is related to only one record in another table. This type of relationship is rare in the world of databases.

You can use the Relationships group on the Database Tools tab to create, view, and modify relationships between the tables in a database. Projects AC-7 and AC-8 provide additional information about setting up and maintaining relationships within the tables of a database.

Figure 11-10

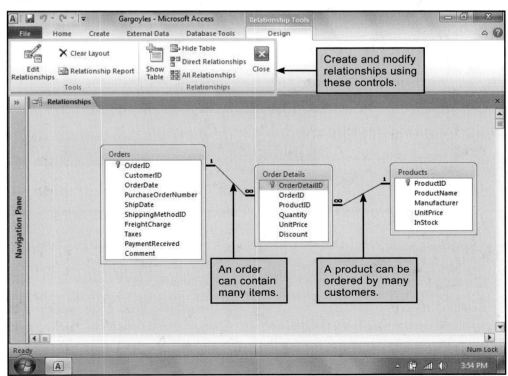

QuickCheck A

1. A database [_____] allows you to display one record at a time, rather than an entire table of data.

2. A database [_____] is typically a formatted printout of some or all of the data contained in a database.

3. True or false? You can use a form to view, edit, and add data to a table. [_____]

4. True or false? Reports are updated each time you display them. [_____]

5. True or false? Access automatically updates the data in Web pages every time you print a report. [_____]

Check It!

QuickCheck B

Indicate the letter of the desktop element that best matches the following:

1. A text field [____]

2. Add a record in Form view [____]

3. Access tools for relationships [____]

4. The *Last record* button [____]

5. Update the corresponding table [____]

Check It!

Skill Tests

A Creating forms

B Creating reports

C Printing reports

D Generating Web page reports

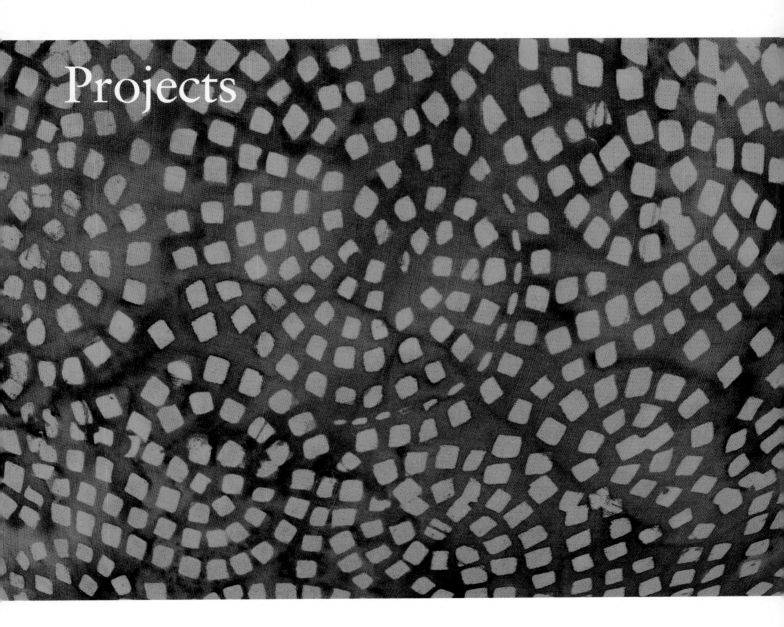

Projects

Projects

● **Presentation Projects**

● **Database Projects**

● **Capstone Projects**

Introduction to Projects

The projects in this section are designed to help you review and develop skills you learned by reading the chapter material and working with Try It! and assessment activities. Projects serve as a valuable intermediate step between the *Practical Microsoft Office* learning environment and working on your own. Even if you are not required to complete the projects for a class, you'll find that trying some of the projects can enhance your ability to use Microsoft Office 2010 software.

Required Software. Although not required for interacting with the Try It! activities in Chapters 1–11, Microsoft Office 2010 must be installed on the computer you use to complete the projects in this section.

To discover if Microsoft Office 2010 software has been installed on your computer, click the Start button, click All Programs, and then look for Microsoft Office on the programs list. Click the Microsoft Office folder. Microsoft Word 2010, Microsoft Excel 2010, Microsoft Access 2010, and Microsoft PowerPoint 2010 should be listed.

Project Help. If you don't remember how to complete a task for a project, refer to Chapters 1–11. They are designed to provide a quick reference to the skills you've learned. Keep the printed book handy as you work on the projects and when working on your own.

Project Files. For many of the projects, you'll start by copying project files from the CD supplied with this book. You can copy a project file from the CD using the Copy It! button on the first page of a project. As another option, you can use the Start menu's Computer button or Windows Explorer to copy the files directly from the CD to a USB flash drive or to your computer's hard disk. We suggest keeping all of the project files together in one location. We will refer to this location as your Project folder.

How to Submit Assignments. At the completion of each project, you will have created a file that demonstrates your ability to apply your skills. To submit a completed project to your instructor, use one of the methods indicated in the instructions at the end of the project. Most projects can be printed, submitted on a USB flash drive, or sent as an e-mail attachment. Your instructor might have a preference for one of these methods. You'll find additional information about printing, saving, and e-mailing projects on the next two pages.

Submitting an Assignment as a Printout or on a Removable Storage Device

You can print or save your project files using the File tab, as shown in the figure below.

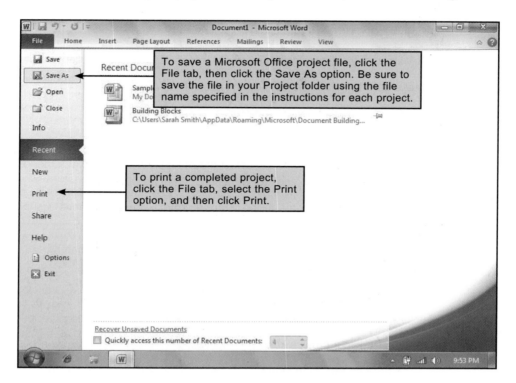

• To print a project file:

1. Make sure that a printer is attached to your computer and that it is turned on.

2. In Microsoft Office, click the File tab, select the Print option, and then click Print. When using other software, such as Paint or WordPad, click the leftmost tab, select the Print option, and then click Print.

3. If the printout doesn't already include your name, student ID number, class section number, date, and project name, be sure to write this information on the printout.

• To save your file on a removable storage device, such as a USB flash drive:

1. In Microsoft Office, click the File tab, then click the Save As option. When using other software, such as Paint or WordPad, click the leftmost tab, then select Save As.

2. When the Save As dialog box appears, navigate to the removable storage device.

3. In the *File name* box, enter the name specified by the project instructions.

4. Click the Save button to complete the process.

5. Before submitting a USB flash drive to your instructor, make sure that it is labeled with your name, student ID number, class section number, date, and project name.

Note: If you save your file on your computer's hard disk, you can use the Copy command in Windows Explorer to copy it to a USB flash drive.

Submitting an Assignment as an E-mail Attachment

You can typically use either Method 1 or Method 2, as explained below, to submit most projects. Access projects, however, require Method 1.

● Method 1—Add Attachments Manually

With Method 1, you'll send your project file using your local e-mail client or Webmail account.

1. Make sure that you have saved the project file.

2. Start your e-mail software and start a new message.

3. Address the new message to your instructor.

4. Click the Attachment button or select the Attachment option from a menu. If you don't see an Attachment option, look for a File option on the Insert menu.

5. When prompted, navigate to the folder that holds the attachment—usually your Project folder—and select the project file.

6. Click the Send button to send the e-mail message and attachment.

● Method 2—Use Microsoft Office 2010's Send Feature

If Microsoft Office 2010 is set up in conjunction with your e-mail software, you can send your project file directly from Word, Excel, or PowerPoint by using the following steps:

1. After saving your project, keep your application (Word, Excel, or PowerPoint) window open.

2. Click the File tab, then select the Share option. Select Send Using E-mail, then click *Send as Attachment*.

3. Enter your instructor's e-mail address in the To: box, enter the body of the e-mail, and then send it.

● Getting an E-mail Account

You can obtain a free Webmail account from e-mail providers such as Google (www.gmail.com), Hotmail (www.hotmail.com), or Yahoo! (www.yahoo.com). Use your Web browser to connect to the Webmail site and register for an account. You'll be able to use it as soon as you complete the registration process.

When you use a Webmail account, complete your project offline. Then, connect to your Webmail account, create a new message addressed to your instructor, and then attach your project file to the message before sending it.

If you prefer to use local e-mail, you'll need to set up an account with an ISP or some other provider, such as your school. To set up a local e-mail account, you might need to obtain the following information from your ISP:

● The Internet access phone number (dial-up service only)

● Your e-mail address (such as hfinn5678@verizon.net)

● Your e-mail password (such as huck2finn)

● The incoming mail server type (usually POP3)

● Your incoming mail server's name (often the part of your e-mail address that comes after the @ symbol, such as aol.com)

● Your outgoing SMTP mail server's name (such as mailhost.att.net)

● The primary and secondary domain name server (DNS) numbers (such as 204.127.129.1)

Microsoft Office 2010 Configuration

Microsoft Office 2010 provides many ways for you to configure and modify the way its applications look and operate. While this adaptability can be a positive feature, it can potentially cause confusion if your version of Microsoft Office 2010 is not configured to look or work the same way as the version used for the examples in *Practical Microsoft Office 2010*. Here's how to configure your software to match the settings that were used for the instructions and figures in this chapter.

- To configure Microsoft Word, Excel, and PowerPoint:

1. Click the File tab, then select Options. On the General tab, make sure *Show Mini Toolbar on selection* and Enable Live Preview are selected.

- To configure Microsoft Access:

1. The entire ribbon should be visible. If it is not, double-click one of the tabs at the top of the application window.

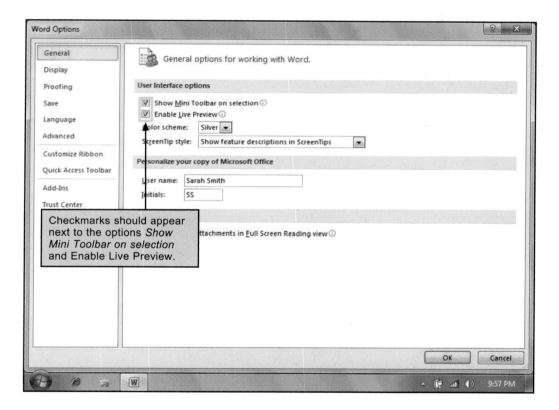

The sample screens were produced on a screen with 1024 x 768 resolution. If your computer's screen resolution is different, the images might appear slightly different, though they will not be incorrect.

- To configure your screen resolution:

1. Right-click any blank area of the Windows desktop.

2. Click *Screen resolution.*

3. Choose 1024 x 768 resolution and then click the OK button.

Project AP-1: Working with Application Windows

In this project, you'll apply what you've learned about application windows to start several programs and arrange your desktop.

Requirements: This project requires Microsoft Windows, WordPad, and Paint.

Project file: No project file is required for this project.

You can write your answers to the questions on a sheet of paper with your name and the title AP-1 Answers. The number for each answer should correspond to the number of the step that contains the question. For example, your first answer will be for Step 5.

1. Start the Paint program. Make sure that the Paint window is maximized.

2. Draw a lightning bolt toward the center of the screen by clicking the lightning shape in the Shapes group. Complete the shape by clicking any blank area of the screen.

3. Click the ▣ Restore button.

4. Minimize the Paint window, then reopen it by clicking its button on the taskbar.

5. Click the ⬚ button in the upper-left corner. What are the menu options? [＿＿＿＿＿＿＿＿]

6. What are the three other buttons on the left side of the titlebar? [＿＿＿＿＿＿＿＿]

7. What happens when you click the down-arrow labeled Customize Quick Access Toolbar? [＿＿＿＿＿＿＿＿]

8. How many tabs are there in the Paint window and what are their names? [＿＿＿＿]

9. Start another instance of the Paint program. Maximize the window.

10. Draw a heart toward the center of the screen. Complete the shape by clicking any blank area of the screen.

11. Type someone's name inside the heart using the Text tool in the Tools Group. Click any blank area of the screen to close the text box.

12. Minimize both Paint windows, then hover over the taskbar to view thumbnails of both windows.

13. Open one Paint window, then open the other window. Right-click a blank area on the taskbar and select *Cascade windows*.

14. View the windows side by side.

15. View the windows stacked.

16. Start the WordPad program by typing wordpad in the Start Menu's Search box.

17. Try viewing all windows three different ways: cascade, side by side, and stacked.

18. Maximize the Paint window containing the lightning bolt. Add a five-point star beside the lightning shape.

19. Choose any two other applications and open them.

20. View all five windows side by side.

•Working with Application Windows (continued)

21. Using the Paint window's side and bottom scroll bars, position all graphics in the windows so you can view them. Your screen should look similar to the one below. The different windows need not be located in the exact same place.

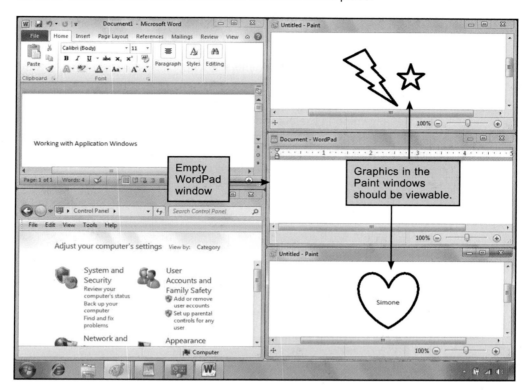

22. Press the PrtSc or Print Screen key on your keyboard.

23. Maximize one of the Paint windows and paste the screenshot.

24. Save the screenshot as a JPEG file in your Project folder and name it PrjAP-1 XXXXX 9999, where XXXXX is your name or student ID number and 9999 is your class section number.

25. Close all open windows.

26. Use one of the following options to submit your project on a USB flash drive, as a printout, or as an e-mail attachment, according to your instructor's directions:

• To submit the project on a USB flash drive, copy the file PrjAP-1 XXXXX 9999 from your Project folder to a USB drive. Make sure your name is on the USB drive.

• To print the project, click the leftmost tab, select the Print option, and then click Print. Write your name, student ID, class section number, date, and PrjAP-1 on the printout.

• To submit the project as an e-mail attachment, use Method 1 as described on page 156. Type your instructor's e-mail address in the To: box. Click the Subject: box, then type PrjAP-1, your student ID number, and your class section number. Click the Send button or perform any additional steps required by your e-mail software to send an e-mail message.

27. Submit your answer sheet. Include your name, student ID number, class section number, date, and PrjAP-1.

Project AP-2: Working with Files

In this project, you'll apply what you've learned about Windows applications to create, save, open, and delete a file.

Requirements: This project requires Microsoft Windows and WordPad.

Project file: No project file is required for this project.

1. Start the WordPad program by typing wordpad in the Start Menu's Search box.

2. Make sure that the WordPad window is maximized.

3. Click anywhere in the blank section of the document window and type the following short memo. Type your own name on the FROM: line and type today's date on the DATE: line. (Hint: Press the Enter key at the end of each line.)

MEMO

TO: Professor Greer

FROM: [Your name]

DATE: [Today's date]

SUBJECT: This week's lesson

I will not be able to attend my music lesson this week.

4. Save the document in your Project folder as PrjAP-2.txt. (Hint: Use the *Save as type* list if necessary to make sure the file is saved as a Text Document.)

5. Stop the WordPad application by closing its window.

6. Start WordPad again. Open the file PrjAP-2.txt from your Project folder.

7. Type the word IMPORTANT so that the first line of the document reads IMPORTANT MEMO. Your document should now look like the one shown on the next page.

• Working with Files (continued)

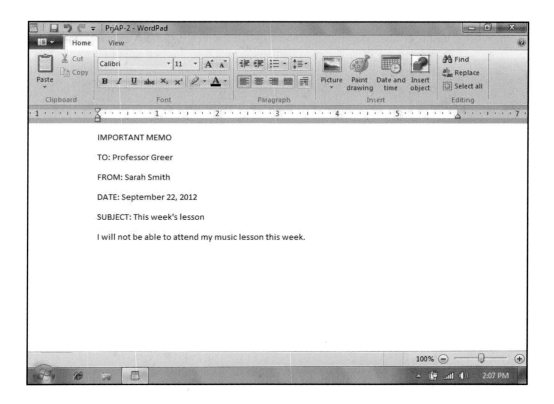

8. Save the new version of your document under a different name in your Project folder. Use PrjAP-2 XXXXX 9999 as the new name, where XXXXX is your name or student ID number and 9999 is your class section number.

9. Use one of the following options to submit your project on a USB flash drive, as a printout, or as an e-mail attachment, according to your instructor's directions:

- To submit the project on a USB flash drive, first close the WordPad window. Copy the file PrjAP-2 XXXXX 9999 from your Project folder to a USB drive. Make sure your name is on the USB drive.

- To print the project, click the leftmost tab, select the Print option, and then click Print. Write your name, student ID number, class section number, date, and PrjAP-2 on the printout.

- To e-mail the memo file, use Method 1 as described on page 156. Type your instructor's e-mail address in the To: box. Click the Subject: box and type PrjAP-2, your student ID number, and your class section number. Click the Send button or perform any additional steps required by your e-mail software to send an e-mail message.

10. Delete the original file, PrjAP-2.txt, from your Project folder.

Project AP-3: Configuration and Navigation Basics

In this project, you'll explore how to use the Word Options dialog box to configure user information and file location settings. You'll also explore some efficient ways to navigate within documents. You'll find out how to use Ctrl End to move to the end of a document in one jump. You'll experiment with the Page Up, Page Down, Home, and End keys, then use the Go To command to jump to a specified page.

Requirements: This project requires Microsoft Word.

Project file: PrjAP-3.docx

1. Copy the file PrjAP-3.docx to your Project folder using the Copy It! button on this page in the BookOnCD.

2. Start Microsoft Word.

3. Open the file PrjAP-3.docx from your Project folder.

4. Click the File tab, and then click the Options button. When the Word Options dialog box appears, click the Save tab on the left and notice the default location set to hold your documents when you save them. Click the Browse button to view the dialog box that allows you to change this location. Unless you want to change the location now, click the Cancel button to return to the Word Options dialog box.

5. Select the General tab. Enter your name in the *User name* text box if it is not already there.

6. Click the OK button to save your User Information and close the Word Options dialog box.

7. Click the View tab, then click the Print Layout button.

8. Press Ctrl End to move to the end of the document. (Hint: Make sure Num Lock is off if you are using the End key on the numeric keypad.)

9. Press Ctrl Enter to insert a page break.

10. Make sure the insertion point is at the top of the new page and type the following:

Breakout Session Evaluation

Please provide comments on the effectiveness of each breakout session. Do not sign your evaluation.

11. Use the scroll bar to scroll to the beginning of the document.

12. Press the Page Down key a few times and notice how this key changes the position of the insertion point. Press the Page Up key to return to the top of the document.

13. Click in the middle of any full line of text in the document. Press the Home key and notice how this key changes the position of the insertion point. Press the End key to see what it does.

14. Click the Home tab and use the Editing Group's GoTo command to jump to page 5. When page 5 is displayed, close the *Find and Replace* dialog box.

• Configuration and Navigation Basics (continued)

15. Add the following line to the end of the memo:

Drop it off on the table at the conference room door before you leave.

The last page of your document should now look like the one shown below.

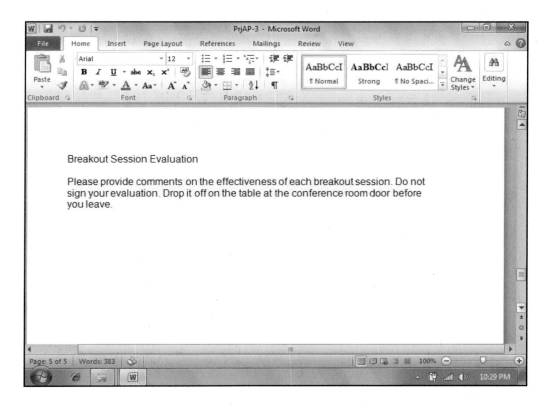

16. Save the new version of your document under a different name in your Project folder. Use PrjAP-3 XXXXX 9999 as the new name, where XXXXX is your name or student ID number and 9999 is your class section number.

17. Use one of the following options to submit your project on a USB flash drive, as a printout, or as an e-mail attachment, according to your instructor's directions:

• To submit the project on a USB flash drive, close Word and then copy the file PrjAP-3 XXXXX 9999 from your Project folder to a USB drive. Make sure your name is on the USB drive.

• To print the project, click the File tab, select the Print option, and then click Print. Write your name, student ID number, class section number, date, and PrjAP-3 on the printout.

• To e-mail the project file, use Method 1 or Method 2, as described on page 156. Type your instructor's e-mail address in the To: box. Click the Subject: box and type PrjAP-3, your student ID number, and your class section number. Click the Send button or perform any additional steps required by your e-mail software to send an e-mail message.

Project WD-1: Creating a Word Document

In this project, you'll apply what you've learned about Microsoft Word to create a document, modify it, and insert a hyperlink.

Requirements: This project requires Microsoft Word.

Project file: No project file is required for this project.

1. Start Microsoft Word.

2. Create a new document containing the text below, placing a blank line between each paragraph:

Dear Marjorie,

Hi! I was happy to receive your letter and learn that all is going well with you, Bob, and the kids. I really miss you all!

Your new job at the bookstore sounds great! How do you manage to keep your mind on work where there are so many fascinating books and magazines just begging to be read?

You mentioned that your first big assignment is to create a display appropriate for the month of February, but without featuring Valentine's Day or Presidents' Day. Did you know that I keep a database of offbeat events, like International Tuba Day and National Accordion Awareness Month? Let me know if you're interested and I'll create a query and send you a list of interesting events.

Sorry for the shortness of this note, but I have to run off to class. I promise to write more soon.

Good luck with the new job!

3. Compare the text that you typed with the text shown above and correct any typing mistakes that you might have made.

4. Use the Delete key to delete the phrase "create a query and" from the last sentence of the third paragraph. The Delete key deletes text without copying it to the Clipboard.

5. Copy the phrase "for the month of February" from the third paragraph. Paste the copied phrase before the period at the end of the sentence that ends with "send you a list of interesting events."

6. Select the sentence "I really miss you all!" in the first paragraph. Drag and drop the sentence after the sentence "Good luck with the new job!" at the end of the document.

7. Delete the fourth paragraph of the document.

8. Use the Undo button to restore the deleted paragraph.

9. While holding down the mouse button, drag the pointer over the phrase "International Tuba Day" to select it.

10. Right-click the selected phrase and select Hyperlink from the shortcut menu. Make sure the *Text to display* box contains "International Tuba Day."

11. In the Address box, enter www.tubaday.com and then click the OK button.

• Creating a Word Document (continued)

12. You've created a hyperlink in your document. To test it, hold down the Ctrl key and click the link. Once you've connected to the International Tuba Day site, you can close your browser and complete the remaining steps in the project.

13. Compare your letter with the document below. Don't worry if the sentences in your document break in different places at the right margin.

Dear Marjorie,

Hi! I was happy to receive your letter and learn that all is going well with you, Bob, and the kids.

Your new job at the bookstore sounds great! How do you manage to keep your mind on work where there are so many fascinating books and magazines just begging to be read?

You mentioned that your first big assignment is to create a display appropriate for the month of February, but without featuring Valentine's Day or Presidents' Day. Did you know that I keep a database of offbeat events, like International Tuba Day and National Accordion Awareness Month? Let me know if you're interested and I'll send you a list of interesting events for the month of February.

Sorry for the shortness of this note, but I have to run off to class. I promise to write more soon.

Good luck with the new job! I really miss you all!

---

14. Add your name as the last line of the letter.

15. Save your document in your Project folder as PrjWD-1 XXXXX 9999, where XXXXX is your name or student ID number and 9999 is your class section number.

16. Use one of the following options to submit your project on a USB flash drive, as a printout, or as an e-mail attachment, according to your instructor's directions:

- To submit the project on a USB flash drive, close Word and then copy the file PrjWD-1 XXXXX 9999 from your Project folder to a USB drive. Make sure your name is on the USB drive.

- To print the project, click the File tab, select the Print option, and then click Print. Write your name, student ID number, class section number, date, and PrjWD-1 on the printout.

- To submit the project as an e-mail attachment, use Method 1 or Method 2, as described on page 156. Type your instructor's e-mail address into the To: box. Click the Subject: box and type PrjWD-1, your student ID number, and your class section number. Click the Send button or perform any additional steps required by your e-mail software to send an e-mail message.

Project WD-2: Using the Mail Merge Wizard

In this project, you'll use Microsoft Word's Mail Merge Wizard to create an address list and perform a mail merge.

Requirements: This project requires Microsoft Word.

Project file: No project file is required for this project.

1. Start Microsoft Word.

2. Click the Mailings tab. Click Start Mail Merge in the Start Mail Merge group, then click *Step by Step Mail Merge Wizard*.

3. In the Mail Merge task pane, select Letters as the type of document, then click *Next: Starting document*.

4. In the Mail Merge task pane, select Start from a template, then click the *Select template* link. Select the Urban Letter template from the Letters tab, then click OK. Click *Next: Select recipients*.

5. In the Mail Merge task pane, select the *Type a new list* option, then click the Create link. Enter the following information in the New Address List dialog box:

First Name	Last Name	Address 1	City	State
Jim	Gallagos	1420 Elm Pass	Springfield	IL
Ed	Zimmerman	1562 River Way	Springfield	IL
Alice	Wegin	523 West Ave	Oak Grove	IL

Use the New Entry button to insert new rows. When you've entered all three names, click the OK button to close the New Address List dialog box.

6. Save the list as Address List in your Project folder. Click the OK button to close the Mail Merge Recipients dialog box. Click *Next: Write your letter*.

7. In the upper-right corner of the letter, delete the name placeholder and then replace the sender company address placeholder with the following return address:

Perfect Pizza
1320 W. Oak Grove Rd.
Springfield, IL

8. Delete the placeholders for the recipient's address and name. Click the *Address block* link from the Mail Merge task pane and then click the OK button to close the Insert Address Block dialog box.

9. Select today's date for the date placeholder.

10. Delete the placeholder for the salutation. Click the *Greeting line* option from the Mail Merge task pane, select any salutation, then click the OK button.

11. Replace the placeholder for the letter's text with:

I'm pleased to announce that Perfect Pizza has opened a new branch in your neighborhood! Stop by any time this week for a free slice of pizza!

12. Delete the placeholder for the name at the bottom of the page. Replace the placeholder for the closing with:

Sincerely,

Paul DiCella

• Using the Mail Merge Wizard (continued)

13. From the Mail Merge task pane, click *Next: Preview your letters*. Use the Forward and Back buttons on the Mail Merge task pane to view the merged letters.

14. From the Mail Merge task pane, click *Next: Complete the merge*. On the task pane, click *Edit individual letters*. Click All, then click the OK button. The mail merge is complete. Scroll down the document. You should have three individually addressed letters.

15. Compare the first letter to the document shown below. Don't worry if the date is different.

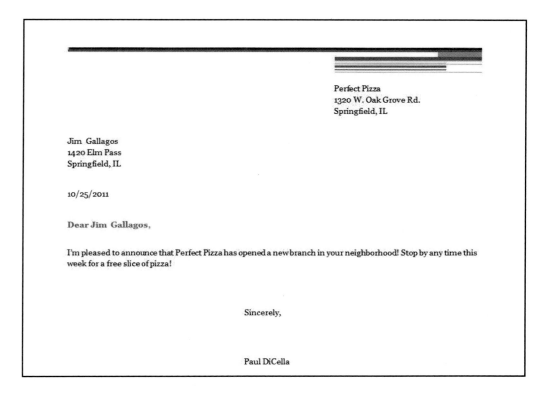

Perfect Pizza
1320 W. Oak Grove Rd.
Springfield, IL

Jim Gallagos
1420 Elm Pass
Springfield, IL

10/25/2011

Dear Jim Gallagos,

I'm pleased to announce that Perfect Pizza has opened a new branch in your neighborhood! Stop by any time this week for a free slice of pizza!

Sincerely,

Paul DiCella

16. Save your document in your Project folder using the file name PrjWD-2 XXXXX 9999, where XXXXX is your name or student ID number and 9999 is your class section number.

17. Use one of the following options to submit your project on a USB flash drive, as a printout, or as an e-mail attachment, according to your instructor's directions:

• To submit the project on a USB flash drive, close Word and then copy the file PrjWD-2 XXXXX 9999 from your Project folder to a USB drive. Make sure your name is on the USB drive.

• To print the project, click the File tab, select the Print option, and then click Print. Write your name, student ID number, class section number, date, and PrjWD-2 on the printouts.

• To submit the project as an e-mail attachment, use Method 1 or Method 2, as described on page 156. Type your instructor's e-mail address in the To: box. Click the Subject: box and type PrjWD-2, your student ID number, and your class section number. Click the Send button or perform any additional steps required by your e-mail software to send an e-mail message.

Project WD-3: Cut, Copy, and Paste

In this project, you'll apply what you've learned about Microsoft Word to copy and paste text, and automatically insert special symbols as well as the date and time.

Requirements: This project requires Microsoft Word and Microsoft Excel.

Project file: PrjWD-3.xlsx

1. Copy the file PrjWD-3.xlsx to your Project folder using the Copy It! button on this page in the BookOnCD.

2. Start Microsoft Word.

3. Create a new document containing the text below, placing a blank line between each paragraph:

MEMO

To: All Staff

Date:

Congratulations to Maria, winner of our quarterly sales bonus! Maria has sold over 1,000 SuperWidgets this year!

Sales totals are as follows:

4. Press the Enter key.

5. Start Microsoft Excel.

6. Click the File tab, then click Open to open the file PrjWD-3.xlsx from your Project folder.

7. Highlight cells A1 through D9. To do this, first click cell A1 where it says "Monthly Sales Totals by Salesperson." Next, hold down the Shift key and click cell D9, which contains $1,004.26.

8. Copy the cells using the Copy button in the Clipboard group on the Home tab. As an alternative, you can use the Ctrl C key combination.

9. Switch back to Microsoft Word.

10. Make sure the insertion point is positioned below the last line of the document.

11. Use the Paste button in the Clipboard group on the Home tab (or press Ctrl V) to paste the spreadsheet data into the document.

12. Switch back to Microsoft Excel. Copy the Congratulations clip art from the spreadsheet. Switch to Microsoft Word and paste the clip art into the document. Use the Text Wrapping options on the Picture Tools contextual tab to size and position the clip art just to the right of the memo heading lines containing: MEMO, To, and Date.

13. If the Paste operation was successful, switch back to Microsoft Excel and close it.

14. In your Microsoft Word document, position the insertion point after the word "Date" on the third line of the memo. If necessary, press the Spacebar to create a space after the colon.

•Cut, Copy, and Paste (continued)

15. Click the Insert tab, then click Insert Date & Time in the Text group. Choose the third option to insert the date in the format March 16, 2012. Click the OK button to insert the date and time.

16. Position the insertion point at the end of the word "SuperWidgets."

17. On the Insert tab, use the Symbols button to insert the ™ trademark sign.

18. Your memo should look similar to the one below.

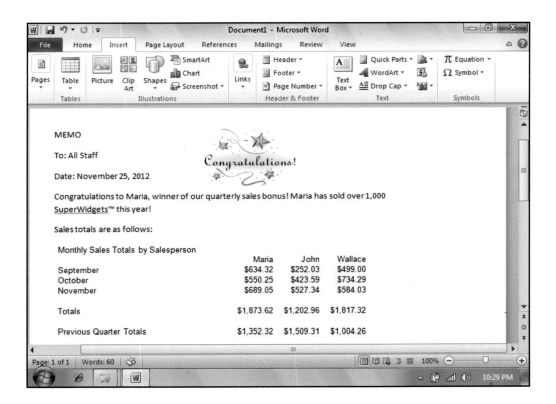

19. Save your memo in your Project folder using the file name PrjWD-3 XXXXX 9999, where XXXXX is your name or student ID number and 9999 is your class section number. Use one of the following options to submit your project:

- To submit the project on a USB flash drive, close Word and then copy the file PrjWD-3 XXXXX 9999 from your Project folder to a USB drive. Make sure your name is on the USB drive.

- To print the project, click the File tab, select the Print option, and then click Print. Write your name, student ID number, class section number, date, and PrjWD-3 on the printouts.

- To submit the project as an e-mail attachment, use Method 1 or Method 2, as described on page 156. Type your instructor's e-mail address in the To: box. Click the Subject: box and type PrjWD-3, your student ID number, and your class section number. Click the Send button or perform any additional steps required by your e-mail software to send an e-mail message.

Project WD-4: Troubleshooting Printing Problems

Sometimes documents fail to print. In this project, you'll experiment with various techniques to troubleshoot common printing problems.

Requirements: This project requires Microsoft Word.

Project file: No files are needed for this project.

1. Start Microsoft Word.

2. Create a new document containing the title below. As you go along, you can add to the document your answers for questions posed in Steps 4–8.

Exploring Printing Problems

3. Before printing, it is important to make sure your printer is plugged in, turned on, and online. On a separate sheet of paper, draw a diagram of the printer currently connected to your computer and label the power switch, power light, online light, and control panel.

4. What is the brand name and model of the printer that is connected to your computer?

5. One of the most common causes of printing problems is selecting the wrong printer. Use the File tab to select Print. What is the name of the printer displayed in the Printer box? Is it the same as the printer you worked with in Step 3? If not, select the correct printer using the arrow button on the Printer box.

6. Microsoft Windows provides help for troubleshooting printing problems. Open Windows Help and Support by clicking *Help and Support* on the Start menu. Enter printer problems in the Search box and press the Enter key. Start the *Printer troubleshooter*. What is the first question asked by the troubleshooter? After you answer this question, what happens?

7. Printers are ultimately controlled by the Windows operating system. Click the *Devices and Printers* button on the Control Panel. What are the names of all the installed printers and faxes? Which device is the default?

8. Check the print queue for the default printer. How many documents are in the print queue? What is their status?

9. You can print a test page to make sure the printer is working properly. Right-click your printer, and then select *Printer properties*. From the General tab, select Print Test Page. The test page might look similar to the figure on the next page.

• Troubleshooting Printing Problems (continued)

Windows
Printer Test Page

Congratulations!

If you can read this information, you have correctly installed your SnagIt 8
Printer on D7SQJZB1.

The information below describes your printer driver and port settings.

```
Submitted Time: 10:03:59 AM 4/22/2012
Computer name:  D7SQJZB1
Printer name:   SnagIt 8
Printer model:  SnagIt 8 Printer
Color support:  Yes
Port name(s):   C:\ProgramData\TechSmith\SnagIt 8\PrinterPortFile
Data format:    RAW
Share name:
Location:
Comment:
Driver name:    UNIDRV.DLL
Data file:      SNAGITP8.GPD
Config file:    UNIDRVUI.DLL
Help file:      UNIDRV.HLP
Driver version: 6.00
Environment:    Windows NT x86

Additional files used by this driver:
  C:\Windows\system32\spool\DRIVERS\W32X86\3\SNAGITD8.DLL        (8.2.1.215)
  C:\Windows\system32\spool\DRIVERS\W32X86\3\STDNAMES.GPD
  C:\Windows\system32\spool\DRIVERS\W32X86\3\UNIRES.DLL   (6.0.6000.16386
(vista_rtm.061101-2205))
  C:\Windows\system32\spool\DRIVERS\W32X86\3\SNAGITP8.INI

This is the end of the printer test page.
```

10. Save your Exploring Printing Problems document in your Project folder using the file name PrjWD-4 XXXXX 9999, where XXXXX is your name or student ID number and 9999 is your class section number.

11. Print your Exploring Printing Problems document and submit it along with your printer sketch and the test printout. Write your name, student ID number, class section number, date, and PrjWD-4 on all the submitted papers.

Project WD-5: Formatting a Document

In this project, you'll apply what you've learned about Microsoft Word to format an existing document.

Requirements: This project requires Microsoft Word.

Project file: PrjWD-5.docx

1. Copy the file PrjWD-5.docx to your Project folder using the Copy It! button on this page in the BookOnCD.

2. Start Microsoft Word.

3. Open the file PrjWD-5.docx from your Project folder.

4. Apply the bold text attribute to the line "Memorandum - Novel-Tea & Coffee, Inc."

5. Apply italics to the phrase "air-tight" in the sentence that begins "Please don't forget."

6. Apply bold and underlining to the phrase "number one" in the last sentence.

7. Select the Memorandum line, then change its font to Book Antiqua, size 18.

8. Center the Memorandum line.

9. Select the word "Memorandum." Use the Change Case button in the Font group on the Home tab to select UPPERCASE.

10. Select the list of items starting with "Bean quality," then format the list as a bulleted list.

11. Indent the first line of the main paragraphs by .4". The three paragraphs that you'll indent begin "Just a reminder," "Please don't forget," and "Thanks for helping."

12. Change the line spacing to 1.5 lines for the paragraphs that begin "Just a reminder," "Please don't forget," and "Thanks for helping."

13. Remove the underlining from the phrase "number one" in the last sentence.

14. Justify the paragraphs that begin "Just a reminder," "Please don't forget," and "Thanks for helping" so that both the left and right margins are straight.

15. For justified paragraphs, hyphenation can reduce some of the extra spacing added between words. On the Page Layout tab, use the Hyphenation button in the Page Setup group to access the Hyphenation dialog box. Place a checkmark in the box for *Automatically hyphenate document*. Uncheck the box for *Hyphenate words in CAPS*.

16. Change the number in the *Hyphenation zone* box to .35" to increase the space allowed between the end of a line and the right margin. This setting produces fewer hyphens in a document, but allows the right margin to become somewhat ragged.

17. Enter the number 1 in the *Limit consecutive hyphens to* box. Professional publishers prefer not to have more than one consecutive line ending with hyphens.

18. Click the OK button to close the Hyphenation dialog box, then compare your document with the document in the figure on the next page.

• Formatting a Document (continued)

MEMORANDUM - Novel-Tea & Coffee, Inc.

To: Tea n' Coffee Shop Managers
From: Food and Beverage Director, Novel-Tea & Coffee
RE: Reminder – Fundamentals of Coffee-making

Just a reminder to all Tea n' Coffee Shop managers that it takes more than our fine beans to make a quality cup of coffee. Sometimes our employees are so busy frothing cream or sprinkling cinnamon that they can forget the five key factors to creating the best possible cup of coffee. Listed below are the five fundamentals of superb coffee creation:

- Bean quality
- Water purity
- Elapsed time from roasting beans to perking
- Cleanliness of equipment
- Elapsed time from grinding beans to perking

Please don't forget to store all beans in clean, glass, *air-tight* containers to retain the freshness and aroma of the coffee beans. Beans from your weekly shipment that you don't anticipate using within the week must be kept in the refrigerator or freezer. This retains flavor by preventing chemical reactions in the beans.

Thanks for helping to make Tea n' Coffee Shops **number one** in the tri-state area.

---

19. Save your document in your Project folder using the file name PrjWD-5 XXXXX 9999, where XXXXX is your name or student ID number and 9999 is your class section number.

20. Use one of the following options to submit your project on a USB flash drive, as a printout, or as an e-mail attachment, according to your instructor's directions:

- To submit the project on a USB flash drive, close Word and then copy the file PrjWD-5 XXXXX 9999 from your Project folder to a USB drive. Make sure your name is on the USB drive.

- To print the project, click the File tab, select the Print option, and then click Print. Write your name, student ID number, class section number, date, and PrjWD-5 on the printout.

- To submit the project as an e-mail attachment, use Method 1 or Method 2, as described on page 156. Type your instructor's e-mail address in the To: box. Click the Subject: box and type PrjWD-5, your student ID number, and your class section number. Click the Send button or perform any additional steps required by your e-mail software to send an e-mail message.

Project WD-6: Using Tabs and Paragraph Alignment

In this project, you'll focus on font formats and tab settings.

Requirements: This project requires Microsoft Word.

Project file: PrjWD-6.docx

CopyIt!

1. Copy the file PrjWD-6.docx to your Project folder using the Copy It! button on this page in the BookOnCD.

2. Start Microsoft Word.

3. Open the file PrjWD-6.docx from your Project folder.

4. Select the document title "How Much Lead is in Your Cup?," then use the Font dialog box to change the title font to size 26, dark blue, bold italic with a shadow effect of Offset Right.

5. Select the list of items starting with "Perked coffee 90-150 mg" and ending with "Tea 30-70 mg." Use the Paragraph Dialog Box Launcher to open the Tabs dialog box and set a left tab at the 1" position. Set another left tab at the 3" position, with a dotted leader. Close the Tab dialog box.

6. Position the insertion point to the left of "Perked coffee," then press the Tab key to move it to the first tab position. Place the insertion point to the left of "90-150 mg," then press the Tab key to move it to the second tab position and display the dotted leader. Use a similar process with the remaining two list items.

7. Position the insertion point at the end of the line that ends with "30-70 mg," then press the Enter key to create a new line. Add this fourth list item, with appropriate tabs: Colas 30-35 mg.

8. Click the ¶ Show/Hide button in the Paragraph group on the Home tab to display non-printing characters. Notice that the locations in which you pressed the Tab key are indicated by arrows. The locations where you pressed the Enter key are indicated by the ¶ symbol.

9. Position the insertion point to the left of any ¶ symbol in the document. Press the Delete key to delete it. By removing this line break symbol, you joined two lines together.

10. To reestablish the original line break, click the Undo button on the Quick Access toolbar. Hide the non-printing characters by clicking the ¶ Show/Hide button.

11. At the top of the document, replace "Juan T. Sposito" with your name.

12. Compare your completed document with the document in the figure on the next page.

• Using Tabs and Paragraph Alignment (continued)

Novel-Tea News
Reporter: Sarah Smith

How Much Lead is in Your Cup?

Caffeine is a product found in many popular beverages. Yet most people are trying to curb their daily caffeine intake. After all, the effects of excessive caffeine have recently received a lot of press coverage.

As employees of Novel-Tea & Coffee, you will often get caffeine-related questions from customers. The following list of common drinks paired with their caffeine content may help you answer many of those questions.

Perked coffee	90-150 mg
Instant coffee	60-80 mg
Tea	30-70 mg
Colas	30-35 mg

Most customers also associate caffeine with chocolate. A typical chocolate bar contains 30 mg of caffeine. Yes, a cup of perked coffee does have three to five times the caffeine of a chocolate bar, but doesn't a chocolate bar have a few more calories than a cup of perked coffee?

So hopefully this information will help you answer commonly asked questions about caffeine and help us better serve our customers.

---

13. Save your document in your Project folder using the file name PrjWD-6 XXXXX 9999, where XXXXX is your name or student ID number and 9999 is your class section number.

14. Use one of the following options to submit your project on a USB flash drive, as a printout, or as an e-mail attachment, according to your instructor's directions:

* To submit the project on a USB flash drive, close Word and then copy the file PrjWD-6 XXXXX 9999 from your Project folder to a USB drive. Make sure your name is on the USB drive.

* To print the project, click the File tab, select the Print option, and then click Print. Write your name, student ID number, class section number, date, and PrjWD-6 on the printout.

* To submit the project as an e-mail attachment, use Method 1 or Method 2, as described on page 156. Type your instructor's e-mail address in the To: box. Click the Subject: box and type PrjWD-6, your student ID number, and your class section number. Click the Send button or perform any additional steps required by your e-mail software to send an e-mail message.

Project WD-7: Finalizing a Document

In this project, you'll apply what you've learned about Microsoft Word to check a document for errors, correct mistakes, set margins, use styles, display document statistics, add headers, and add footers. You'll also add footnotes, endnotes, and citations, plus find out how to assemble citations into a bibliography.

Requirements: This project requires Microsoft Word.

Project file: PrjWD-7.docx

1. Copy the file PrjWD-7.docx to your Project folder using the Copy It! button on this page in the BookOnCD.

2. Start Microsoft Word.

3. Open the file PrjWD-7.docx from your Project folder.

4. Use the Margins button on the Page Layout tab to set the right and left margins of the document to 1.25".

5. Use the right-click method to check the spelling of any words with a wavy red underline. If the spelling checker catches any proper names that you'd like to add to your custom dictionary, right-click and choose *Add to Dictionary*.

6. Use the *Spelling and Grammar* button on the Review tab to correct spelling and grammar errors.

7. Use the thesaurus to select a more appropriate word to replace "serious" in the first sentence of the third paragraph.

8. Add a left-justified header to the document that includes your name and your student ID number on one line; add your class section number and PrjWD-7 on a second line.

9. Add a right-justified footer that shows the word Page followed by the page number.

10. Apply the Heading 1 style to the first line in the document.

11. Click the File tab and then click the Options button. Select the Proofing option and make sure that the boxes for checking grammar and showing readability statistics are checked. Return to the document and perform a spelling check to view readability statistics.

12. Use the Find button on the Home tab to locate the word "BAR." Select the Reference tab and then add the endnote Browning Automatic Rifle.

13. Position the insertion point at the end of the paragraph on the first page that ends "...shot as spies." Use the Insert Citation button to add the following citation to the book: Insights into History by Jefferson MacGruder, published in 2008 by Random House (New York).

14. Go to the end of the document and right-click the endnote. Select *Convert to Footnote*, which moves it to the bottom of the page on which it is referenced.

15. Go to the end of the document once again. Press the Enter key and then click the Bibliography button on the References tab. Select the Works Cited option. Make sure that the Works Cited section of your document looks like the sample on the next page.

• Finalizing a Document (continued)

> In the big picture of World War II, Art and Ron were part of a desperate effort to repulse a last-ditch German attack that began on December 16. Many historians (Jones, 1998) now note that the Axis was on the brink of collapse and further struggle simply prolonged the course of the war and needlessly increased the number of casualties on both sides of the struggle.
>
>
> **Works Cited**
> Jones, G. (1998). *World War II Reconstructed.* Boston: Little Brown.
> MacGruder, J. (2008). *Insights into History.* New York: Random House.

16. Save your document in your Project folder using the file name PrjWD-7 XXXXX 9999, where XXXXX is your name or student ID number and 9999 is your class section number.

17. Click the File tab and select the Share option. Click the *Save to SkyDrive* option. SkyDrive is a Microsoft Windows Live online service for sharing documents and photos. You would need to sign up for a Windows Live ID to use this service. You do not need to use this option now. Just take note that this service is available to you.

18. Now notice the *Publish as Blog Post* option that would let you post this document directly to your blog. To use this option, however, you would have to sign up for a blog and then configure Word with the name and location of your blog. It is not necessary to post this document to a blog for this project.

19. Review your document. Make sure it contains citations in parentheses for MacGruder on page 1 and Jones on page 3, a footnote at the bottom of page 1, and a Works Cited section at the end of the document.

20. Use one of the following options to submit your project on a USB flash drive, as a printout, or as an e-mail attachment, according to your instructor's directions:

- To submit the project on a USB flash drive, copy the file PrjWD-7 XXXXX 9999 from your Project folder to a USB drive. Make sure your name is on the USB drive.

- To print the project, click the File tab, select the Print option, and then click Print. Write your name, student ID number, class section number, date, and PrjWD-7 on the printout.

- To submit the project as an e-mail attachment, use Method 1 or Method 2, as described on page 156. Type your instructor's e-mail address in the To: box. Click the Subject: box and type PrjWD-7, your student ID number, and your class section number. Click the Send button or perform any additional steps required by your e-mail software to send an e-mail message.

Project WD-8: Creating a Table

In this project, you'll apply what you've learned about Microsoft Word to create a table in a document.

Requirements: This project requires Microsoft Word.

Project file: PrjWD-8.docx

1. Copy the file PrjWD-8.docx to your Project folder using the Copy It! button on this page in the BookOnCD.

2. Start Microsoft Word.

3. Open the file PrjWD-8.docx from your Project folder.

4. Insert a table before the paragraph that starts "Because of the special nature." The table should consist of four columns and seven rows, and have a fixed column width.

5. Enter the following four labels into the first row of the table:

COFFEE (16 oz.)   TOTAL CALORIES   CALORIES   FROM FAT

6. Select all of the cells in the leftmost column. Resize the column by using the Table Tools Layout contextual tab. Change Width in the Cell Size group to 2.5". Center just the label using the Align Top Center button in the Alignment group.

7. You can combine two cells into one cell. Select the cells containing the labels "CALORIES" and "FROM FAT." Click Merge Cells in the Merge group. Fix the label so that it fits on one line.

8. With the merged cell still selected, create a new cell next to the merged cell by clicking Split Cells in the Merge group. Select 2 for number of columns and 1 for number of rows.

9. Enter the label FAT (grams) in the new cell.

10. Your labels should look similar to the example below. Enter the following data into the cells of the table, under the appropriate labels:

COFFEE (16 oz.)	TOTAL CALORIES	CALORIES FROM FAT	FAT (grams)
Black Coffee	0	0	0
Café Latte (non-fat milk)	126	0	0
Café Latte (whole milk)	204	99	11
Cappuccino (non-fat milk)	75	0	0
Cappuccino (whole milk)	120	54	6
Café Mocha (non-fat milk)	174	18	2

11. Insert one more row into the table and enter the following data:

Café Mocha (whole milk)	234	90	10

12. You can split a table if you need to. Select the cell in the first column, fifth row, and click Split Table in the Merge group. Click the Undo button on the Quick Access toolbar to go back to your original table.

13. Using the Table Tools Layout contextual tab, delete the row containing "Black Coffee."

• Creating a Table (continued)

14. Click Sort in the Data group of the Table Tools Layout contextual tab to sort the data in ascending order, first by TOTAL CALORIES, then by COFFEE. Select the number type for TOTAL CALORIES and the text type for COFFEE.

15. Click the Table Tools Design contextual tab. Highlight all the labels in the top row, click Shading in the Table Styles group, and select the Light Green standard color.

16. With all the top-row labels still highlighted, click Borders in the Table Styles group and select No Border. Click the Undo button on the Quick Access toolbar to restore the borders.

17. To automatically format the table, use the Table Styles group on the Table Tools Design contextual tab. Select the Medium List 2 - Accent 2 format.

18. If needed, insert a blank line so that the table is separated from the paragraphs above and below it.

19. At the top of the document, replace the reporter's name with your own name.

20. Compare your document to the figure below.

Novel-Tea News
Reporter: Sarah Smith

How Much Fat Is in Your Cup?

As employees of Novel-Tea & Coffee, you may be asked about the calories and the fat content of some of our standard and specialty drinks. The following list of standard drinks with their caloric and fat contents may help you answer those questions.

COFFEE (16 oz.)	TOTAL CALORIES	CALORIES FROM FAT	FAT (grams)
Cappuccino (non-fat milk)	75	0	0
Cappuccino (whole milk)	120	54	6
Café Latte (non-fat milk)	126	0	0
Café Mocha (non-fat milk)	174	18	2
Café Latte (whole milk)	204	99	11
Café Mocha (whole milk)	234	90	10

Because of the special nature of our monthly spotlight drinks, they are likely to be higher in both calories and fat content than any of the above drinks. We'll try to get you the data on a spotlight drink when we announce the drink.

If a customer is troubled by the calories or fat content of a particular drink, suggest a drink that's similar, but with fewer calories or less fat. For example, suggest a cappuccino instead of a café latte, or recommend using non-fat milk instead of whole milk. Hopefully this information will help you answer commonly asked questions and help us better serve our customers.

---

21. Save your document in your Project folder using the file name PrjWD-8 XXXXX 9999, where XXXXX is your name or student ID number and 9999 is your class section number. Submit your project on a USB flash drive, as a printout, or as an e-mail attachment, according to your instructor's directions.

Project WD-9: Using SmartArt Graphics

In this project, you'll use the SmartArt Graphics options to customize a document.

Requirements: This project requires Microsoft Word.

Project file: PrjWD-9.docx

CopyIt! **1.** Copy the file PrjWD-9.docx to your Project folder using the Copy It! button on this page in the BookOnCD.

2. Start Microsoft Word.

3. Open the file PrjWD-9.docx from your Project folder.

4. Position the insertion point in the text box that contains the text "SmartArt," then delete the text.

5. With the insertion point still in the text box, click the Insert tab, then click the SmartArt button in the Illustrations group.

6. From the List tab, select the Basic Block List option, then click the OK button.

7. Insert the following items in the text boxes:

   Sledding
   Skating
   Sled Dog Racing
   Ice Sculptures

8. Delete any extra text boxes by selecting them, then pressing the Delete key on your keyboard.

9. From the Layouts group on the SmartArt Tools Design contextual tab, select the Vertical Box List layout. Adjust the size of the SmartArt so it fits properly in the text box.

10. From the SmartArt Styles group on the SmartArt Tools Design contextual tab, select the Subtle Effect Style.

11. Compare your document to the one on the next page.

• Using SmartArt Graphics (continued)

12. Save your document in your Project folder using the file name PrjWD-9 XXXXX 9999, where XXXXX is your name or student ID number and 9999 is your class section number. Use one of the following options to submit your project on a USB flash drive, as a printout, or as an e-mail attachment, according to your instructor's directions:

• To submit the project on a USB flash drive, close Word and then copy the file PrjWD-9 XXXXX 9999 from your Project folder to a USB drive. Make sure your name is on the USB drive.

• To print the project, click the File tab, select the Print option, and then click Print. Write your name, student ID number, class section number, date, and PrjWD-9 on the printout.

• To submit the project as an e-mail attachment, use Method 1 or Method 2, as described on page 156. Type your instructor's e-mail address in the To: box. Click the Subject: box and type PrjWD-9, your student ID number, and your class section number. Click the Send button or perform any additional steps required by your e-mail software to send an e-mail message.

Project EX-1: Creating a Worksheet

In this project, you'll apply what you've learned to create a worksheet using Microsoft Excel.

Requirements: This project requires Microsoft Excel.

Project file: No file is required for this project.

1. Start Microsoft Excel.

2. Click the File tab and select Options to open the Excel Options dialog box. Use the General and Save tabs to make sure the user name and default file locations are correct. Click the OK button to save these settings if you have permission to modify them. Otherwise, click the Cancel button.

3. Enter the labels and values shown below. Adjust column widths if necessary.

	A	B	C	D	E	F
1	Phone Charges Per Roommate for February					
2	Basic Monthly Service Rate		20.44			
3	Long Distance Charges for Each Roommate:					
4			Jamesson	Coleman	Depindeau	Struthers
5			5.65	0.25	1.35	3.75
6			0.45	0.65	2.15	0.88
7			1.68	0.56	3.78	1.23
8				4.15	5.77	0.95
9				1.25		0.88
10				3.67		1.95
11						3.88
12	Total Long Distance					
13	Share of Basic Rate					
14	Total					

4. In cell C12, use the AutoSum button to calculate the sum of the cells in column C. Use a similar procedure to calculate the long distance call totals for Coleman, Depindeau, and Struthers in cells D12, E12, and F12.

5. In cell C13, create a formula to calculate Jamesson's share of the $20.44 basic monthly service rate by dividing the contents of cell D2 by 4. Create a similar formula for each roommate in cells D13, E13, and F13.

6. In cell C14, create a formula to calculate Jamesson's share of the total phone bill by adding the contents of cell C12 to the contents of cell C13. Create a similar formula for each roommate in cells D14, E14, and F14.

7. Change the contents of Cell A1 to Feb Phone.

8. Use the Undo button to change the label in cell A1 back to the original wording.

9. Compare your worksheet to the one shown in the figure on the next page.

• Creating a Worksheet (continued)

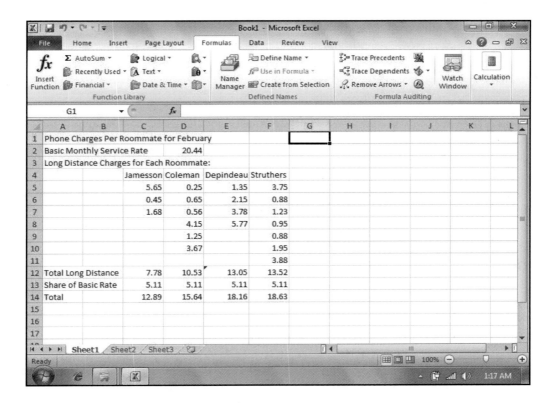

10. Save your worksheet in your Project folder using the file name PrjEX-1 XXXXX 9999, where XXXXX is your name or student ID number and 9999 is your class section number.

11. Use one of the following options to submit your project on a USB flash drive, as a printout, or as an e-mail attachment, according to your instructor's directions:

• To submit the project on a USB flash drive, close Excel and then copy the file PrjEX-1 XXXXX 9999 from your Project folder to a USB drive. Make sure your name is on the USB drive.

• To print the project, click the File tab, select the Print option, and then click Print. Write your name, student ID number, class section number, date, and PrjEX-1 on the printout.

• To submit the project as an e-mail attachment, use Method 1 or Method 2, as described on page 156. Type your instructor's e-mail address in the To: box. Click the Subject: box and type PrjEX-1, your student ID number, and your class section number. Click the Send button or perform any additional steps required by your e-mail software to send an e-mail message.

Project EX-2: Using Functions

In this project, you'll apply what you've learned about AutoSum plus the MAX, MIN, AVERAGE, and IF functions to complete a Microsoft Excel worksheet.

Requirements: This project requires Microsoft Excel.

Project file: PrjEX-2.xlsx

CopyIt!

1. Copy the file PrjEX-2.xlsx to your Project folder using the Copy It! button on this page in the BookOnCD.

2. Start Microsoft Excel.

3. Open the file PrjEX-2.xlsx from your Project folder. When completing the rest of the steps for this project, you can use the *fx* Fx button on the formula bar, or you can use the Function Library buttons on the Formulas tab. You might want to experiment a bit with both methods to discover the one you like best.

4. Use the AutoSum button to display the total number of flights in cells B11 and C11.

5. In cell B12, use the MIN function to display the lowest number of Mango Air flights from the list that begins in cell B4 and ends in cell B10. Enter a similar function in cell C12 for Econo Air flights. (Hint: On the Formulas tab, try clicking the arrow button next to AutoSum for a list of frequently used statistical functions.)

6. In cell B13, use the MAX function to display the highest number of Mango Air flights from the list that begins in cell B4 and ends in cell B10. Enter a similar function in cell C13 for Econo Air flights.

7. In cell B14, use a function to display the average number of Mango Air flights from the list that begins in cell B4 and ends in cell B10. Enter a similar function in cell C14 for Econo Air flights.

8. In cell D3, enter the label Most Flights and adjust the column width so the label fits in a single cell.

9. In cell D4, use the IF function to compare the number of flights for Mango Air and Econo Air, based on the numbers that appear in cells B4 and C4. The IF function should display Econo Air in cell D4 if that airline has the most flights for Costa Rica. It should display Mango Air in cell D4 if that airline has the most flights. (Hint: Place quotation marks around "Econo Air" and "Mango Air" when you create the function, and remember that the Insert Function dialog box provides help and examples.)

10. Use the Fill handle to copy the IF function from cell D4 down to cells D5 through D10.

11. In cell B16, use the Count function to display the number of destination countries for Mango Air flights from the list that begins in cell B4 and ends in cell B10. Enter a similar function in cell C16 for Econo Air flights.

12. Enter your name in cell E1.

13. Change the number in cell C9 to 85.

14. Compare your worksheet to the one shown in the figure on the next page.

• Using Functions (continued)

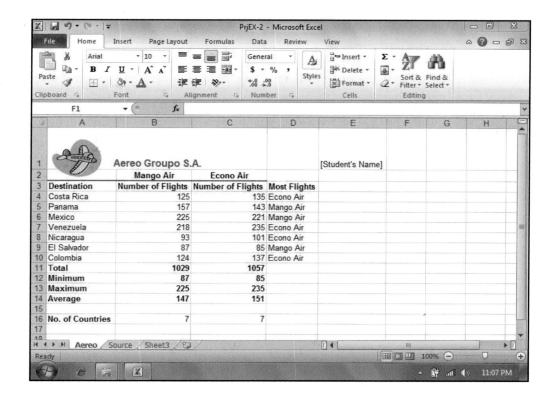

15. Save your worksheet in your Project folder using the file name PrjEX-2 XXXXX 9999, where XXXXX is your name or student ID number and 9999 is your class section number.

16. Use one of the following options to submit your project on a USB flash drive, as a printout, or as an e-mail attachment, according to your instructor's directions:

• To submit the project on a USB flash drive, close Excel and then copy the file PrjEX-2 XXXXX 9999 from your Project folder to a USB drive. Make sure your name is on the USB drive.

• To print the project, click the File tab, select the Print option, and then click Print. Write your name, student ID number, class section number, date, and PrjEX-2 on the printout.

• To submit the project as an e-mail attachment, use Method 1 or Method 2, as described on page 156. Type your instructor's e-mail address in the To: box. Click the Subject: box and type PrjEX-2, your student ID number, and your class section number. Click the Send button or perform any additional steps required by your e-mail software to send an e-mail message.

Project EX-3: Formatting a Worksheet

In this project, you'll apply what you've learned about Microsoft Excel to complete and format a worksheet.

Requirements: This project requires Microsoft Excel.

Project file: PrjEX-3.xlsx

1. Copy the file PrjEX-3.xlsx to your Project folder using the Copy It! button on this page in the BookOnCD.

2. Start Microsoft Excel.

3. Open the file PrjEX-3.xlsx from your Project folder.

4. Click the  empty block between the "A" and "1" labels in the upper-left corner of the worksheet to select the entire worksheet.

5. Change the font size of the entire worksheet to 12 point.

6. Use the Fill handle to copy the formula from cell C6 to cells D6 and E6.

7. Copy the formula from cell C15 to cells D15 and E15.

8. Copy the formula from cell F4 to cells F5 through F6, and cells F9 through F15.

9. Insert a new, empty row before row 15.

10. Change the color of the text in cell A1 to dark blue.

11. Change the font in cell A1 to Times New Roman, size 14, bold.

12. Using the *Merge and Center* button in the Alignment group to merge the contents of cells A1 through F1 so that the title is centered across those columns.

13. In cell A2, enter today's date.

14. Click cell A2 and use the Dialog Box Launcher in the Number group to open the Format Cells dialog box. Select a date format that displays dates in the format Wednesday, March 14, 2001.

15. Merge the contents of cells A2 through F2 so that the date is centered.

16. Format cells A3 through F3 as bold text. Format cells A8 and A16 as bold text.

17. Format the numbers in cells C4 through E16 as currency using buttons in the Number group on the Home tab.

18. Format the numbers in cells F4 through F16 as percentages (no decimal places).

19. Right-align the labels in cells C3 through F3.

20. Add both inside and outside borders (All Borders) to two cell ranges: B4 through F5 and B9 through F13. (Hint: Look at the Font group on the Home tab.)

21. Adjust the width of all columns so that all labels and values fit within the cells.

22. Now, explore what happens when you align some of the worksheet labels at a 90-degree angle. Select cells C3 through F3. Click the Orientation button in the Alignment group, then select Rotate Text Up.

• Formatting a Worksheet (continued)

23. Aligning column headings at a 90-degree angle is useful for worksheets that have many narrow columns. On this worksheet, however, the labels looked better at the normal angle, so use the Undo button on the Quick Access toolbar to undo the 90-degree angle.

24. Compare your worksheet to the one shown below.

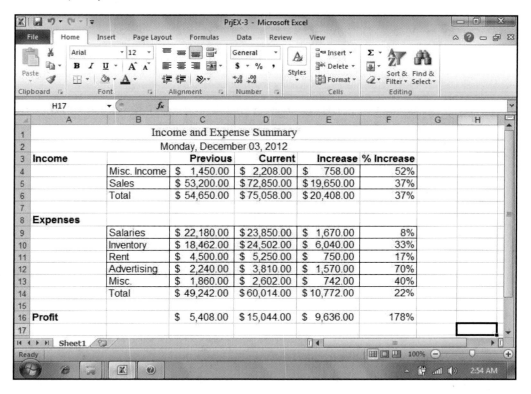

25. Save your worksheet in your Project folder using the file name PrjEX-3 XXXXX 9999, where XXXXX is your name or student ID number and 9999 is your class section number.

26. Use one of the following options to submit your project on a USB flash drive, as a printout, or as an e-mail attachment, according to your instructor's directions:

- To submit the project on a USB flash drive, close Excel and then copy the file PrjEX-3 XXXXX 9999 from your Project folder to a USB drive. Make sure your name is on the USB drive.

- To print the project, click the File tab, select the Print option, and then click Print. Write your name, student ID number, class section number, date, and PrjEX-3 on the printout.

- To submit the project as an e-mail attachment, use Method 1 or Method 2, as described on page 156. Type your instructor's e-mail address in the To: box. Click the Subject: box and type PrjEX-3, your student ID number, and your class section number. Click the Send button or perform any additional steps required by your e-mail software to send an e-mail message.

Project EX-4: Using Absolute and Relative References

In this project, you'll apply what you've learned about absolute and relative references to complete a sales commission worksheet.

Requirements: This project requires Microsoft Excel.

Project file: PrjEX-4.xlsx

1. Copy the file PrjEX-4.xlsx to your Project folder using the Copy It! button on this page in the BookOnCD.

2. Start Microsoft Excel.

3. Open the file PrjEX-4.xlsx from your Project folder.

4. Notice that cell B2 contains a sales commission rate. Each salesperson receives a commission equal to his or her total sales multiplied by the commission rate. The commission rate changes periodically. The worksheet is set up so that if the sales manager changes the rate in cell B2, all the sales commissions will be recalculated.

5. Create a formula in cell B10 to calculate the sales commission for column B by multiplying the Total Sales in cell B9 by the Commission Rate in cell B2. (Hint: You must use an absolute reference for the Commission Rate in the formula.)

6. Copy the formula from cell B10 to cells C10 through E10.

7. Check the results of the copied formulas to make sure that they show the correct results. If cells C10 through E10 contain zeros, you did not use the correct absolute reference for the formula that you entered in Step 5. If necessary, modify the formula in B10, then recopy it to cells C10 through E10.

8. Compare your worksheet to the one shown in the figure on the next page, but don't save it until you complete Steps 9 and 10.

•Using Absolute and Relative References (continued)

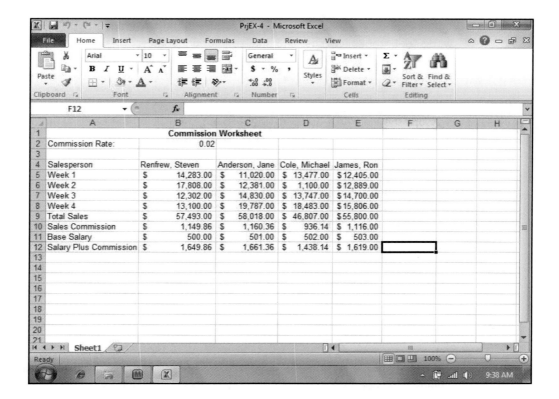

9. Change the contents of cell B2 to 0.03.

10. Enter your name in cell B4.

11. Save your worksheet in your Project folder using the file name PrjEX-4 XXXXX 9999, where XXXXX is your name or student ID number and 9999 is your class section number.

12. Use one of the following options to submit your project on a USB flash drive, as a printout, or as an e-mail attachment, according to your instructor's directions:

● To submit the project on a USB flash drive, close Excel and then copy the file PrjEX-4 XXXXX 9999 from your Project folder to a USB drive. Make sure your name is on the USB drive.

● To print the project, click the Microsoft Office button, then click Print. Click the OK button. Write your name, student ID number, class section number, date, and PrjEX-4 on the printout.

● To submit the project as an e-mail attachment, use Method 1 or Method 2, as described on page 156. Type your instructor's e-mail address in the To: box. Click the Subject: box and type PrjEX-4, your student ID number, and your class section number. Click the Send button or perform any additional steps required by your e-mail software to send an e-mail message.

Project EX-5: Finalizing a Worksheet

In this project, you'll apply what you've learned about Microsoft Excel to complete a worksheet, freeze its titles, and finalize it for printing.

Requirements: This project requires Microsoft Excel.

Project file: PrjEX-5.xlsx

1. Copy the file PrjEX-5.xlsx to your Project folder using the Copy It! button on this page in the BookOnCD.

2. Start Microsoft Excel and open the file PrjEX-5.xlsx from your Project folder.

3. Notice that when you scroll the worksheet, the title and column headings are no longer visible. To freeze the titles at the top of the screen, click cell A3. You've clicked this cell because you want the titles above row 3 to remain fixed in place when you scroll.

4. Click the View tab, click Freeze Panes in the Window group, then select Freeze Panes. Now scroll the worksheet and make sure that rows 1 and 2 remain in view.

5. Scroll down the worksheet and notice that data for the miniature gargoyles is not complete. Select cells B43 and B44, then use the Fill handle to consecutively number the products. (Hint: To check your work, make sure that the Miniature Dragon Gargoyle has a product number of 359 and the Miniature War Horse has 381.)

6. All of the miniatures are the same size, weight, price, and shipping cost. Use the Fill command to duplicate the information from cells C43 through F43 for all miniature gargoyles.

7. Select cell B2. Use the Dialog Box Launcher in the Alignment group to wrap the text.

8. Adjust the width of column B so that "Product Number" fits on two lines.

9. Right-justify the data in column C and center the titles in columns B through F.

10. Sort the data in cells A3 through F68 in A to Z order by Description.

11. Check the spelling of the worksheet and correct misspellings as needed.

12. Unfreeze the panes so that you can scroll the entire worksheet.

13. Add a right-justified header to the worksheet that includes your name, your student ID number, your class section number, today's date, and PrjEX-5.

14. Add a centered footer to the worksheet that includes the word Page followed by the page number. (Hint: If you can't see header and footer elements such as Page Number, select the Design tab.)

15. Switch back to Normal View. Click the File tab and look at the print preview to see how this worksheet is set up to print. Does it print all the miniature gargoyles? What's printed on the second page?

16. Go back to the worksheet and look at the current print area, A1:I43. Part of the sheet is not included. To clear the print area so the entire sheet will be printed, click the Page Setup Dialog Box Launcher in the Sheet Options group on the Page Layout tab.

17. Use the File tab's Print settings to adjust the scaling option so that the worksheet will be printed on a single sheet of paper. Print your worksheet.

• Finalizing a Worksheet (continued)

18. The text on the single-page printout is quite small. Let's suppose that you don't want to print the Discount Schedule. On the Page Layout tab, change the width and height to Automatic, and the scale to 100%.

19. Select cells A1 through F68. Using the Layout tab, designate this range as the print area so that the Discount Schedule is not printed.

20. Use the Print Titles button to designate cells A1 through F2 as the title to print on every page.

21. Specify that you want to print gridlines and headings so that you can see the row numbers and column letters on the printout. Click OK to apply all selected settings and close the Page Setup dialog box.

22. Set a page break at row 33. (Hint: Select cell G33 before you click the Breaks button.)

23. Look at a print preview of your worksheet. It should look similar to the two pages below.

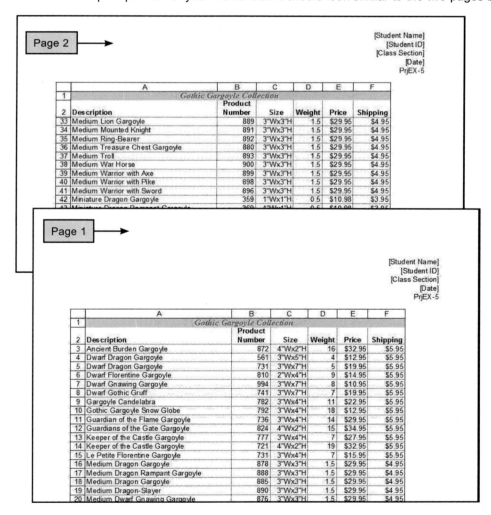

24. Save your worksheet in your Project folder using the file name PrjEX-5 XXXXX 9999, where XXXXX is your name or student ID number and 9999 is your class section number.

25. Submit your project on a USB flash drive, as a printout, or as an e-mail attachment, according to your instructor's directions.

Project EX-6: Creating Charts

In this project, you'll apply what you've learned about Microsoft Excel to create a column chart and a pie chart for an e-commerce worksheet.

Requirements: This project requires Microsoft Excel.

Project file: PrjEX-6.xlsx

1. Copy the file PrjEX-6.xlsx to your Project folder using the Copy It! button on this page in the BookOnCD.

2. Start Microsoft Excel.

3. Open the file PrjEX-6.xlsx from your Project folder.

4. Select the data in cells B3 through C6. Use the Insert tab to create a 3D pie chart. Select Layout 6 in the Chart Layouts group on the Design contextual tab. Enter Which Activities Lead? in the Chart Title box. Move the chart to a new sheet and name the sheet Comparison Chart.

5. Change the style of the chart to Style 12 in the Chart Styles group on the Design contextual tab.

6. Change the chart background color to Subtle Effect - Red, Accent 2 in the Shape Styles group on the Format contextual tab.

7. Select the data in cells H4 through H9. Use the Insert tab to create a Clustered Column chart.

8. Click the Select Data button in the Data group on the Design contextual tab. Click the Edit button for the Horizontal (Category) Axis Labels. Select cells G4 through G9, then click the OK button to close the Axis Labels dialog box. Click the OK button to close the Select Data Source dialog box.

9. Use the Labels group on the Layout contextual tab to add the chart title, U.S. Projections, above the chart. Add a vertical Y-axis title, $ Billions. Remove the legend from the chart. Move the chart to a new sheet and name the sheet Growth Chart.

10. Change the chart type to Line with markers in the Type group on the Design contextual tab. Click the OK button to apply the chart type.

11. Examine the charts to ensure that the spreadsheet data is accurately represented. One easy verification technique is to identify a data trend and see if the trend is shown both in the data and on the chart. A trend in this data is the trend for projected growth to increase from one year to the next. Verify that the line chart corresponds to this trend by making sure the line moves up as it moves to the right.

Use care when identifying trends; make sure the conclusions you draw are accurate. Be aware of what can and can't be concluded from data. For example, although this data shows that 52% of e-commerce business activity is from business to consumer, it would be incorrect to assume that 52% of monetary transactions on a given day are between businesses and consumers.

12. Copy both charts to the E-Commerce tab.

13. Size and position the pie chart so that the upper-left corner of the chart is in cell A10 and the lower-right corner is in cell E23.

• Creating Charts (continued)

14. Size and position the line chart so that the upper-left corner of the chart is in cell G11 and the lower-right corner is in cell L23.

15. Click a blank cell in the worksheet, then display a print preview. Use Settings options to change the page orientation to Landscape and fit the worksheet on one page. The worksheet preview should look like the one shown in the figure below.

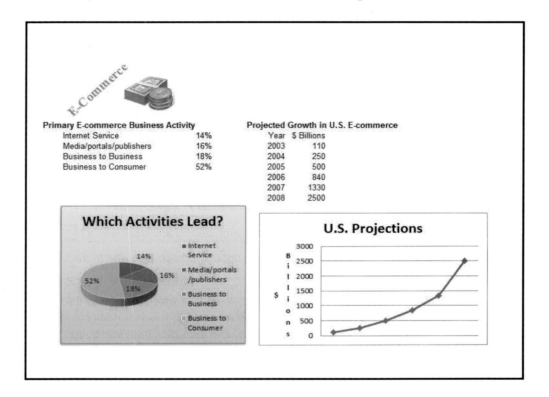

16. Save your worksheet in your Project folder using the file name PrjEX-6 XXXXX 9999, where XXXXX is your name or student ID number and 9999 is your class section number.

17. Use one of the following options to submit your project on a USB flash drive, as a printout, or as an e-mail attachment, according to your instructor's directions:

- To submit the project on a USB flash drive, close Excel and then copy the file PrjEX-6 XXXXX 9999 from your Project folder to a USB drive. Make sure your name is on the USB drive.

- To print the project, click the File tab, select the Print option, and then click Print. Write your name, student ID number, class section number, date, and PrjEX-6 on the printout.

- To submit the project as an e-mail attachment, use Method 1 or Method 2, as described on page 156. Type your instructor's e-mail address in the To: box. Click the Subject: box and type PrjEX-6, your student ID number, and your class section number. Click the Send button or perform any additional steps required by your e-mail software to send an e-mail message.

Project EX-7: Interpreting Worksheets and Charts

In this project, you'll practice identifying simple trends and drawing conclusions based on tabular information and charts. You'll also try your hand at sorting, ranking, and filtering data.

Requirements: This project requires Microsoft Excel.

Project file: PrjEX-7.xlsx

1. Copy the file PrjEX-7.xlsx to your Project folder using the Copy It! button on this page in the BookOnCD.

2. Start Microsoft Excel and open the file PrjEX-7.xlsx from your Project folder.

3. The worksheet contains raw data from the National Climatic Data Center. It is a 100-year record (1910–2009) of mean temperatures in the U.S. for the month of January. Examine the data. What would you guess is the average temperature for this 100-year period? Can you tell if temperatures seem to be increasing or decreasing? [_____]

4. To make it easier to analyze the data, highlight cells A3:B102 and use the Data tab's Sort button to arrange the temperatures in order from smallest to largest. The lowest temperature should be 22.57 in 1979. If your results are different, undo the sort and try it again, making sure to highlight both columns A and B.

5. Which year had the highest mean temperature and what was it? [_____]

6. Do all of the highest temperatures appear to have occurred in the last 50 years? [_____]

7. Suppose you'd like to answer the question "In which years was the average temperature greater than 34 degrees?" Select cells A2 and B2, which contain the Year and Temperature labels, respectively. Click the Data tab, and then click the Filter button. Click the arrow button in column B, select Number Filters, and then click Greater Than. Enter 34 and then click the OK button. How many years had temperatures above 34 degrees? [_____]

8. Clear the filter by clicking the Filter button again.

9. Now, sort columns A and B by year from smallest to largest.

10. In cell E3, calculate the average temperature and write it down. Do temperatures before 1920 appear to be above or below average? [_____]

11. To identify trends in the temperatures, enter formulas in column E to compute the average January temperatures for each of the ten-year intervals listed in the Decade column. Which decade appears to have the highest average January temperatures? [_____]

12. Excel can automatically rank the decades so that you can easily see which decade was the warmest, which was the second warmest, and so on. Click cell F6 and enter the formula =RANK(E6, $E$6:$E$15). That formula should produce the number 8 to indicate that 1910–1919 was the eighth warmest decade. Copy the formula down through row 15. Which decade is ranked ninth? [_____]

13. Create a pie chart of the data in cells D6 through E15. Does that chart make sense? Change the chart type and look at the data formatted as a column chart, a scatter chart, and a line chart. Which chart best shows the temperature trends over time, and which one best lets you compare temperatures from one decade to the next? [_____]

• Interpreting Worksheets and Charts (continued)

14. Select the clustered column chart type once again. Use the Layout tab to add the chart title, Average Temperatures Per Decade, above the chart.

15. Add a vertical Y-axis title, Degrees Fahrenheit, using the Rotated Title option. Remove the "Series 1" legend from the chart. Format the vertical axis so the temperatures are displayed without decimal places. (Hint: Click the vertical axis, then select Format Selection in the Current Selection group on the Format tab.) Compare your chart to the example below.

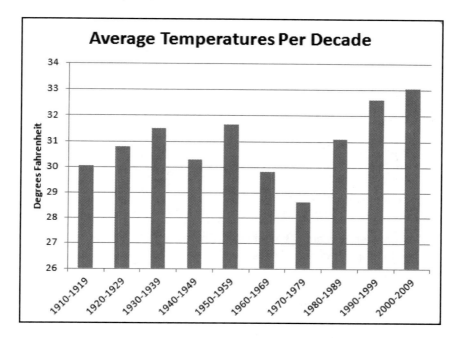

16. Place the chart on Sheet2 and rename Sheet2 Chart by Decade.

17. Examine the chart to ensure that the spreadsheet data is accurately represented. One easy verification technique is to identify a data trend and see if the trend is shown both in the data and on the chart. A trend in this data is the trend for the lowest temperatures in the 1960s and 1970s, and the highest in the last 20 years. Verify that the column chart corresponds to this trend.

18. You can add a trendline to your chart using the Trendline button in the Analysis group on the Layout tab. Select Linear Trendline. According to this trendline, how would you characterize the temperature differences now compared to a hundred years ago?

[   ]

19. To forecast trends based on your chart, right-click the line, then select Format Trendline to display the Format Trendline dialog box. Under Forecast, enter 2 in the Forward box. Based on the result, what would you expect as the average temperature for the decade 2020–2029? [   ]

20. Add your name to cell G1 on the first worksheet. Save your project using the file name PrjEX-7 XXXXX 9999, where XXXXX is your name or student ID number and 9999 is your class section number. Submit your project on a USB flash drive, as a printout, or as an e-mail attachment, according to your instructor's directions.

ject PP-1: Creating a Presentation

ect, you'll apply what you've learned to create a PowerPoint presentation about
orts.

ts: This project requires Microsoft PowerPoint.

.. No file is required for this project.

1. Start Microsoft PowerPoint.

2. Create a new presentation using any theme. The example on the next page shows the Newsprint theme.

3. Add a title slide, then enter Extreme Sports as the title. Enter Taking it to the Limit as the subtitle.

4. Add a Title and Content slide. Enter What are Extreme Sports? as the slide title. Enter the following items as bullets:

> Beyond traditional sports
> High level of physical exertion
> Inherent danger
> Adrenaline rush
> Young demographic
> Individuals rather than teams

5. Add another Title and Content slide. Enter History of Extreme Sports as the slide title. Add the following items as bullets:

> Might be traced back to rock-climbing, marathon running in the 70's, but opinions vary
> Evolved from traditional sports due to advances in sports technology
> A modern rite of passage, according to some sociologists
> Popularized by media attention and marketing trends
> Guaranteed to continue to evolve

6. Add another Title and Content slide. Enter Extreme Sports Examples as the slide title. Add the following items as bullets:

> Bouldering (rock climbing without rope)
> BASE jumping (from buildings, bridges, cliffs)
> Barefoot skiing
> Bungee jumping

7. Add whatever clip art you decide is appropriate. Click the Clip Art logo in the Content box. In the Clip Art pane, put a checkmark in the checkbox for *Include Office.com content* to display more samples.

8. Experiment with changing the slide background by clicking Background Styles in the Background group on the Design tab. Select Format Background, then click the Picture Color option. Click the Presets arrow button under Recolor. Change the background color to Dark Red, Accent color 1 Light. Close the Format Background dialog box.

9. Use the Undo button on the Quick Access toolbar to display the original background.

10. Compare your slides to those shown in the figure on the next page.

• Creating a Presentation (continued)

Extreme Sports

Taking it to the Limit

- Beyond traditional sports
- High level of physical exertion
- Inherent danger
- Adrenaline rush
- Young demographic
- Individuals rather than teams

What are Extreme Sports?

- Might be traced back to rock-climbing, marathon running in the 70's, but opinions vary
- Evolved from traditional sports due to advances in sports technology
- A modern rite of passage, according to some sociologists
- Popularized by media attention and marketing trends
- Guaranteed to continue to evolve

History of Extreme Sports

- Bouldering (rock climbing without rope)
- BASE jumping (from buildings, bridges, cliffs)
- Barefoot skiing
- Bungee jumping

Extreme Sports Examples

11. Save your presentation using the file name PrjPP-1 XXXXX 9999, where XXXXX is your name or student ID number and 9999 is your class section number.

12. Use one of the following options to submit your project on a USB flash drive, as a printout, or as an e-mail attachment, according to your instructor's directions:

- To submit the project on a USB flash drive, close PowerPoint and then copy the file PrjPP-1 XXXXX 9999 from your Project folder to a USB drive. Make sure your name is on the USB drive.

- To print the project, click the File tab, select the Print option, and then click Print. Use the Full Page Slides pull-down list to specify Handouts with 6 slides per page in horizontal order. Also, make sure that the *Scale to Fit Paper* checkbox contains a checkmark. Close the pull-down list. Write your name, student ID number, class section number, date, and PrjPP-1 on the printout.

- To submit the project as an e-mail attachment, use Method 1 or Method 2, as described on page 156. Type your instructor's e-mail address in the To: box. Click the Subject: box and type PrjPP-1, your student ID number, and your class section number. Click the Send button or perform any additional steps required by your e-mail software to send an e-mail message.

Project PP-2: Creating Slides with Charts and Tables

In this project, you'll apply what you've learned about charts and tables to create PowerPoint slides for a fitness center.

Requirements: This project requires Microsoft PowerPoint.

Project file: PrjPP-2.pptx

1. Copy the file PrjPP-2.pptx to your Project folder using the Copy It! button on this page in the BookOnCD.

2. Start Microsoft PowerPoint.

3. Open the file PrjPP-2.pptx from your Project folder.

4. Add a Title and Content slide. Enter Target Heart Rates as the slide title. Add a table consisting of three columns and four rows. Select the table style called Themed Style 1 - Accent 1.

5. Enter the following data into the table:

Age	Minimum Rate	Maximum Rate
20	120	170
30	114	162
40	108	163

6. Set the height of each cell to 1".

7. Select the slide you just made in the pane that contains the Slides and Outline tabs. Right-click the slide and select Duplicate Slide in the shortcut menu. Suppose you realize that you need a slide with a different layout. Click the Undo button on the Quick Access toolbar.

8. Add a Title and Content slide. Enter Caloric Expenditures by Body Weight as the slide title.

9. Create a clustered column chart that shows the following data:

	Jogging	Swimming
125 Lbs.	7.3	6.9
175 Lbs.	10.4	9.8

Make sure you have the weight categories as the labels for the X-axis, and enlarge the font so it is easier to read.

10. Compare your slides to those shown in the figure on the next page.

•Creating Slides with Charts and Tables (continued)

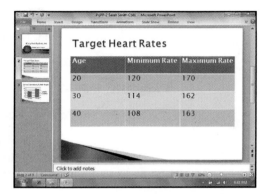

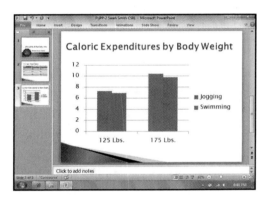

11. Save your presentation in your Project folder using the file name PrjPP-2 XXXXX 9999, where XXXXX is your name or student ID number and 9999 is your class section number.

12. Use one of the following options to submit your project on a USB flash drive, as a printout, or as an e-mail attachment, according to your instructor's directions:

• To submit the project on a USB flash drive, close PowerPoint and then copy the file PrjPP-2 XXXXX 9999 from your Project folder to a USB drive. Make sure your name is on the USB drive.

• To print the project, click the File tab, select the Print option, and then click Print. Use the Full Page Slides pull-down list to specify Handouts with 6 slides per page in horizontal order. Also, make sure that the *Scale to Fit Paper* checkbox contains a checkmark. Close the pull-down list. Write your name, student ID number, class section number, date, and PrjPP-2 on the printout.

• To submit the project as an e-mail attachment, use Method 1 or Method 2, as described on page 156. Type your instructor's e-mail address in the To: box. Click the Subject: box and type PrjPP-2, your student ID number, and your class section number. Click the Send button or perform any additional steps required by your e-mail software to send an e-mail message.

Project PP-3: Using Animations, Transitions, and Sounds

In this project, you'll apply what you've learned to add animations, transitions, and sounds to a PowerPoint presentation.

Requirements: This project requires Microsoft PowerPoint.

Project file: PrjPP-3.pptx

1. Copy the file PrjPP-3.pptx to your Project folder using the Copy It! button on this page in the BookOnCD.

2. Start Microsoft PowerPoint.

3. Open the file PrjPP-3.pptx from your Project folder.

4. On the first slide, change the subtitle text "The time is right!" to size 44, bold, and italic.

5. Add the Uncover transition to the second slide.

6. Suppose you want the second slide to appear from the bottom of the first slide instead of from the right side, which is the default. Use the Effect Options pull-down list to achieve your desired effect.

7. Add the Shred transition to the third slide.

8. Add the Drum Roll transition sound effect to the same slide.

9. Add the Fly In animation (coming from the left) to the bulleted list on the third slide in the presentation. (Hint: Use Effect Options to specify the direction.)

10. Notice that the bullets appear in two groups. Suppose you want the bullet items to appear one at a time when the presenter clicks the mouse. Click the arrow button of the Start box in the Timing group and select On Click.

11. View the presentation to see how the transition and animation effects work together. Click the mouse, press Enter, or click the right-arrow button to display each bullet item.

12. Do you think the combination of the Drum Roll sound effect and the Shred transition is more distracting than effective? Perhaps selecting a less flashy transition would be better. Switch back to Normal View and change the transition on the third slide to something more subdued.

13. View the presentation once more to see if you're satisfied with the new combination of transition and animation effects. If not, go back and select another transition for the third slide.

14. When you're done, switch to Slide Sorter View. You should see ⭐ Play Animations icons under slides 2 and 3, as shown on the next page.

• Using Animations, Transitions, and Sounds (continued)

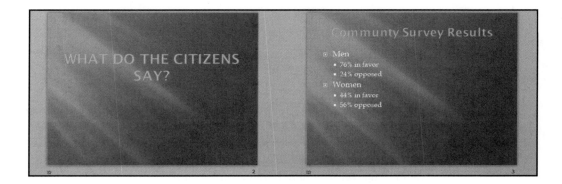

15. Save your presentation in your Project folder using the file name PrjPP-3 XXXXX 9999, where XXXXX is your name or student ID number and 9999 is your class section number.

16. Use one of the following options to submit your project on a USB flash drive, as a printout, or as an e-mail attachment, according to your instructor's directions:

• To submit the project on a USB flash drive, close PowerPoint and then copy the file PrjPP-3 XXXXX 9999 from your Project folder to a USB drive. Make sure your name is on the USB drive.

• To print the project, click the File tab, select the Print option, and then click Print. Use the Full Page Slides pull-down list to specify Handouts with 6 slides per page in horizontal order. Also, make sure that the *Scale to Fit Paper* checkbox contains a checkmark. Close the pull-down list. Write your name, student ID number, class section number, date, and PrjPP-3 on the printout.

• To submit the project as an e-mail attachment, use Method 1 or Method 2, as described on page 156. Type your instructor's e-mail address in the To: box. Click the Subject: box and type PrjPP-3, your student ID number, and your class section number. Click the Send button or perform any additional steps required by your e-mail software to send an e-mail message.

Project PP-4: Finalizing a Presentation

In this project, you'll apply what you've learned as you finalize a version of the Microsoft PowerPoint presentation that you worked with in Project PP-3.

Requirements: This project requires Microsoft PowerPoint.

Project file: PrjPP-4.pptx

1. Copy the file PrjPP-4.pptx to your Project folder using the Copy It! button on this page in the BookOnCD.

2. Start Microsoft PowerPoint.

3. Open the file PrjPP-4.pptx from your Project folder.

4. Use Slide Sorter View to move the "Questions & Answers?" slide to the end of the presentation.

5. Move the "Best Site" slide so that it comes immediately after the "Potential Sites" slide.

6. In Normal View, add the following speaker note to the first slide in the presentation: Introduce team members Jill Smith, David Byrne, and Tom Woods.

7. Add the following speaker note to the last slide in the presentation: Let's get a general idea of your reaction to the proposed golf course... raise your hand if you would like the project to proceed.

8. Delete the slide titled "We need to proceed as quickly as possible!"

9. Check the spelling of all slides and make any necessary corrections.

10. Select the View tab and then click the Slide Master button. Select the first (and largest) master slide. Select *Click to edit Master title style*. Go back to the Home tab and select a bright yellow color for the title text.

11. Look through the list of master slides and make sure that all the titles are bright yellow.

12. Switch back to Normal View and double-check the color of all the titles. If you need to make adjustments to the title colors, go back to Slide Master View.

13. Bullets should use consistent grammar and sentence structure. Modify the bullets on slide 5 so that all are either full sentences with periods at the end, or sentence fragments with no periods.

14. In Slide Sorter View, compare your presentation to the one shown on the next page.

•Finalizing a Presentation (continued)

15. Save your presentation in your Project folder using the file name PrjPP-4 XXXXX 9999, where XXXXX is your name or student ID number and 9999 is your class section number.

16. Use one of the following options to submit your project on a USB flash drive, as a printout, or as an e-mail attachment, according to your instructor's directions:

• To submit the project on a USB flash drive, close PowerPoint and then copy the file PrjPP-4 XXXXX 9999 from your Project folder to a USB drive. Make sure your name is on the USB drive.

• To print the project, click the File tab, select the Print option, and then click Print. Use the Full Page Slides pull-down list to specify Handouts with 3 slides per page in horizontal order. Also, make sure that the *Scale to Fit Paper* checkbox contains a checkmark. Close the pull-down list. Write your name, student ID number, class section number, date, and PrjPP-4 on the printout.

• To submit the project as an e-mail attachment, use Method 1 or Method 2, as described on page 156. Type your instructor's e-mail address in the To: box. Click the Subject: box and type PrjPP-4, your student ID number, and your class section number. Click the Send button or perform any additional steps required by your e-mail software to send an e-mail message.

Project PP-5: Creating an Organization Chart

In this project, you'll explore the graphics capabilities of PowerPoint to create a presentation that includes an organization chart.

Requirements: This project requires Microsoft PowerPoint.

Project file: No file is required for this project.

1. Start Microsoft PowerPoint.

2. Create a new blank presentation. Select the first slide and change the layout to Title and Content.

3. Add the title Company Hierarchy.

4. Select the Insert SmartArt Graphic content icon. Select the Organization Chart option from the Hierarchy category.

5. Delete all boxes except the top tier by selecting the box, then clicking the Delete key. Add the title President to the top of the organization chart.

6. Click the arrow button on the Add Shape button in the Create Graphic group on the SmartArt Tools Design contextual tab to create a second tier with three boxes containing the following text: VP Marketing, VP Research, and VP Operations.

7. Click any blank area of the President box. If you click the text and see an insertion bar, try again until the box itself is selected, not the text inside the box. Click the arrow button on the Add Shape button to create an assistant for the President.

8. Add the text Administrative Assistant to the new box.

9. Add four subordinates to the VP Marketing box. Type Marketing Rep in each subordinate box.

10. Select the VP Marketing box, select Layout in the Create Graphic group, and then select Left Hanging.

11. Remove one Marketing Rep box by selecting it, then clicking the Delete key.

12. Compare your slide to the one shown in the figure on the next page.

• Creating an Organization Chart (continued)

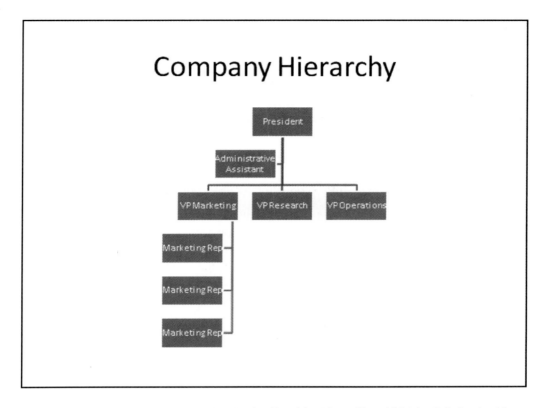

13. Add your name as a second line in the President box. To add text, click the text in the box. Use the End key to jump to the end of the line, and then press the Enter key. When the insertion point is on a new line, type the additional text.

14. Use the SmartArt Styles group to change the style for the organization chart to Subtle Effect.

15. Save your presentation in your Project folder using the file name PrjPP-5 XXXXX 9999, where XXXXX is your name or student ID number and 9999 is your class section number.

16. Use one of the following options to submit your project on a USB flash drive, as a printout, or as an e-mail attachment, according to your instructor's directions:

• To submit the project on a USB flash drive, close PowerPoint and then copy the file PrjPP-5 XXXXX 9999 from your Project folder to a USB drive. Make sure your name is on the USB drive.

• To print the project, click the File tab, select the Print option, and then click Print. Write your name, student ID number, class section number, date, and PrjPP-5 on the printout.

• To submit the project as an e-mail attachment, use Method 1 or Method 2, as described on page 156. Type your instructor's e-mail address in the To: box. Click the Subject: box and type PrjPP-5, your student ID number, and your class section number. Click the Send button or perform any additional steps required by your e-mail software to send an e-mail message.

Project PP-6: Working with Slide Graphics

In this project, you'll explore how to use Microsoft PowerPoint to add simple graphical elements to slides and change existing slide graphics.

Requirements: This project requires Microsoft PowerPoint.

Project file: PrjPP-6.pptx

1. Copy the file PrjPP-6.pptx to your Project folder using the Copy It! button on this page in the BookOnCD.

2. Start Microsoft PowerPoint.

3. Open the file PrjPP-6.pptx from your Project folder.

4. Display the first slide, which is titled Nitrogen Cycling. Select the chart by clicking the area just above the legend that contains Ammonia, Nitrite, and Nitrate. Now that the chart is selected, you can change various formats, such as the background color. Right-click any blank background area of the chart, then select Format Chart Area. When the Format Chart Area dialog box appears, select *Solid fill*. Click the arrow button for Color, and then select Dark Red under Standard Colors. Click the Close button to close the Format Chart Area dialog box and apply the new color.

5. Suppose you want to change the color of the Ammonia line to light blue. Click anywhere inside the legend. Now that the legend is selected, click Ammonia, then right-click it. Select Format Data Series from the shortcut menu. When the Format Data Series dialog box appears, select Line Color in the left pane, then select *Solid line*. Click the arrow button for Color, then select Light Blue under standard colors. Click the Close button.

6. Switch to the slide titled Losses in Fish Hatch. Suppose you decide that a different chart type would be more appropriate for displaying the information. Select the chart to change its chart type. Click Change Chart Type in the Type group on the Design tab. When the Change Chart Type dialog box appears, select a 3D pie chart. Click the OK button to apply the new chart type. Click Style 2 in the Chart Styles group on the Design tab.

7. Suppose you want to position the pie chart toward the center of the slide, with the legend to the right of it. Click the blank area to the left of the chart. When the chart box appears, hold down the left mouse button and drag the box toward the center of the slide. (Hint: Make sure your pointer is in the box, but not on the chart, when you drag the box.) Change the color of each pie slice by right-clicking the slice and then selecting a color.

8. Now, suppose you want to duplicate this chart on another slide. Make sure the chart is selected. Click Copy in the Clipboard group on the Home tab. Switch to the slide titled Causes of Mortality and click Paste in the Clipboard group on the Home tab to paste the chart and legend on the slide. Position and size the chart on the right side of the slide so it visually balances the bullets. Move the legend below the chart so it doesn't overlap the chart.

•Working with Slide Graphics (continued)

9. You can use elements in the Drawing group on the Home tab to draw your own graphics that tie slide elements together. Switch to the slide titled Biological Cycling. You can follow the next set of steps to make the slide look like the one below.

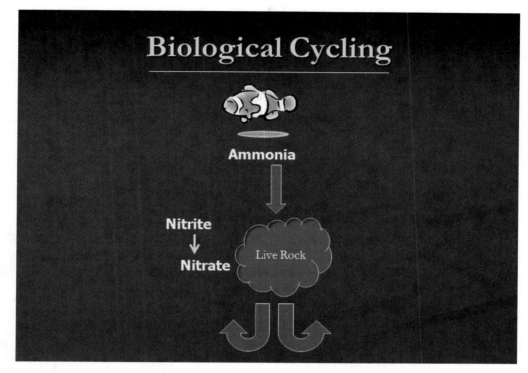

10. You can draw a line under the slide title by clicking the Line icon in the Drawing group. Position the pointer under the first letter of the title. While holding down the left mouse button, draw the line across the bottom of the title. Release the mouse button.

11. To draw the arrow that points down from "Ammonia," click the Down Arrow icon in the Drawing group. Drag the pointer in the area under "Ammonia." Resize and reposition the arrow as necessary.

12. Now, to add the thin arrow between "Nitrite" and "Nitrate," click the thin Arrow icon in the Drawing group. Position the cursor below the word "Nitrite." While holding down the left mouse button, draw an arrow to the word "Nitrate," and then release the mouse button. Position the arrow so it is centered between the two text items.

13. Suppose you want to change the format of the thin arrow. Click the arrow, then click Shape Outline in the Shape Styles group of the Format tab. Select Yellow under Standard Colors. You can also change the line thickness using the Shape Outline option. Select Weight from the pull-down list, and then select the 3 pt option.

14. Suppose you want to duplicate a drawn object. Click the U-Turn arrow and click Copy in the Clipboard group on the Home tab. Now click Paste in the Clipboard group to paste the duplicate U-Turn arrow on the slide. To flip the arrow, click the left square (sizing handle) on the side of the arrow and hold your mouse pointer down to drag it to the right without changing the size of the arrow. Position the flipped arrow so it is right beside the original arrow, as illustrated above.

•Working with Slide Graphics (continued)

15. To add text to the slide, click the Text Box in the Text group on the Insert tab. Position the pointer just above the two U-Turn arrows. Drag a box shape and then type Live Rock.

16. To draw the cloud, click its shape under Basic Shapes in the Illustrations group. Position the pointer just above your new text box. While holding the left mouse button, draw a cloud large enough to cover the new text box.

17. Notice that the new object is covering the text box. To change the order of your objects so that the text box is on top and the cloud moves to the back, double-click the cloud, then click Send Backward in the Arrange group of the Format tab.

18. Suppose you want to change the style of the cloud. To apply a shadow effect, make sure the cloud is selected, then click Shape Effects in the Shape Styles group of the Format tab. Select Shadow, then click Inside Diagonal Top Left in the Inner options list.

19. Make sure the slides in your presentation look like the slides below, then save the presentation in your Project folder using the file name PrjPP-6A XXXXX 9999, where XXXXX is your name or student ID number and 9999 is your class section number.

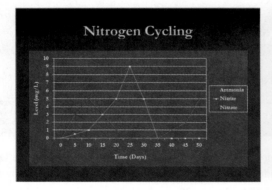
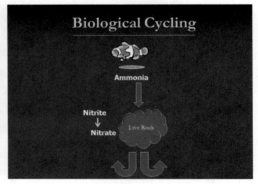
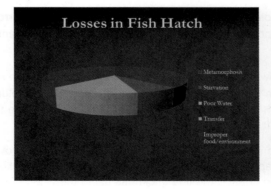
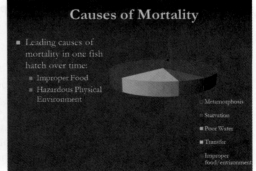

•Working with Slide Graphics (continued)

20. Now, create an Executive Summary presentation using any theme you like. The presentation should contain one title slide and one blank slide. Enter Biological Cycling as the title for slide 1.

21. Next, copy the objects from slide 2 of the PrjPP-6A presentation to slide 2 of the new presentation. To do so, switch to the PrjPP-6A presentation and display slide 2. Hold down the Shift key as you click each object you want to copy. Click Copy in the Clipboard group of the Home tab. Switch to slide 2 of the Executive Summary presentation and click Paste in the Clipboard group to paste the objects on the blank slide.

22. Make any adjustments to the title and objects, if necessary, and then select a background style from the Background group on the Design tab.

23. Save the Executive Summary in your Project folder using the file name PrjPP-6B XXXXX 9999, where XXXXX is your name or student ID number and 9999 is your name or class section number.

24. Use one of the following options to submit your project files on a USB flash drive, as printouts, or as e-mail attachments, according to your instructor's directions:

- To submit the project on a USB flash drive, close PowerPoint and then copy the files PrjPP-6A XXXXX 9999 and PrjPP-6B XXXXX 9999 from your Project folder to a USB drive. Make sure your name is on the USB drive.

- To print the two project files, click the File tab, select the Print option, and then click Print. Write your name, student ID number, class section number, date, and PrjPP-6A and PrjPP-6B, respectively, on the printouts.

- To submit the project as an e-mail attachment, use Method 1 or Method 2, as described on page 156, attaching both files to one e-mail message. Type your instructor's e-mail address in the To: box. Click the Subject: box and type PrjPP-6A and PrjPP-6B, your student ID number, and your class section number. Click the Send button or perform any additional steps required by your e-mail software to send an e-mail message.

Project PP-7: Working with Slide Text

In this project, you'll explore how to zoom in or zoom out to view a slide, and how to use the PowerPoint Options dialog box to configure user information and file location settings. You'll also explore how to copy, cut, and paste clip art and text; and you'll experiment with text formatting, and Undo and Redo options.

Requirements: This project requires Microsoft PowerPoint.

Project file: PrjPP-7.pptx

1. Copy the file PrjPP-7.pptx to your Project folder using the Copy It! button on this page in the BookOnCD.

2. Start Microsoft PowerPoint and open the file PrjPP-7.pptx from your Project folder.

3. Let's explore what happens when you adjust the magnification level. Use the Zoom control in the lower-right corner of the PowerPoint window to view the maximum zoom level. Depending on your computer's screen resolution, the slide might now be too big to fit in the window. Click the button to the right of the Zoom control to select the most practical zoom level.

4. To explore how to configure a presentation's author information, click the File tab, then click Options. When the PowerPoint Options dialog box appears, enter your name and initials in the boxes provided.

5. To adjust the Save options, click Save in the left pane. Typically, PowerPoint is configured to save presentations in the My Documents folder. If you want to change this setting, use the *Default file location* box to do so now.

6. To apply your new settings and close the PowerPoint Options dialog box, click the OK button.

7. Add a new slide at the end of the presentation. Select the *Title and Content* layout. Enter Top Three Sponsors as the slide title. Add the following items as three bullets:

Titleist

PepsiCo

PGA

8. Select the bullets and change them to a numbered list using the Numbering button in the Paragraph group on the Home tab.

9. Make sure all the bullets are selected, and then use the Line Spacing button to double-space the bullets.

10. Switch to the slide titled *We need to proceed as quickly as possible*. Copy the clip art from this slide to the slide titled Top Three Sponsors. Adjust the position of the graphic so that it looks visually pleasing.

11. Switch back to the slide titled *We need to proceed as quickly as possible*. Suppose you would rather have this clip art image on the slide titled *What do the citizens say?* Move the clip art image to the slide titled *What do the citizens say?* Adjust the position of the graphic so that it looks visually pleasing.

12. To explore the best alignment for the quoted text, click the Align Text Left button in the Paragraph group. Next, click the Align Text Right button. Finally, click the Center button.

• Working with Slide Text (continued)

13. Use the Undo button on the Quick Access toolbar to change back to right alignment. Use the Redo button to return the alignment to centered.

14. Make sure the rectangular quote text box is selected by clicking on the border of the text box. Move the entire text box to the Top Three Sponsors slide. You might need to reposition the text box just below the bullets.

15. Suppose you want to use the contents of this slide for another presentation. To select the entire contents of the slide, position the cursor in the upper-right corner, hold down the left mouse button, and drag the box to the lower-left corner. When you release the mouse button, all the objects should be selected. Click the Copy button in the Clipboard group on the Home tab. Now, create a new, blank PowerPoint presentation and select the blank layout for the first slide. Paste the contents of the golf slide into the new presentation. Use the Solstice theme. Your slide should look similar to the one shown in the figure below.

16. Switch to the Advantages of a New Golf Course slide in the original presentation. Use Cut in the Clipboard group on the Home tab to delete this slide from the presentation. Switch to your new presentation and paste the slide there. Your new presentation should now contain two slides.

17. Save the original presentation in your Project folder using the file name PrjPP-7A XXXXX 9999, where XXXXX is your name or student ID number and 9999 is your class section number. Save the new presentation in your Project folder as PrjPP-7B XXXXX 9999.

18. Submit both presentations for this project on a USB flash drive, as printouts, or as e-mail attachments, according to your instructor's directions.

Project PP-8: Final Presentation Details

In this project, you'll explore how to add footers to slides and how to change slide setup.

Requirements: This project requires Microsoft PowerPoint.

Project file: PrjPP-8.pptx

1. Copy the file PrjPP-8.pptx to your Project folder using the Copy It! button on this page in the BookOnCD.

2. Start Microsoft PowerPoint and open the file PrjPP-8.pptx from your Project folder.

3. Suppose you would like all the slides to display the date they were created, slide numbers, and your name. Select any slide, then select Header & Footer on the Insert tab. When the *Header and Footer* dialog box appears, click the Slide tab.

4. To add the date the slides were created, click the *Date and time* checkbox. Make sure the Fixed option is selected and then type today's date in the box.

5. To add sequential numbers to every slide, place a checkmark in the *Slide number* box.

6. To add your name to a footer, place a checkmark in the Footer box and type your name in the box. Place a checkmark in the *Don't show on title slide* box. This step prevents the footer from appearing on the title page.

7. Click the *Apply to All* button to add the footer to all the slides and close the *Header and Footer* dialog box. Look through the slides to make sure your footer appears on every slide except the title slide.

8. Suppose that you want to display the current date on the title slide each time the presentation is given. Select the title slide, then click *Header and Footer*. Click *Update automatically*. To change the date format, click the arrow button on the date box and select the second option (e.g., Monday, February 22, 2012).

9. Remove the checkmarks from the two checkboxes at the bottom of the dialog box. You do not want this slide numbered, nor do you want your name on it. To apply this footer to just the title slide and close the *Header and Footer* dialog box, click the Apply button. Today's date now appears in the lower-left corner of the title slide.

• Final Presentation Details (continued)

10. Now, suppose you want to print the presentation on 8.5" x 11" paper and you would like to stretch each slide to fit the entire page. Click the Design tab and then click the Page Setup button. When the Page Setup dialog box appears, click the arrow button for the *Slides sized for* box and select *Letter Paper (8.5 x 11 in)*. Change the orientation of the slides to Portrait and then click the OK button. Your title slide should look similar to the one shown in the figure below.

11. Save your presentation in your Project folder using the file name PrjPP-8 XXXXX 9999, where XXXXX is your name or student ID number and 9999 is your class section number.

12. Use one of the following options to submit your project on a USB flash drive, as a printout, or as an e-mail attachment, according to your instructor's directions:

• To submit the project on a USB flash drive, close PowerPoint and then copy the file PrjPP-8 XXXXX 9999 from your Project folder to a USB drive. Make sure your name is on the USB drive.

• To print the project, click the File tab, select the Print option, and then click Print. Use the Full Page Slides pull-down list to specify Handouts with 4 slides per page in vertical order. Also, make sure that the *Scale to Fit Paper* checkbox contains a checkmark. Close the pull-down list. Write your name, student ID number, class section number, date, and PrjPP-8 on the printout.

• To submit the project as an e-mail attachment, use Method 1 or Method 2, as described on page 156. Type your instructor's e-mail address in the To: box. Click the Subject: box and type PrjPP-8, your student ID number, and your class section number. Click the Send button or perform any additional steps required by your e-mail software to send an e-mail message.

Project AC-1: Creating a Database Table

In this project, you'll apply what you've learned about Microsoft Access to create a database, create a table, and enter data into the table. You'll also explore data formats and validation rules.

Requirements: This project requires Microsoft Access.

Project file: No project file is required for this project.

1. Start Microsoft Access.

2. Create a new blank database in your Project folder. (Hint: Click the folder on the right side of the File Name box to select your Project folder.)

3. Name the database PrjAC-1 XXXXX 99999, where XXXXX is your name or student ID number and 9999 is your class section number. Click the Create button under the File Name box to complete the create operation.

4. Suppose you have a personal library filled with books that you like to lend out to friends. You can keep track of your books by creating a simple library database.

5. Enter the following fields: Title, Author, Publisher, Quantity, Lend Date, Borrower, and E-mail. Specify the Text data type for all the fields except Quantity and Lend Date. Specify Number as the data type for the Quantity field. Specify the Date & Time data type for the Lend Date field.

6. Change the name of the ID field to ISBN and change the data type to Number. (Hint: The data type setting is in the Formatting group.)

7. Select the Quantity field, then set its default value to 1. (Hint: Look for the Default Value button in the Properties group.)

8. Select the Lend Date field, then use the Format option in the Properties group to change the field's format to Short Date.

9. Delete the Quantity field.

10. Add a field called Book Value and specify currency as its data type. Drag the field so it is between the Publisher and Lend Date fields.

11. Choose any five books that you own and fill in all the fields except Lend Date, Borrower, and E-mail. If you can't see the full text for a field, drag the dividing line between field headers to resize the column.

12. Sort the records by Author in A to Z order.

13. Select any record and add data for the Borrower, Lend Date, and E-mail fields.

14. Select another record and add data for the Borrower, Lend Date, and E-mail fields.

15. Sort the data by the Borrower field in Z to A order.

•Creating a Database Table (continued)

16. The fields in your table should be arranged like those in the figure below.

17. Close the table, save it, and name it Book List.

18. Use one of the following options to submit your project on a USB flash drive, as a printout, or as an e-mail attachment, according to your instructor's directions:

• To submit the project on a USB flash drive, close Access and then copy the file PrjAC-1 XXXXX 9999 from your Project folder to a USB drive. Make sure your name is on the USB drive.

• To print the file, make sure that the Book List table is open. Click the File tab, select the Print option, and then click Print. Write your name, student ID number, class section number, date, and PrjAC-1 on the first page of the printout.

• To submit the project as an e-mail attachment, exit Access and start your usual e-mail program. Type your instructor's e-mail address in the To: box. Type PrjAC-1, your student ID number, and your class section number in the Subject: box. Attach the file PrjAC-1 XXXXX 9999 from your Project folder to the e-mail message and send it.

Project AC-2: Creating Queries

In this project, you'll apply what you've learned about Microsoft Access to find specific records and create queries for finding specific information in a database.

Requirements: This project requires Microsoft Access.

Project file: PrjAC-2.accdb

1. Copy the file PrjAC-2.accdb to your Project folder using the Copy It! button on this page in the BookOnCD.

2. Start Microsoft Access.

3. Open the file PrjAC-2.accdb from your Project folder.

4. Select the Contacts table and delete it.

5. Suppose you hadn't intended to delete that table. If you remember to click the Undo button right away, you can easily restore the table to the database. Click the Undo button on the Quick Access toolbar.

6. Open the Products table and right-click the Product Number field, and then sort it from smallest to largest.

7. Sort the data by price from largest to smallest.

8. Use the Query Wizard on the Create tab to create a simple query that includes all fields from the Products table. Name the query Products Under $10. Specify that you want to modify the query design before you click the Finish button that closes the Simple Query Wizard.

9. Add the query criterion <10 to the Price field to limit the query results to products that cost less than $10. Click the Run button in the Results group to view your results. Compare your results to those shown in the figure below.

Products Under $10			✕
ID ▾	Product Number ▾	Description ▾	Price ▾
1	72838	8 oz Coffee Mug	$3.45
2	82892	12 oz Coffee Mug	$4.15
3	18372	Cup Holder	$2.85
5	83827	Auto Trash Bag	$7.95
7	23702	Lock De-icer	$2.89
8	37027	Windshield Scraper	$3.25
* (New)	0		$0.00

10. Right-click the Products Under $10 tab and save this query. Right-click it again and close the query.

11. Open the Contacts table and use the Query Wizard to create a query that includes only the State/Province and EmailName fields. Name the query Ohio E-mail Addresses. Specify that you want to modify the query design before you close the wizard.

• Creating Queries (continued)

12. Add criteria to limit the query results to records of people located in the state of Ohio (OH). Run the query and compare your results to those shown in the figure below.

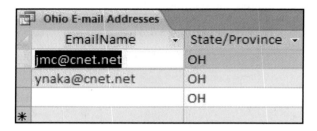

EmailName	State/Province
jmc@cnet.net	OH
ynaka@cnet.net	OH
	OH

13. Save and close the updated query.

14. Delete the query named E-mail Address List by right-clicking its title and then selecting Delete from the shortcut menu.

15. Save your database in your Project folder using the file name PrjAC-2 XXXXX 9999, where XXXXX is your name or student ID number and 9999 is your class section number.

16. Use one of the following options to submit your project on a USB flash drive, as a printout, or as an e-mail attachment, according to your instructor's directions:

• To submit the project on a USB flash drive, close Access and then copy the file PrjAC-2 XXXXX 9999 from your Project folder to a USB drive. Make sure your name is on the USB drive.

• To print the project, make sure that the Products Under $10 query is open. Click the File tab, select the Print option, and then click Print. Close the Products Under $10 query, then open the Ohio E-mail Addresses query. Follow the previous instructions for printing a query. Staple the pages together, then write your name, student ID number, class section number, date, and PrjAC-2 on the first page.

• To submit the project as an e-mail attachment, exit Access and start your usual e-mail program. Type your instructor's e-mail address in the To: box. Type PrjAC-2, your student ID number, and your class section number in the Subject: box. Attach the file PrjAC-2 XXXXX 9999 from your Project folder to the e-mail message and send it.

Project AC-3: Creating Forms

In this project, you'll apply what you've learned about Microsoft Access to create forms that would allow a data entry person to easily update the Products and Contacts tables.

Requirements: This project requires Microsoft Access.

Project file: PrjAC-3.accdb

 1. Copy the file PrjAC-3.accdb to your Project folder using the Copy It! button on this page in the BookOnCD.

2. Start Microsoft Access.

3. Open the file PrjAC-3.accdb from your Project folder and make sure the Products table is displayed.

4. Use the Form Wizard on the Create tab to create a form containing all the fields from the Products table. Specify the Columnar layout. Enter Product Inventory as the form title.

5. Click the Finish button and compare your form to the one shown below.

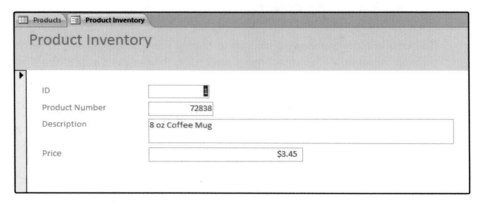

6. Use the Product Inventory form to add a new record for product number 54431, which is Fix-a-Flat priced at $1.89. (Hint: Click the 🔲 *new(blank) record* button on the navigation bar at the bottom of the window.) Note that the ID field is automatically filled in for you.

7. Close the Product Inventory form.

8. Open the Products table and use the Refresh All button to make sure the new record for Fix-a-Flat has been added to the table.

9. Use the Form Wizard to create a form containing the following fields from the Contacts table: LastName, FirstName, and EmailName. Use the Justified layout. Enter E-Mail List as the form title.

10. Compare your form to the one shown below.

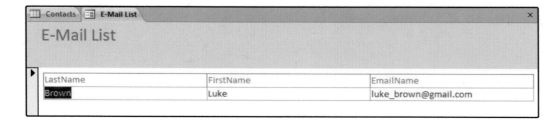

• Creating Forms (continued)

11. Suppose you would like the date and time on a header for each form. Switch to Layout View. Select *Date and Time* in the Header/Footer group on the Design tab. In the *Date and Time* dialog box, check the format you prefer, then click the OK button. The form should now have the date and time in its upper-right corner.

12. Switch to Design View and edit the title so that it says E-Mail Address List instead of "E-Mail List." Resize the text box so that the title is displayed on one line. Save the changes to your form and return to Form View to view the new form with the revised title.

13. Forms are usually displayed on the screen for data entry and editing. You can print one or more forms. For example, you might print and mail a form to a client so that he or she can verify the data it contains. To print the form you are viewing, click the File tab, select the Print option, and then click Print.

14. When working with small forms, such as the E-Mail Address List, you might want to print all the forms on a single page. To do so, make sure the Print dialog box has a Print Range set to All.

15. Add the e-mail address of a friend or relative to the E-Mail Address List form, then close the form. Use the Refresh All button to make sure the new record is added to the Contacts table.

16. Sometimes forms become obsolete and should be deleted. Delete the form called Client Addresses.

17. Save your database in your Project folder using the file name PrjAC-3 XXXXX 9999, where XXXXX is your name or student ID number and 9999 is your class section number.

18. Use one of the following options to submit your project on a USB flash drive, as a printout, or as an e-mail attachment, according to your instructor's directions:

• To submit the project on a USB flash drive, close Access and then copy the file PrjAC-3 XXXXX 9999 from your Project folder to a USB drive. Make sure your name is on the USB drive.

• To print the data as it appears in the form, make sure that the Product Inventory form is open. Click the File tab, select the Print option, and then click Print. Close the Product Inventory form and open the E-Mail Address List form. Follow the previous instructions for printing a form. Staple the pages together, then write your name, student ID number, class section number, date, and PrjAC-3 on the first page.

• To submit the project as an e-mail attachment, exit Access and start your usual e-mail program. Type your instructor's e-mail address in the To: box. Type PrjAC-3, your student ID number, and your class section number in the Subject: box. Attach the file PrjAC-3 XXXXX 9999 from your Project folder to the e-mail message and send it.

Project AC-4: Creating Reports

In this project, you'll apply what you've learned about Microsoft Access to generate printed reports.

Requirements: This project requires Microsoft Access.

Project file: PrjAC-4.accdb

1. Copy the file PrjAC-4.accdb to your Project folder using the Copy It! button on this page in the BookOnCD.

2. Start Microsoft Access.

3. Open the file PrjAC-4.accdb from your Project folder and make sure that all the database objects are displayed on the left side of the Access window. To do so, click the ⊙ button in the navigation pane and make sure that All Access Objects is selected.

4. Use the Report Wizard to create a report containing only the LastName, FirstName, and EmailName fields from the Contacts table. Do not add any grouping levels. Sort the records by last name in ascending order. Use the Tabular layout for the report. Enter Contact E-mail Addresses for the report title.

5. Compare your report to the one shown in the figure below, then close the report.

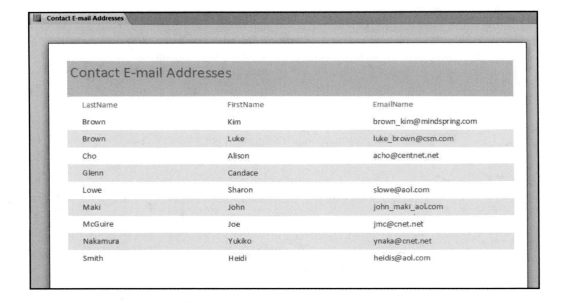

• Creating Reports (continued)

6. Use the Report Wizard to create a report for the query *Products Under $10* that contains all fields except the ID field. Group by department. Sort the records by Description in ascending order. Use the Stepped layout for the report. Enter Products Under $10 by Department for the report title.

7. Compare your report to the one shown in the figure below, then close the report.

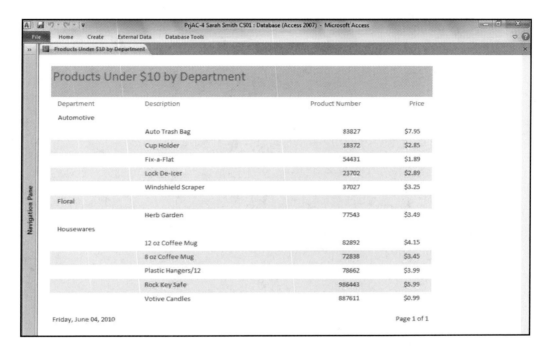

8. Save your database in your Project folder using the file name PrjAC-4 XXXXX 9999, where XXXXX is your name or student ID number and 9999 is your class section number.

9. Use one of the following options to submit your project on a USB flash drive, as a printout, or as an e-mail attachment, according to your instructor's directions:

• To submit the project on a USB flash drive, close Access and then copy the file PrjAC-4 XXXXX 9999 from your Project folder to a USB drive. Make sure your name is on the USB drive.

• To print the project, open the Contact E-mail Addresses report, click the File tab, select the Print option, and then click Print. Close the Contact E-mail Addresses report and open the Products Under $10 by Department report. Follow the previous instructions for printing a report. Staple the pages together, then write your name, student ID number, class section number, date, and PrjAC-4 on the first page.

• To submit the project as an e-mail attachment, exit Access and start your usual e-mail program. Type your instructor's e-mail address in the To: box. Type PrjAC-4, your student ID number, and your class section number in the Subject: box. Attach the file PrjAC-4 XXXXX 9999 from your Project folder to the e-mail message and send it.

Project AC-5: Indexing and Filtering

In this project, you'll explore how indexes can be used to make databases more efficient. You'll also find out how to use filters to create a quick query by example.

Indexes are used to find and sort records quickly. The field used as a primary key should always be indexed. It is a good idea to index any other fields commonly used for searching and sorting. In Access, index settings can also be used to restrict fields to unique values. For example, a customer number field must contain only unique customer numbers because no two customers can share a customer number. A "No Duplicate" index restricts values entered into the field to only unique values.

Requirements: This project requires Microsoft Access.

Project file: PrjAC-5.accdb

1. Copy the file PrjAC-5.accdb to your Project folder using the Copy It! button on this page in the BookOnCD.

2. Start Microsoft Access.

3. Open the file PrjAC-5.accdb from your Project folder. Open the Contacts table and then click the Fields tab on the ribbon so that you can modify the fields.

4. Suppose you'd like to create an index on the State/Province field to speed up sorts and searches. Click the State/Province field, then click the Indexed checkbox in the Field Validation group.

5. The ID field is the primary key, so the data it contains must be unique for each record. To verify that this is the case, select the ID field and make sure that the Unique box in the Field Validation group contains a checkmark.

6. Access includes filters that help you quickly sift through a table to find records. Click the arrow button on the column header in the State/Province field. Remove the checkmarks from all of the selections except OH, then click the OK button.

7. Compare your results to the example below.

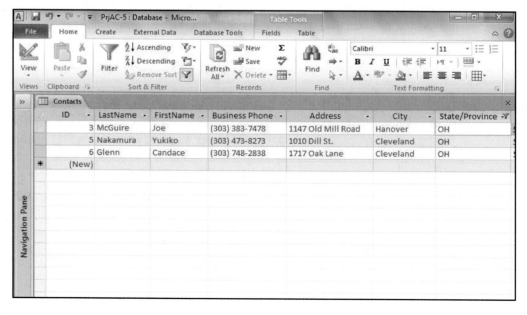

• Indexing and Filtering (continued)

8. Cancel the OH filter by clicking the State/Province arrow button and selecting *Clear filter from State/Province.*

9. Now use a filter to display only contacts located in Canada. Compare your results to those shown below.

ID	LastName	FirstName	Business Phone	Address	City	State/Province	Zip/PostalCode	Country/Region
10	Garceau	Jayden	(514) 723-5498	556 d'Youville	Montreal	Quebec	H3C 1W7	Canada
11	Eagleton	Liam	(514) 856-2242	3402 Saint-Denis	Montreal	Quebec	H3C 1W7	Canada
12	Dufaye	Sophie	(604) 781-7275	Stanley Park Drive	Vancouver	British Columbia	V6H 3J4	Canada
13	Lamarre	Maya	(416) 965-5022	51 Benvenuto Pl.	Toronto	Ontario	M4V 1L1	Canada
	(New)							

10. Save your database in your Project folder using the file name PrjAC-5 XXXXX 9999, where XXXXX is your name or student ID number and 9999 is your class section number.

11. Use one of the following options to submit your project on a USB flash drive, as a printout, or as an e-mail attachment, according to your instructor's directions:

• To submit the project on a USB flash drive, close Access and then copy the file PrjAC-5 XXXXX 9999 from your Project folder to a USB drive. Make sure your name is on the USB drive.

• To print the project, open the Contacts table, set the filter, click the File tab, select the Print option, and then click Print. Write your name, student ID number, class section number, date, and PrjAC-5 on the printout.

• To submit the project as an e-mail attachment, exit Access and start your usual e-mail program. Type your instructor's e-mail address in the To: box. Type PrjAC-5, your student ID number, and your class section number in the Subject: box. Attach the file PrjAC-5 XXXXX 9999 from your Project folder to the e-mail message and send it.

Project AC-6: Working with Lookup Fields

Access includes a Lookup data type that can be used to streamline and standardize data entry. Let's suppose you are working with two tables that pertain to the work of artist Jackson Pollock. One table contains a list of his significant paintings. The other table contains a list of art galleries that sometimes display his work.

A gallery curator uses two tables for this data because some galleries own more than one Pollock painting. You can use a lookup field to easily enter the name of the gallery that displays or owns each Jackson Pollock painting.

Requirements: This project requires Microsoft Access.

Project file: PrjAC-6.accdb

1. Copy the file PrjAC-6.accdb to your Project folder using the Copy It! button on this page in the BookOnCD.

2. Start Microsoft Access.

3. Open the file PrjAC-6.accdb from your Project folder. Open each of the tables and familiarize yourself with the fields each one contains.

4. Suppose you want to keep track of the galleries in which these paintings are located. The Paintings table will need an additional field. To avoid entering long gallery names, you can create a lookup field based on the galleries that are listed in the Galleries table.

5. While looking at the Paintings table, click the *Click to Add* field heading to select it.

6. Select the Lookup & Relationship option to start the Lookup Wizard.

7. Select the button for *I want the lookup field to get the values from another table or query*, then click Next to continue.

8. Select Table: Galleries, and then click the Next button.

9. Select the Gallery field and then click Next.

10. Sort by Gallery in Ascending order.

11. On the next window, drag the field border so you can see the entire contents of all fields. Click Next.

12. Enter Gallery as the label for the lookup field and then click Finish.

13. Increase the width of the Gallery field.

14. When you click a cell in the Gallery field, a Lookup button appears so that you can view a list of galleries and select one.

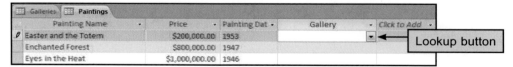

15. Click the Lookup button in the Gallery field for the painting *Easter and the Totem*, and then select *Museum of Modern Art*.

16. Use the arrow button to enter these galleries for the next three paintings:
Enchanted Forest   Peggy Guggenheim Collection
Eyes in the Heat   Peggy Guggenheim Collection
Full Fathom Five   Museum of Modern Art

• Working with Lookup Fields (continued)

17. Pollock's Mural painting is at the Figge Art Museum, which is not one of the galleries in the lookup list. To add this gallery, switch to the Galleries table and add the following record:

    Figge Art Museum   Davenport IA

18. Make sure you've pressed the Enter key or Tab key so that the record is added.

19. Now switch back to the Paintings table and click the Refresh All button on the Home tab.

20. Use the Lookup button in the Gallery field to enter Figge Art Museum for the Mural painting.

21. Add the Museum of Fine Arts in Boston to the Galleries table.

22. Complete the Paintings table by entering the following galleries:

Number 10	Museum of Fine Arts
Number 7	National Gallery of Art
One: Number 31	Museum of Modern Art
Shimmering Substance	Museum of Modern Art
Stenographic Figure	Museum of Modern Art
Summertime: Number 9A	Tate Modern
The She-Wolf	Museum of Modern Art

23. Compare your table with the figure below.

Painting Name	Price	Painting Date	Gallery
Easter and the Totem	$200,000.00	1953	Museum of Modern Art
Enchanted Forest	$800,000.00	1947	Peggy Guggenheim Collec
Eyes in the Heat	$1,000,000.00	1946	Peggy Guggenheim Collec
Full Fathom Five	$200,000.00	1947	Museum of Modern Art
Mural	$200,000.00	1943	Figge Art Museum
Number 10	$300,000.00	1949	Museum of Fine Arts
Number 7	$850,000.00	1951	National Gallery of Art
One: Number 31	$200,000.00	1950	Museum of Modern Art
Shimmering Substance	$500,000.00	1946	Museum of Modern Art
Stenographic Figure	$150,000.00	1942	Museum of Modern Art
Summertime: Number 9A	$2,000,000.00	1948	Tate Modern
The She-Wolf	$500,000.00	1943	Museum of Modern Art

24. Save your database in your Project folder using the file name PrjAC-6 XXXXX 9999, where XXXXX is your name or student ID number and 9999 is your class section number.

25. Use one of the following options to submit your project on a USB flash drive, as a printout, or as an e-mail attachment, according to your instructor's directions:

• To submit the project on a USB flash drive, close Access and then copy the file PrjAC-6 XXXXX 9999 from your Project folder to a USB drive. Make sure your name is on the USB drive.

• To print the project, print the Galleries table and the Paintings table. Write your name, student ID number, class section number, date, and PrjAC-6 on the first page.

• To submit the project as an e-mail attachment, exit Access and start your usual e-mail program. Type your instructor's e-mail address in the To: box. Type PrjAC-6, your student ID number, and your class section number in the Subject: box. Attach the file PrjAC-6 XXXXX 9999 from your Project folder and send the e-mail message.

Project AC-7: Creating Relationships

In this project, you'll learn how to create and use relationships. A relationship links a record from one table to one or more records in another table. For example, suppose a college offers a series of workshops for students. A many-to-many relationship exists between students and workshops. Each workshop can be attended by many students; and a student can attend more than one workshop.

To complete this project, you'll create a relationship between the Students table and the Workshops table so that you can use the data from both tables in a single report. Many-to-many relationships require a third table containing links between the two tables in the relationship. The database contains a table called Rosters that contains the student ID for each student who is enrolled in each workshop.

Requirements: This project requires Microsoft Access.

Project file: PrjAC-7.accdb

1. Copy the file PrjAC-7.accdb to your Project folder using the Copy It! button on this page in the BookOnCD.

2. Start Microsoft Access. Open the file PrjAC-7.accdb from your Project folder.

3. The database contains three tables. Open each table and familiarize yourself with the data in each table. From the data in these tables, can you find the name of at least two students who are enrolled in the Volunteering workshop? The process becomes much easier when you establish relationships between tables.

4. Click the Database Tools tab, then click the Relationships button. The Relationships tab now displays three field lists—one for each of the tables.

5. Note that the Workshops table and the Rosters table both include a WorkshopID field. To create a relationship between these tables, drag WorkshopID from the Workshops table and drop it on WorkshopID in the Rosters table.

6. When the Edit Relationships window appears, make sure it says *One-to-Many* as the Relationship Type, and then click the Create button. If the window says *One-to-One*, click the Cancel button, then repeat Step 5, making sure to drop on the word "WorkshopID."

7. Next, create a one-to-many relationship between the Rosters table and the Students table using the StudentID field.

8. Close the Relationships window and save the changes.

9. With the relationships created, you can generate a query to easily see the names of students enrolled in each workshop. To begin, click the Query Wizard button on the Create tab.

10. From the Workshops table, add the WorkshopTitle to the Selected Fields list. From the Students table, add the LastName and FirstName fields. Name the query Students Enrolled in Each Workshop.

11. Scroll down to view the students enrolled in the Volunteering workshop. If your query does not produce the expected results, delete it and try Steps 9 and 10 again.

•Creating Relationships (continued)

12. You can also create a database report for the workshop rosters. Use the Report Wizard to create a report with the following specifications:

- Fields: Add all fields from the Workshops table and only the LastName and FirstName fields from the Students table.

- View data: Select *by Workshops* for the data view.

- Grouping levels: Do not add any.

- Sort order: Sort the records by LastName in ascending order.

- Layout: Use the Outline layout for the report.

- Title: Enter Workshop Rosters for the report title.

13. Compare your results to the report shown below. Be sure to look at page 2 of the report. Is it now easier to determine the names of students enrolled in the Volunteering workshop?

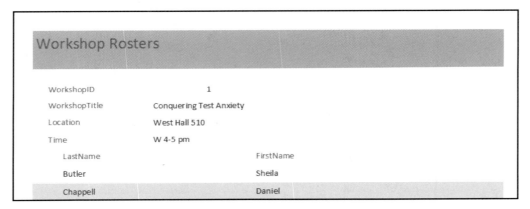

14. Save your database in your Project folder using the file name PrjAC-7 XXXXX 9999, where XXXXX is your name or student ID number and 9999 is your class section number.

15. Use one of the following options to submit your project on a USB flash drive, as a printout, or as an e-mail attachment, according to your instructor's directions:

- To submit the project on a USB flash drive, close Access and then copy the file PrjAC-7 XXXXX 9999 from your Project folder to a USB drive. Make sure your name is on the USB drive.

- To print the Workshop Rosters report, open it, click the File tab, select the Print option, and then click Print. Close the report. To print the relationships, open the Relationships window. Click the Relationship Report button in the Tools group on the Relationship Tools Design contextual tab. Click the Print button in the Print group on the Print Preview tab, then click OK. Close the Print Preview. Save and close the relationships report using the default report name. Write your name, student ID number, class section number, date, and PrjAC-7 on the printouts.

- To submit the project as an e-mail attachment, exit Access and start your usual e-mail program. Type your instructor's e-mail address in the To: box. Type PrjAC-7, your student ID number, and your class section number in the Subject: box. Attach the file PrjAC-7 XXXXX 9999 from your Project folder to the e-mail message and send it.

Project AC-8: Managing Tables and Relationships

In this project, you'll explore basic database management techniques, such as viewing tables in different ways and deleting old or obsolete items from the database.

Requirements: This project requires Microsoft Access.

Project file: PrjAC-8.accdb

1. Copy the file PrjAC-8.accdb to your Project folder using the Copy It! button on this page in the BookOnCD.

2. Start Microsoft Access and open the file PrjAC-8.accdb from your Project folder.

3. Open the Student Names table and the Students table. Click Switch Windows in the Window group on the Home tab. Select Tile Horizontally to arrange both tables as shown below so that they do not overlap.

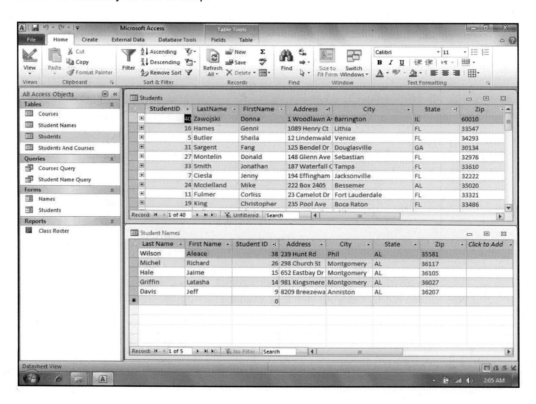

4. Does data in one of these tables simply duplicate data in the other table? The Student Names table seems to include only students from Alabama. To more easily see if the same students are in the Students table, sort the Students table in A to Z order by state.

5. Examine the data in the two tables. The records in the Student Names table also appear to be in the Students table. Are their student numbers the same? Students in the Student Names table are sorted in descending order by Student ID. To match this order, sort the Students table in descending order by Student ID.

• Managing Tables and Relationships (continued)

6. It is still a bit difficult to compare the data. You can apply a filter to show only the students in Alabama in the Students table. In the Students table, click any state field that contains "AL." Click Selection in the Sort & Filter group on the Home tab. Select Equals AL. Now Access displays only students who live in Alabama, sorted by Student ID. Compare the two tables. The data in the Student Names table is already stored in the Students table.

7. Remove the filter on the Students table by clicking Filter in the Sort & Filter group. Select *Clear filter from State*.

8. Close both tables. Click No if you are asked if you want to save the changes.

9. Assume you've seen enough to convince yourself that the Student Names table is not needed. You can delete the table, but first you should check if the table is related to any other tables. Click Relationships on the Database Tools tab. Click the All Relationships button. Notice the relationship between Student Names and Students and Courses. Right-click the relationship and select Delete. Click the Yes button when prompted to delete the relationship. Close the Relationships window and save your changes.

10. The Student Name query is based on data from the table you want to eliminate. To delete the query, right-click the Student Name query, and select Delete. Click the Yes button to complete the deletion.

11. Now that you have deleted the relationships and queries associated with the Student Names table, you can delete the table itself. Right-click Student Names, and choose Delete.

12. Save your database in your Project folder using the file name PrjAC-8 XXXXX 9999, where XXXXX is your name or student ID number and 9999 is your class section number.

13. Use one of the following options to submit your project on a USB flash drive, as a printout, or as an e-mail attachment, according to your instructor's directions:

• To submit the project on a USB flash drive, close Access and then copy the file PrjAC-8 XXXXX 9999 from your Project folder to a USB drive. Make sure your name is on the USB drive.

• To print the relationships, open the Relationships window. Click the All Relationships button. Click the Relationship Report button in the Tools group on the Relationship Tools Design contextual tab. Click the Print button in the Print group on the Print Preview tab, then click OK. Close the Print Preview. Save and close the relationships report using the default report name. Write your name, student ID number, class section number, date, and PrjAC-8 on the first page.

• To submit the project as an e-mail attachment, exit Access and start your usual e-mail program. Type your instructor's e-mail address in the To: box. Type PrjAC-8, your student ID number, and your class section number in the Subject: box. Attach the file PrjAC-8 XXXXX 9999 from your Project folder to the e-mail message and send it.

Project AC-9: Grouped Reports

In this project, you'll explore how to use Microsoft Access to create reports containing "control breaks" that group, summarize, and total data.

Requirements: This project requires Microsoft Access.

Project file: PrjAC-9.accdb

CopyIt!

1. Copy the file PrjAC-9.accdb to your Project folder using the Copy It! button. Start Microsoft Access and open the file PrjAC-9.accdb from your Project folder.

2. Open the table called Mutual Fund. Notice that it contains a list of funds, such as American Value, that are managed by various companies, such as Dean Witter. Each record includes the fund's current value, and its performance over the past year and past five years.

3. Print this table by clicking the File tab, selecting the Print option, and then clicking Print. Click OK in the Print Dialog box.

4. Next, highlight just the Dean Witter records. To print just these records, open the Print dialog box and click Selected Record(s) before you click the OK button. Printing the raw data contained in a table does not provide much flexibility for formatting and organizing report data, so it is rarely done. The Reporting features provided by Access offer much more flexibility.

5. Use the Report Wizard to create a report based on data in the Mutual Fund table. Respond to the wizard prompts with the following specifications and compare your report to the one shown in the figure below:
• For Tables/Queries, select Mutual Fund.
• Select Company, Fund Name, and Net Asset Value fields.
• Group by Company and sort by Fund Name in ascending order.
• Use the Summary Options button to select Sum.
• Use the Stepped layout.
• Title the report Net Asset Value By Company.

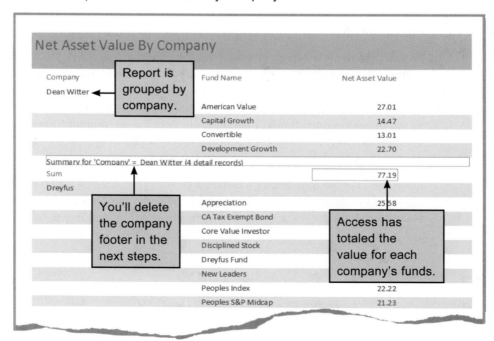

• Grouped Reports (continued)

6. The report contains a Company Footer that starts "Summary for 'Company'..." This footer detracts from the readability of the report, so it should be deleted. Right-click the report and select Design View. Locate the block containing ="Summary for " & "'Company'... and delete it.

7. Switch back to Report View and make sure the Company Footer has been removed, then close and save the report.

8. Now, suppose you want to create a report that contains the average, minimum, and maximum 1-year and 5-year statistics for each fund management company. Use the Report Wizard to create a report based on data in the Mutual Fund table with the following specifications:
* Include Company, One Year, and Five Years fields.
* Group by Company (no sort field).
* Use the Summary Options button to select Avg, Min, and Max for One Year and Five Years.
* Use the Summary Options button to select Summary Only.
* Use the Stepped Layout.
* Title the report 1-Year and 5-Year Fund Performance Summary.

9. Right-click the report and select Design View. Locate the block containing the Company Footer and delete it.

10. Compare your report to the one shown in the figure below.

11. Submit the four printed reports you produced.

1-Year and 5-Year Fund Performance Summary

Company	One Year	Five Years
Dean Witter		
Avg	12.6	11.0
Min	10.5	5.0
Max	17.0	15.1
Dreyfus		
Avg	17.1	12.1
Min	-2.6	5.5
Max	25.7	15.3
Evergreen		
Avg	15.0	12.8
Min	5.0	8.9
Max	23.8	16.9

Project AC-10: Exporting Information

In this project, you'll practice exporting Access data to a spreadsheet, to a Word document, and into comma-delimited format.

Requirements: This project requires Microsoft Access, Microsoft Excel, Microsoft Word, and NotePad.

Project file: PrjAC-10.accdb

1. Copy the file PrjAC-10.accdb to your Project folder using the Copy It! button on this page in the BookOnCD.

2. Start Microsoft Access and open the file PrjAC-10.accdb from your Project folder.

3. Open the Products table.

4. Suppose you'd like to work with this data in a spreadsheet. You can export the data from Access to Excel.

5. Click the External Data tab, then look in the Export group. Click the Excel button. (Hint: Make sure you select the Excel button in the Export group.)

6. Use the Browse button to navigate to your Project folder and then enter the file name PrjAC-10A.

7. Select the export option *Export data with formatting and layout*. Also select the option *Open the destination file after the export operation is complete*, and then click the OK button.

8. After the data is transferred, Excel opens and displays the data as shown in the figure below.

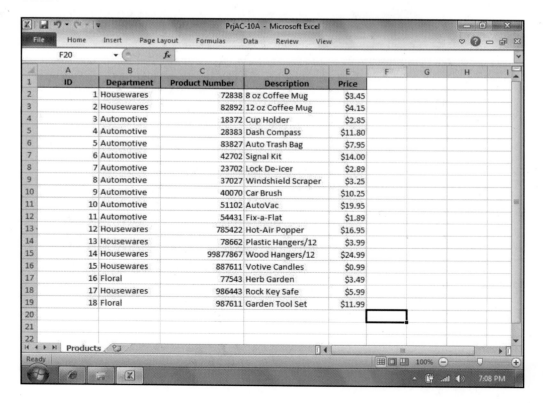

ID	Department	Product Number	Description	Price
1	Housewares	72838	8 oz Coffee Mug	$3.45
2	Housewares	82892	12 oz Coffee Mug	$4.15
3	Automotive	18372	Cup Holder	$2.85
4	Automotive	28383	Dash Compass	$11.80
5	Automotive	83827	Auto Trash Bag	$7.95
6	Automotive	42702	Signal Kit	$14.00
7	Automotive	23702	Lock De-icer	$2.89
8	Automotive	37027	Windshield Scraper	$3.25
9	Automotive	40070	Car Brush	$10.25
10	Automotive	51102	AutoVac	$19.95
11	Automotive	54431	Fix-a-Flat	$1.89
12	Housewares	785422	Hot-Air Popper	$16.95
13	Housewares	78662	Plastic Hangers/12	$3.99
14	Housewares	99877867	Wood Hangers/12	$24.99
15	Housewares	887611	Votive Candles	$0.99
16	Floral	77543	Herb Garden	$3.49
17	Housewares	986443	Rock Key Safe	$5.99
18	Floral	987611	Garden Tool Set	$11.99

• Exporting Information (continued)

9. Close Excel, go back to Microsoft Access, and click the Close button in the Export dialog box without saving the export steps.

10. Use the Report Wizard to create a report containing only the LastName, FirstName, BusinessPhone, City, and State/Province from the Contacts table. Group by State/Province. Sort the records by LastName in ascending order. Use the Stepped layout. Enter Phone Contacts for the report title. Click the Finish button.

11. You can export reports to Microsoft Word, where you can add explanatory text. You can also export tables, queries, and forms to Word. All data is exported to Word in Rich Text Format (rtf). To export the Phone Contacts report, switch to Report View, click the External Data tab, then click More in the Export group. Select Word.

12. Use the Browse button to navigate to your Project folder, enter the file name PrjAC-10B, and click the Save button. Select the export option *Open the destination file after the export operation is complete*, then click the OK button. Your Word document should look very similar to the Phone Contacts report.

13. Close Word, close the Export dialog box, and close the Phone Contacts report.

14. You can also export Access data for processing by programs such as Notepad that work with ASCII text in comma-delimited format. Open the Contacts table, click the External Data tab, then click Text File in the *Export* group.

15. Use the Browse button to navigate to your Project folder, enter the file name PrjAC-10C, and click the Save button.

16. Do not select any of the export options. Click the OK button.

17. The next window displays a preview of your data. Notice that fields are separated by commas. Click the Next button.

18. Make sure Comma is selected as the choice of delimiter, then click the Next button. Click the Finish button. Close the Export dialog box.

19. Your file has been saved. To view its contents, use Windows Explorer to locate the PrjAC-10C file in your Project folder. Double-click the file and it will open in Notepad.

20. Use one of the following options to submit the three project files on a USB flash drive, as printouts, or as e-mail attachments, according to your instructor's directions:

• To submit the project files on a USB flash drive, close Access and then copy the files PrjAC-10A, PrjAC-10B, and PrjAC-10C from your Project folder to a USB drive. Make sure your name is on the USB drive.

• To print each project file, double-click the file to open it. The correct application program should start. In Excel or Word, click the File tab, select the Print option, and then click Print. In Notepad, click the File menu, then select Print. Staple the pages together, then write your name, student ID number, class section number, date, and PrjAC-10 on the first page.

• To submit the project files as e-mail attachments, exit Access and start your usual e-mail program. Type your instructor's e-mail address in the To: box. Type PrjAC-10, your student ID number, and your class section number in the Subject: box. Attach the project files PrjAC-10A, PrjAC-10B, and PrjAC-10C. Click the Send button or perform any additional steps required by your e-mail software to send an e-mail message.

Project CP-1: Word Processing

In this project, you'll apply all that you've learned about Microsoft Word.

Requirements: This project requires Microsoft Word.

Project files: Capstone1.docx, Marquee.jpg

1. Copy the file Capstone1.docx to your Project folder using the Copy It! button on this page in the BookOnCD.

2. Copy the file Marquee.jpg to your Project folder.

3. Start Microsoft Word and open the file Capstone1.docx from your Project folder. You will use the file Capstone1.docx as the basis for this project, making the modifications shown on pages 235–237. The following steps will help you implement the modifications.

4. Add The History of the Drive-In Theater as a left-justified header, and your name as a right-justified header.

5. Add page numbers as centered footers on all pages, including the title page.

6. Search for theatre and replace it with theater.

7. Use the Formal style for the document.

8. Format the title with the Title style and the line containing the author's name with the Subtitle style.

9. Insert Marquee.jpg between the title and byline, and center it.

10. Set a right-justified tab at 6" and use it to align the numbers in the Table of Contents.

11. Format the heading "Table of Contents" as white, bold, 14 point font with a dark gray background. Format all the headings in the same style using the Format Painter.

12. Delete and move paragraphs as shown on page 235.

13. Add a footnote as shown on page 235.

14. Insert page breaks as shown on pages 235–237.

15. Highlight all the text in Figure 1 and adjust the margin to .5" from the left.

16. In Figure 1, use the Show/Hide Characters button and modify the list so that instead of spaces, there is only one tab between each item. Set a right-justified tab at 2". Set a left-justified tab at 2.5".

17. Change the text in Figures 2 and 3 to tables. Format the column headings as white, 12 pt. text with a dark gray background. Adjust the columns so the cells all contain only one line of text.

18. Format the Figure titles using the Quote style at 8 point.

19. In the Unusual Drive-In Theaters section of the document, find synonyms for the words "occupy," "gaudy," and "necessities."

20. Make the wording changes indicated on page 236.

•Word Processing (continued)

21. Add the Wikipedia reference shown on page 237 and make sure it is an active hyperlink.

22. Set the top and bottom margins to 1"; the right and left margins to 1.25".

23. Check your work against the document shown on pages 238 and 239. Save the project as Capstone1-[Your Name]. You will use parts of this project again when you work on the third Capstone project.

24. Submit your project on a USB flash drive, as a printout, or as an e-mail attachment according to your instructor's preference.

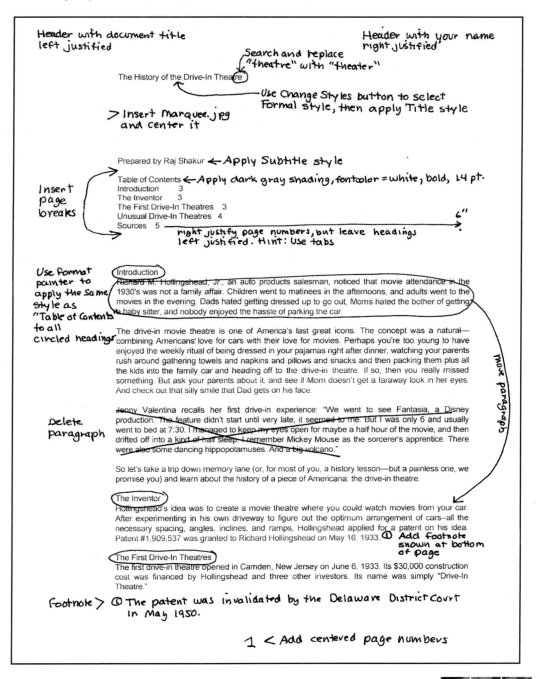

• Word Processing (continued)

Admission to that first drive-in was 25 cents for the car, plus 25 cents per person, with a limit of $1.00 total—certainly an affordable family entertainment option.

Drive-in theatres caught on slowly at first, with three theatres opening in 1934: one each in Pennsylvania, Texas, and California. In 1936, Massachusetts got its first drive-in. Michigan, Ohio, Rhode Island, Florida, and Maine soon followed, with one or at most two drive-in theatres in an entire state. By 1948, fifteen years after the first drive-in opened, there were 820 drive-in theatres in the United States.

Insert page break

The number of drive-ins peaked in the late 1950's, as shown in Figure 1. Although their numbers dwindled after that date, their decline wasn't significant until the 1980's when home video and DVDs offered an even more convenient way to view movies.

change spaces to a tab

Make sure margin is only ½" in from regular margin

1945 102	Radio is the most popular entertainment medium
1955 3855	Black and white television in 65% of U.S. homes
1965 3454	First affordable color televisions available
1975 3075	Betamax format allows home videotaping
1985 1451	VHS gaining popularity
1995 695	VHS is standard video format; DVDs gaining popularity
2005 419	New movie releases in DVD format only

set a right-justified tab at 1½"

Figure 1: Number of Drive-In Theatres by Year 1945-2005 *← Use Quote style 8 pt.*

(Unusual Drive-In Theatres)

Find synonyms for underlined words

In time, most drive-in theatres featured playgrounds to occupy children while they waited for dusk to fall and the movie to start. Almost every drive-in theatre included a gaudy concession stand that stocked such movie-watching necessities as candy, popcorn, hot dogs, ice cream, and beverages.

One of the The largest drive-in theatres *located which was* in Copaigue, New York, covered 28 acres and had a shuttle train to take customers from their cars to other areas *such* and back. Notably large drive-ins are listed in Figure 2 below. *of the theater*

Name	Location	# of Cars
Troy Drive-In	Detroit, Michigan	3,000
Panther Drive-In	Lufkin, Texas	3,000
All-Weather Drive-In	Copaigue, New York	2,500
110 Drive-In	Melville, New York	2.500
Newark Drive-In	Newark, New Jersey	2,400
Belair Drive-In	Cicero, Illinois	2.300
Timonium Drive-In	Timonium, Maryland	2,479
Los Altos Drive-In	Long Beach, California	2,150

Convert into a table. Column headings should be white 12 point text with a dark gray background. Adjust column width so no cell contains 2 lines of text.

Figure 2: The Eight Largest Drive-In Movie Theatres *← Use Quote style 8 pt.*

Insert page break

Most drive-in theatres had room for approximately 500 cars. A few drive-in theatres were significantly smaller, however. Figure 3 lists the five smallest drive-in theatres.

• Word Processing (continued)

Name	Location	# of Cars	
Harmony Drive-In		Harmony, Pennsylvania	50
Highway Drive-In		Bamberg, South Carolina	50
Ponce DeLeon Drive-In		Ponce DeLeon, Florida	60
Twilite Drive-In		Nakina, North Carolina	60
Norwood Drive-In		Norwood, Colorado 64	

Convert to a table with the same format as previous table

Figure 3: The Five Smallest Drive-In Movie Theatres ← Use Quote style 8 pt.

According to Wikipedia, 2001 marked the beginning of "Do-It-Yourself Drive-ins" and "Guerrilla drive-ins" where films are unofficially shown in parking lots and other vacant urban or rural venues using DVDs and LCD projectors. Any blank wall can serve as a screen. Film showings are often organized online via e-mail,Twitter, or social networking sites.

So the drive-in theatre lives on. Perhaps not in all its former glory, but in a modern mashup version made possible by today's technology.

Final margins: Top 1" Left 1.25" Bottom 1" Right 1.25"

Sources

"After Sunset: The Life & Times of the Drive-In Theatre" (updated 1 Nov., 1996) http://www.janson.com/aftersunset.html

Carpenter, Erich. *Drive-In Movie Theatres.* New York: Heflin Connors Press, 1985

"Welcome to the Drive-In Theatre: The Drive-In Theatre History Page" (updated 24 Oct., 1996) http://www.driveintheatre.com

> Wikipedia http://en.wikipedia.org/wiki/Drive-in_theater

• Word Processing (continued)

THE HISTORY OF THE DRIVE-IN THEATER

Table of Contents

Introduction

The drive-in movie theater is one of America's last great icons. The concept was a natural—combining Americans' love for cars with their love for movies. Perhaps you're too young to have enjoyed the weekly ritual of being dressed in your pajamas right after dinner, watching your parents rush around gathering towels and napkins and pillows and snacks and then packing them plus all the kids into the family car and heading off to the drive-in theater. If so, then you really missed something. But ask your parents about it, and see if Mom doesn't get a far away look in her eyes. And check out that silly smile that Dad gets on his face.

So let's take a trip down memory lane (or, for most of you, a history lesson—but a painless one, we promise you) and learn about the history of a piece of Americana: the drive-in theater.

The Inventor

Richard M. Hollingshead, Jr., an auto products salesman, noticed that movie attendance in the 1930's was not a family affair. Children went to matinees in the afternoons, and adults went to the movies in the evening. Dads hated getting dressed up to go out, Moms hated the bother of getting a baby sitter, and nobody enjoyed the hassle of parking the car.

Hollingshead's idea was to create a movie theater where you could watch movies from your car. After experimenting in his own driveway to figure out the optimum arrangement of cars--all the necessary spacing, angles, inclines, and ramps, Hollingshead applied for a patent on his idea. Patent #1,909,537 was granted to Richard Hollingshead on May 16, 1933.[1]

The First Drive-In Theaters

The first drive-in theater opened in Camden, New Jersey on June 6, 1933. Its $30,000 construction cost was financed by Hollingshead and three other investors. Its name was simply "Drive-In Theater."

Admission to that first drive-in was 25 cents for the car, plus 25 cents per person, with a limit of $1.00 total—certainly an affordable family entertainment option.

Drive-in theaters caught on slowly at first, with three theaters opening in 1934: one each in Pennsylvania, Texas, and California. In 1936, Massachusetts got its first drive-in. Michigan, Ohio, Rhode Island, Florida, and Maine soon followed, with one or at most two drive-in theaters in an entire state. By 1948, fifteen years after the first drive-in opened, there were 820 drive-in theaters in the United States.

---

[1] The patent was invalidated by the Delaware District Court in May 1950.

3

• Word Processing (continued)

The History of the Drive-In Theater   Jane Student

The number of drive-ins peaked in the late 1950s, as shown in Figure 1. Although their numbers dwindled after that date, their decline wasn't significant until the 1980s when home video and DVDs offered an even more convenient way to view movies.

1945	102	Radio is the most popular entertainment medium
1955	3855	Black and white television in 65% of U.S. homes
1965	3454	First affordable color televisions available
1975	3075	Betamax format allows home videotaping
1985	1451	VHS gaining popularity
1995	695	VHS is standard video format; DVDs gaining popularity
2005	419	New movie releases in DVD format only

Figure 1: Number of Drive-In Theaters by Year 1945-2005

Unusual Drive-In Theaters

In time, most drive-in theaters featured playgrounds to engage children while they waited for dusk to fall and the movie to start. Almost every drive-in theater included a garish concession stand that stocked such movie-watching provisions as candy, popcorn, hot dogs, ice cream, and beverages.

One of the largest drive-in theaters, located in Copaigue, New York, covered 28 acres and had a shuttle train to take customers from their cars to other areas of the theater and back. Notably large drive-ins are listed in Figure 2 below.

Name	Location	# of Cars
Troy Drive-In	Detroit, Michigan	3,000
Panther Drive-In	Lufkin, Texas	3,000
All-Weather Drive-In	Copaigue, New York	2,500
110 Drive-In	Melville, New York	2,500
Newark Drive-In	Newark, New Jersey	2,400
Belair Drive-In	Cicero, Illinois	2,300
Timonium Drive-In	Timonium, Maryland	2,479

The History of the Drive-In Theater   Jane Student

Most drive-in theaters had room for approximately 500 cars. A few drive-in theaters were significantly smaller, however. Figure 3 lists the five smallest drive-in theaters.

Name	Location	# of Cars
Harmony Drive-In	Harmony, Pennsylvania	50
Highway Drive-In	Bamberg, South Carolina	50
Ponce DeLeon Drive-In	Ponce DeLeon, Florida	60
Twilite Drive-In	Nakina, North Carolina	60
Norwood Drive-In	Norwood, Colorado	64

Figure 3: The Five Smallest Drive-In Movie Theaters

According to Wikipedia, 2001 marked the beginning of "Do-It-Yourself Drive-ins" and "Guerrilla drive-ins" where films are unofficially shown in parking lots and other vacant urban or rural venues using DVDs and LCD projectors. Any blank wall can serve as a screen. Film showings are often organized online via e-mail, Twitter, or social networking sites.

So the drive-in theater lives on. Perhaps not in all its former glory, but in a modern mashup version made possible by today's technology.

Sources

"After Sunset: The Life & Times of the Drive-In Theater" (updated 1 Nov., 1996) http://www.janson.com/aftersunset.html

Carpenter, Erich. *Drive-In Movie Theaters.* New York: Heflin Connors Press, 1985

"Welcome to the Drive-In Theater: The Drive-In Theater History Page" (updated 24 Oct., 1996) http://www.driveintheater.com

Wikipedia http://en.wikipedia.org/wiki/Drive-in theater

Project CP-2: Spreadsheets

In this project, you'll apply all that you've learned about Microsoft Excel.

Requirements: This project requires Microsoft Excel.

Project file: DIClipArt.bmp

1. Copy the file DIClipArt.bmp to your Project folder using the Copy It! button on this page in the BookOnCD.

2. Start Microsoft Excel.

3. Look at the worksheet on the next page as a guide for constructing your worksheet and completing the rest of the steps.

4. Use WordArt to enter the title Drive-In Theaters.

5. Use the picture DIClipArt.bmp for the image in the upper-left corner of the worksheet. Shrink it to about 1" in size. Expand row 1 to the bottom of the picture.

6. In Row 3, enter the column headings shown on page 241 and format the text as bold, 14 pt., and with a dark red standard color. Make the text wrap to a second line in the cells.

7. "Year" should be left justified. The other headings should be right justified.

8. Enter the years and format them as text, not numbers.

9. Enter the numbers in the remaining two columns. Format the numbers in column B to display numbers with commas, but no decimal places. Format the numbers in column C for dollars and cents.

10. In cell C19, use a function to calculate the average for column C. In cell D19, enter the label Average in bold.

11. Create a 3D area chart showing the number of operating drive-ins from 1945–2010.

12. Title the chart U.S. Drive-Ins (18 pt. bold) and add Number in Operation as a title for the vertical axis (9 pt. bold).

13. Display vertical and horizontal gridlines in the chart area. (Hint: Look for the Gridlines button on the Layout tab of the Chart Tools contextual tab.)

14. Right-click the data series to format it with a gradient fill of the color Late Sunset.

15. Delete the text "Series 1" from the chart key and baseline.

• Spreadsheets (continued)

16. Create a 3D line chart showing the trend in drive-in admission prices. Move this chart below the first chart.

17. Add the title Admission Price per Car (18 pt. bold).

18. Format the data series with a similar gradient as you used for the first chart.

19. Format the plot area of both charts with a light gray color.

20. Save the worksheet as Capstone2-[Your Name]. You will use parts of this project again when you work on the third Capstone project.

21. Submit your project on a USB flash drive, as a printout, or as an e-mail attachment according to your instructor's preference.

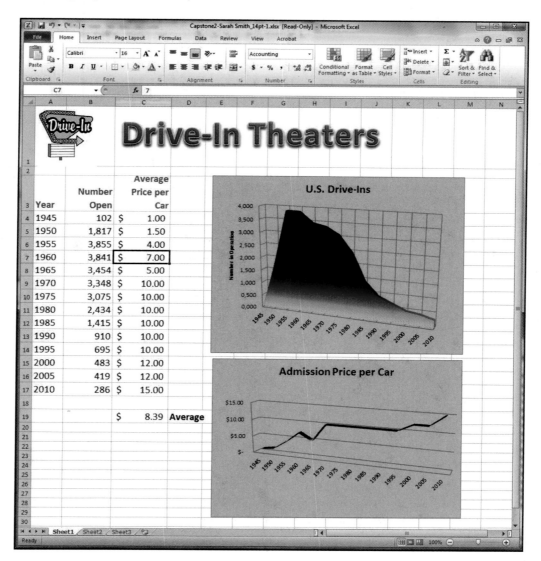

Project CP-3: PowerPoint

In this project, you'll apply all that you've learned about Microsoft PowerPoint.

Requirements: This project requires Microsoft PowerPoint.

Project file: Drivein1.jpg, Snackbar.jpg

 1. Copy the file Drivein1.jpg to your Project folder using the Copy It! button on this page in the BookOnCD.

 2. Copy the file Snackbar.jpg to your Project folder.

3. Start PowerPoint and create a presentation containing seven slides, as shown below and on the next pages.

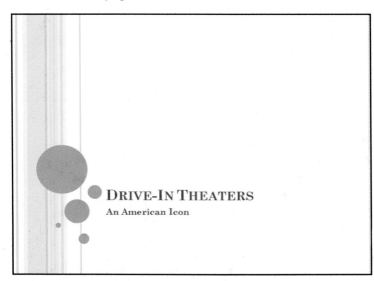

Slide 1:

• Use the Oriel theme.

• Add the title and subtitle as shown.

• PowerPoint (continued)

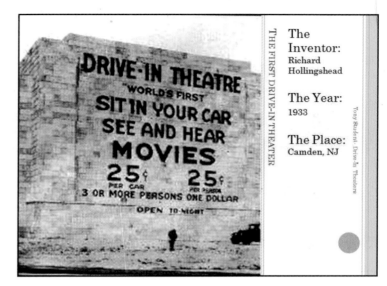

Slide 2:

- Use the *Picture with Caption* layout.

- Use the photo Drivein1.jpg.

- Add the vertical caption as shown.

- Add the text as shown.

- Add a footer containing your name and "Drive-In Theaters", which will appear on the right side of all slides except the title slide.

Slide 3:

- Use the *Title and Content* layout.

- Add the title and bullets as shown.

- Add the image Snackbar.jpg and position it as shown.

• PowerPoint (continued)

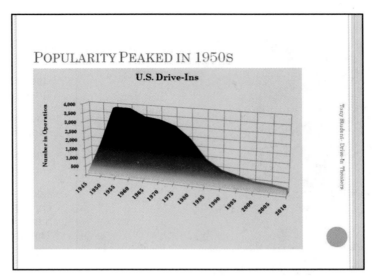

Slide 4:

- Use the *Title and Content* layout.

- Add the title shown.

- Copy the chart from Capstone Project 2 and paste it onto the slide.

- Adjust the size and position of the chart.

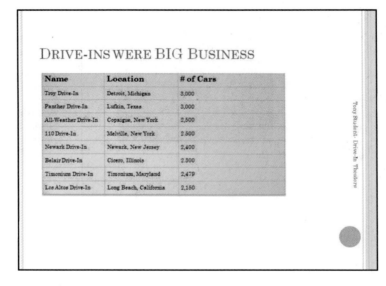

Slide 5:

- Use the *Title and Content* layout.

- Add the title shown.

- Copy the table in Figure 2 from Capstone Project 1. (Hint: Click the box with the plus sign that hovers just above the upper-left corner of the table to copy the entire table.)

- Paste the table onto the slide.

- Use the Table tools to apply the orange format to the table.

- Enlarge the font for the column headings to 16 pt.

- Center the text vertically in the cells. (Hint: Vertical centering places the text equidistant between the top and bottom of the cell; it is not the same as centering from left to right.)

• PowerPoint (continued)

Slide 6:

- Search the Web for photos and clip art pertaining to drive-in theaters.

- Copy and paste several photos to create a collage.

- List the Web sites where you obtained the photos under Photo Credits:.

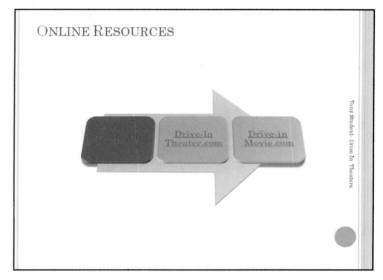

Slide 7:

- Use the Blank layout.

- Add the SmartArt shown from the Process group.

- Change the SmartArt Style to the Flat Scene style.

- Change colors by selecting one of the options from Accent 2 variations.

- Add the following Web links:
  Wikipedia: http://en.wikipedia.org/wiki/Drive-in_theater
  Drive-In Theater.com: www.driveintheater.com
  Drive-inMovie.com: www.driveinmovie.com

4. Save the project as Capstone3-[Your Name].

5. Submit your project on a USB flash drive, as a printout, or as an e-mail attachment according to your instructor's preference.